C000160766

A Journey to Remember

AN AUTOBIOGRAPHY

David Hughes

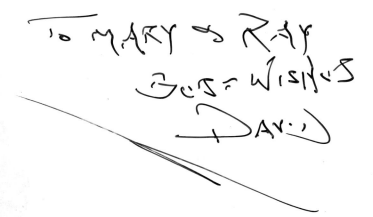

County Durham Books

© David Hughes 2000
The right of David Hughes to be identified as author of this work has been asserted by him in accordance with the Copyright Designs and Patent Act 1988.

Published by County Durham Books

Typeset by Sumner Type, London SE22

Printed by Trade Union Printing Services,
            Newcastle upon Tyne NE1 2PQ

ISBN 1-897585-61-6

THE NORTH OF ENGLAND OPEN AIR MUSEUM

A Journey to Remember

by David Hughes

Big business, ruthlessness, intrigue, power and everyday North Eastern folk – these are all elements in David Hughes' meticulous account of his experiences, from early days in the army in Cyprus, from shop boy to Chief Executive Officer of a Co-operative Society and then he was North East trouble shooter for the Co-operative Wholesale Society.

This is compulsive reading, written in a humorous and informative style. The book covers a fascinating period in the history of the Co-operative movement in the North East of England from bankruptcies, through store closures to the modernising and opening of brand new supermarkets. It is a very human account of the characters and methods involved and is an important contribution to recording this untold piece of history of our well known institution – the Store.

Rosemary E Allan
Senior Keeper

The Mark of an Outstanding Museum

Beamish, County Durham DH9 0RG
Tel. 01207 231811 Fax. 01207 290933 Email museum@beamish.org.uk
European Museum of the Year   British Museum of the Year
Beamish is a major development sponsored since 1970
by the local authorities of the North East of England

24 May 2000

With Best Wishes
Davd Hughes

CONTENTS

ACKNOWLEDGEMENTS

This autobiography was written over a period of four years and would not have been completed without the help and encouragement of my wife May. This is as much her story as mine.

My son David and daughter Sheila—to whom I apologise for giving time to the Co-op when I should have been with them in their early years.

Bill Fish—my friend, colleague and motivator in the publishing and publicising of this book.

Lord Graham of Edmondton—he encouraged me to publish when I had doubts.

Neil Arnold, CEO, North Eastern Co-op—gave total support in publication and book launch.

Durham County Council—provided full professional support.

Beamish Museum believed in my story from the beginning and provided massive help.

All those people throughout my career who helped me to do something new, do something different, and change things.

Sunderland Echo
Evening Chronicle
The Journal—Thank you for permission to use relevant news
Self Service Magazine—reports
The Grocer
Co-op News
All other unidentified newspapers

§

*This book is lovingly dedicated
to the memory of my wife May*

§

PROLOGUE

Headlines in newspapers on 19 December 1985 read *'Retail rebel checks out'* … *'Former chief retires'* … *'Co-op says goodbye Mr Cut Price'*. The stories continued with:

> 'He changed the shopping habits of a generation'
> 'Masterminded the amalgamation of North East Co op Societies'
> 'He was first in Britain to cut the price of bread'
> '… first to advertise Co-op Stores on T.V.'
> '… the first to install self-service in the North East'
> 'He was the first to cut the price of cigarettes'
> 'First to open a shop without fixtures'
> '… first manager in the North East to introduce "Management Trainees" '

As we approach the Millennium these are the expected items in retailing, but someone had to be first, and it was in the late 1950s that the revolution in retailing was launched. The war had been long ended, but regulations still remained as rigid as ever and retail systems hadn't changed in decades.

The names Superstore, Computer, Internet, Television, hadn't even been installed in the dictionary. Thousands of today's products hadn't even been thought of. It was a totally different world.

Reliving those days, it seems that one man had the foresight and vision to begin a revolution. Maybe it was newspaper hype. Maybe the press stories were nowhere near the truth. Maybe they were talking about someone else. Now that I'm in my seventies with nothing better to do, I'm writing my story, re-reading headlines with the realisation that it's *me* they were reporting on.

Such excitement, so much animosity and such glorious satisfaction, I look forward to reliving those days. Read on and enjoy.

BOOK 1

THE
IMPETUOSITY
OF YOUTH

1

LIFE IN THE 1920s AND 1930s

On Saturday 19 December 1925 I was born in my grandparent's miner's cottage at Ryhope Street, Ryhope, Co. Durham. My father was a coal miner, my mother an ex-nurse. I was called David after my grandfather who had been 'Mine Host' in the Times Inn pub at Dalton-le-Dale. I say 'had been' because he had died from drink when only 37 years old.

Our home was two upstairs rooms in a house at Murton, but it was too small, consequently my mother had returned 'home' for my birth.

How space was created at Ryhope I've never known, but being the first grandchild with two uncles and four aunts in the same house, I was given ample attention. Eleven months later my mother returned home to give birth to twins. Sadly, Frank died; my brother Ted survived.

It was 1926, the miners' strike had been going some weeks and things were desperate (not that I was aware, being one year old). We moved to a council house at Cutting Street, Seaham, which was a palace to mother and father, compared to the two rooms at Murton. It had three bedrooms, a front room and a large kitchen. In addition there was a garden back and front. The end house of Cutting Street faced on to a huge field that was the playground of every child in the area. The Mitchell family were our next-door neighbours. Bill Mitchell's pit wage had to support a family of six, yet they were the street's happiest family.

We had been in the house only a few months and I had just had my second birthday, when I fell down the stairs from top to bottom and hit my forehead on the concrete step inside the door. The cut, bruise and blood were eventually healed, but I was left with a double squint, that was devastating for my father and mother, particularly when told that there was no cure other than strong spectacles that might eventually pull them straight.

Prior to marriage, my father had developed a hobby for drinking and gambling on the horses; the acquisition of a house and family didn't diminish his hobby. Consequently, even though he was a 'face' worker, we were always badly off and, without help from my Ryhope grandmother, I'm sure the situation would have been desperate.

Mother was determined that her family would get the best she could provide. Pit wages would never satisfy her and in 1930 she converted part of our kitchen into a shop. Still in her early twenties, with no retail or business experience, she became buyer and owner of her own grocery shop. Father made wood fixtures and a counter; the kitchen window was now the shop window. Jopling, the wholesaler at Sunderland, supplied most of the stock; my aunt Nora baked bread and cakes. At the weekend I accompanied my aunt Bella, pushing a wheelbarrow round the streets selling meat pies (they were Nora's speciality). Mother made home-made toffee of every flavour imaginable, and toffee apples by the hundred.

Ryhope Cottage, 1925

Father's job—collier, 1925

Our family activity was divided between the shop and father's work. They only converged when he was in a shift that ended during the day. He arrived home black from the pit, had a meal and was ready for his bath. The front room was definitely out of bounds (this was only for special occasions) and, in any case, the hot water was boiling on the kitchen fire. He would be in full view of customers, so there was no alternative: the shop closed until he finished his bath. Customers patiently waited and usually gave a little cheer when he emerged, clean-faced and dressed. So long as there was trade, we kept the shop open, and in the evening we sat in the kitchen having a meal or listening to the wireless with constant interruptions.

I learned to serve customers at a very early age. Father refused to have anything to do with the shop—in any case it would interrupt him studying the racing form.

He never had a drink during the week. Apart from being too tired, he couldn't afford to and there was no way that mother would finance his drinking from the shop, although she would often give him a shilling to have a bet and a packet of Woodbines.

For the first few years my brother Ted was very weak, constantly being examined by the doctor. As I got older, I was always warned by my mother to 'look after Ted' when we were out playing, which was very difficult because I got into so many fights.

Wearing glasses with both eyes in the corner I was constantly taunted, and I always retaliated. At least twice a week I'd go home bloodied and with broken glasses in my hand, only to get told off by my mother for leaving Ted on his own outside.

But it was a good environment to be reared in. It was a close-knit community and we made our own entertainment. Violence, muggings and robbery didn't exist, for the good reason there was nothing to take.

During the week the men were going to or coming from the pit. When the weekend arrived the whole atmosphere in our house and in the whole community changed. It seemed as if father was determined to enjoy every single minute.

The tin bath and pit clothes were put away in an outhouse until Monday, as if 'out of sight was out of mind'. If the weather was good, Saturday morning saw my father sitting outside talking to Bill Mitchell and other neighbours discussing football, racing or the pit. They occasionally joined us on the 'square' for a game of football or cricket, depending on the season.

Ted and I kept pigeons in a shed at the bottom of the garden, but father wasn't really interested in them. Although we had a large garden and many of our neighbours grew every vegetable imaginable, for my father, gardening was a one-day-a-year activity. Regardless of the weather, he spent all day, Easter Monday, in the garden. He dug over every spare inch of soil and filled the whole garden with potatoes, after laying down some stinking manure from Davidson's farm at Seaton. He never touched the garden from that day until the next Easter Monday.

His Saturday afternoon routine was always the same. First stop was the betting shop, followed by a walk to Seaham football ground to see the Red Stars play. When they weren't playing at home, he made his way to a field behind the Dun Cow at Seaton to see the whippet racing and have a bet. Occasionally he took me with him, but mother never let Ted go—she was too afraid he'd take ill.

On Saturday evening he always left the house at seven o'clock. It took him an age to brush his hair, and get dressed in his dark suit, white shirt and trilby hat and, finally, display his father's Albert watch chain on his waistcoat.

Ted and I were usually fast asleep when he returned except when we were awakened by my father and mother arguing, always about money and drink. Their fights were at times horrendous. Ted and I just lay in bed, listening and waiting for the inevitable. My mother would storm upstairs, get us out of bed and dressed, saying we were leaving and going to Ryhope. By the time we got to the front door (it was cold and dark) she would have calmed down, and would say she would give him one more chance—and we all went back to bed.

In the eleven years in that house, the episode must have been re-enacted twice a month. She never did get past the front door and she always dressed us on top of our pyjamas, always as if anticipating our return to bed. Throughout it all Ted and I didn't utter a sound.

One night in the year we could stay up all night (if we could keep our eyes open). New Year's Eve was the special night of the year. We always had a party. Preparations began beforehand, making cakes, pies, jelly etc. My aunts and uncles from Ryhope would help. It was a strong superstition that if you had a full table of food on New Year's Eve, you'd never go hungry the following year. Aunt Nora baked cakes, neighbours contributed, and the table was bulging as the hour reached midnight. Ever since we could walk, Ted and I had been joint first-foots, with father insisting we each placed a foot at the door at exactly the same time and put our pieces of coal on the fire together. We than had to proceed amid kisses and handshaking to wish every single person in the house a 'Happy New Year'.

We loathed it.

However, the entertainment soon began, while everyone devoured the food and drink. The door was never closed and every new arrival was greeted with more kisses, handshakes and cries of 'Happy New Year'.

I always took my place at the side of the piano. I never did find out when my father learned to play the piano, but he could play anything without a note of music. I thought he was brilliant and would have given anything to be as good. (In fact I did begin piano lessons when I was seven). Almost everyone except my mother did a turn. Tom played the bones, Mat was a good tap dancer and always sang: 'I'm going back to Him-as-Has!'

Ted was usually in bed within an hour, I always fell asleep where I was sitting and never heard the party break up.

During school holidays mother opened the shop to suit the weather. When the sun was shining it was 'beach day'. A huge crowd of us would walk down Byron's Way, through the dene to Seaham Beach. There we would stay until late in the afternoon, our mothers sitting gossiping and ladling out lettuce sandwiches and diluted lemonade, while we played on the rocks, paddled, and had a great time. Tired out, our weary legs got us back home, where mother usually had one or two people waiting for her opening the shop. When I was about eight years old, my aunt Bella was taken into Seaham Hall sanatorium with tuberculosis. My mother never missed a visiting time and on our way back from the beach the whole group of us made a detour to give her an enthusiastic wave. Mother was desperately concerned: Bella was the baby of the family and her favourite.

About this time we were given some good news. I had been to the eye infirmary for some stronger glasses when the doctor told my mother that some work was well advanced on straightening eyes and he was confident that my eyes would be straight one day. Little did we realise in our delight that another three years would elapse before they were ready to try on a human being, and that I'd be the first.

My grandmother (father's mother) never visited our house and only on very rare occasions did my mother get Ted and me dressed in our best to visit her. We'd been so conditioned by my mother's vitriolic comments over the years that we never looked forward to a visit. There was always an atmosphere and we were under instructions to 'speak when you are spoken to and don't move off the seat'.

The regular visits to our other grandmother were eagerly anticipated. It was a long walk from Seaham to Ryhope, but our tiredness was forgotten with the warmth of our reception. Ted and I were smothered with love and affection, we were free of restrictions, and my mother seemed to be totally relaxed the minute she saw my grandmother. The kitchen was tiny, the brasses gleamed and the stove was black-leaded once a week. With so many to feed there was a constant smell of baking. It was a good 'meat' house, everyone crowded in the kitchen, the front room was dark with velvet curtains and covers. A huge bed dominated the room where my grandparents slept.

Ted and I were utterly spoilt with ice-cream and attention. My grandfather delighted in having us down the garden with him, feeding his ducks, hens and pigeons. Occasionally father would accompany us to

Ryhope (if he was in the right shift) but it always ended up with mother waiting for him returning from the Poplars with my grandfather, and their inevitable argument when we returned home.

One Saturday we had a memorable change to our routine. Father had a win on the horses. It must have been a good win, because Ted and I were called into the house to be told that next Saturday we would all be away for the day. This was incredible news—never, ever did my father join us on a day out. We were ready in good time to catch the train from Seaton Station to Sunderland. We couldn't believe my mother had actually closed the shop on a Saturday and we were going as a family for a day out. Ted and I were dressed in our best clothes, with strict instructions on behaviour.

As we all walked to Seaton station, mother made certain she spoke to everyone in sight—no way would she allow this day out to be a secret. On our arrival at Sunderland my mother, Ted and I went window shopping. We visited the old market down the east end, which was fascinating, with its fortune tellers, market stalls and roundabouts.

We were to meet up with father later in the day after he had inspected the Sunderland pubs. We'd finished our sandwiches by the time father met up with us in Mowbray Park, behind the museum. He didn't want anything to eat. We then made our way to the Havelock cinema and stood in a queue to see a Charlie Chaplin film. Father laughed throughout the show—he thought Chaplin was hilarious. We even had an ice-cream in the interval while the organ was played.

Our journey home was in a slow train, stopping at Grangetown and Ryhope. We had had a great day out. My mother didn't even object to father leaving us at the station to visit the Dun Cow while we made our way home.

I was swotting for the exam to go to the grammar school, very near to my eleventh birthday, when my mother received a letter, asking her to take me to see a specialist at Sunderland Eye Infirmary.

We were told that tests were completed and they were ready to do the first operation and I could be first to have an operation to straighten my eyes. My mother didn't hesitate and within a week, exams forgotten, I found myself being settled into a children's ward. From the minute I arrived I seemed to be the centre of attention. I lost count of the number of photographs taken of my eyes from every angle and a constant stream of doctors visited and examined my eyes. It was explained that for some technical reason I wouldn't be unconscious during the operation—I would see all that went on but would feel nothing.

They were right, I didn't feel a thing, I could see all their movements and didn't feel nervous or afraid. Afterwards, I had to have bandages on my eyes for ten days, which seemed forever. In those days they used leeches to clean the wound, but they had no feeling, except I had to keep still when they were used.

On the day of unveiling my father and mother had been invited to be present. The doctor told me to keep my eyes closed when he took the bandages off and then slowly open them. This I did to discover the bed surrounded by doctors and nurses, my father and mother weren't in my line of vision. The doctor who'd operated was looking in my eyes, then bent close and whispered: 'We'll have another try, David.' I wasn't sure what he meant until my father and mother came to the bed. Between her tears she told me I was no different. The operation had failed.

They wanted to try once more, if I wanted. Everyone was leaving the decision to me. I immediately said yes and after another ten days of darkness and leeches the bandages came off. Everyone was delighted: my eyes were normal. I couldn't stop looking in the mirror, every minute. I expected them to be going back into the corner.

Although my father had visited me at some time every day, the day the bandages came off he was down the pit, but I'll not forget his beaming smile when he walked into the ward that night.

After a few days I was allowed home to be a minor celebrity: everyone wanted to look at my eyes. I didn't need to wear glasses—it was fantastic to be normal. I'd missed my chance for grammar school, but I couldn't care less. I was now eleven years old. Ted and I would soon move to a school at Seaham Harbour.

For some time father and mother had talked about moving back to Murton to be nearer the pit, and they decided that now would be the right time. It was a nice house in Western Terrace, very near the Co-op. My father's uncle Dick had rented it to us. My mother felt like a queen with teachers as neighbours.

The year was 1937. I had two more years at school—then I'd be a working man. Father was working long hours and, although bacon cuttings were still on our menu, we seemed better off than ever before. Ted and I even received bicycles at Christmas and, to our surprise, father arrived from the pub one day with a bicycle for himself. That was one of the happiest periods of my life. The three of us were up at seven o'clock every Sunday morning and cycled for miles. During these rides we found a field near Trimdon, full of mushrooms. We filled a carrier bag and mushrooms were on the menu once a month until the season ended.

When summer arrived, someone in the street always seemed to be going to or returning from holiday. We'd never been away on holiday, so my father considered it was time we had a family holiday. We were on cloud nine! We were actually going away, but we didn't know where until two weeks later, he announced our destination. We were going to Crimdon Dene—camping. Ted and I thought a camping holiday, any holiday, was fantastic. The only concern for my mother was: 'What would the neighbours think?' They went to places like Scarborough and Whitley Bay. Nevertheless 1937 was to be our holiday year, under canvas, for one whole week.

According to father, the tent was quite large, already erected and on loan from a workmate. The week before our holiday we collected everything we needed. Grandmother sent a load of pies, cakes and bread—we wouldn't starve. Ted and I sorted out cricket gear, a football, and anything else for our entertainment. Mother insisted we would sleep in a proper bed and eat at a table with chairs. Our iron-framed brass bed was to be dismantled and transported with mattress and bedding to Crimdon. Four chairs and a table were borrowed from the big club (where else!). They were made of cast iron. Crockery, cutlery, even a clippy mat to cover the ground—absolutely nothing was forgotten.

Billy Brass, the fruiterer, had been hired to get everything to the campsite. He arrived early on Saturday morning with a flat cart and a very small pony. He couldn't believe we were going for only one week. It took a lot of persuasion to get him to take the load, but eventually it was secure. It was twice the height of the pony and there was no room for Ted and me to get a ride. My two uncles from Ryhope were helping. Ted and I set off walking at the side of the cart, Billy Brass led the way, with his small pony heaving to pull the load. Slowly we made our way through Murton with some of father's mates asking if we were going for a month or if we'd 'forgot the kitchen sink'.

Then we were on the open road and going through Hesledon and Blackhall. In 1937 the amount of motor traffic was not too heavy and Ted and I enjoyed running ahead then sitting waiting for the load to catch up. Approaching Crimdon Dene is a very steep hill. We were half way up, the pony struggling with its load, when suddenly its four feet slowly left the ground, the load slipped backwards, and our travels came to a grinding halt. The scene was hilarious, but no one was laughing. Billy Brass was cursing, father and my two uncles were taking the load off the cart and stacking it on the roadside. As the load lightened, the pony gradually returned to earth and was calmed down by Billy. Half of the load was taken to the top of the hill and unloaded. Billy then returned for the remainder, all the while cursing the brass bed and the iron table. It was a long time before we continued the journey. The holiday atmosphere had evaporated, Billy never said another word and, after unloading at the camp site, he demanded his money and then announced he wouldn't be available for the return journey.

We had just unloaded everything, erected the bed, set up the table and chairs outside the tent and laid down the clippy mat, when my mother made a grand entrance, having travelled in the comfort of a bus. Thankfully she didn't find fault with anything and we settled down to a life under canvas. My two uncles had a small tent nearby, without any of the trappings of civilisation.

We had a lovely holiday: the weather was good, and we had father's exclusive attention for a whole week. With regret Ted and I helped to load a lorry that father had hired to get us back home. Mother again elected to return by bus.

Our holiday had been over only a couple of weeks when the family was plunged into panic. Everyone in the school heard the pit buzzer and we were all aware that it indicated something was seriously wrong at the pit, but school continued. I thought no more until Ted and I were walking home and realised something was wrong by the number of people standing outside in small groups. When we got home, a number of neighbours were in our house, all talking in whispers, with my mother sitting near the fire in a terrible state. We were told there had been a fall down in the pit and my father and a dozen other miners were trapped. They had already been there four hours and contact had been made. Some were still alive, how many or who wasn't known. The police asked everyone to stay at home and they were relaying bulletins every hour.

Ted and I were shattered. My mind went berserk, thinking of the possibilities of what had happened down below, but all we could do was wait.

Midnight came and still no good news. People were saying the longer it went, the less their chances, although I don't think my mother heard the comments. Then about three o'clock in the morning the police called to take my mother to the pit. The rescue men had got through and were bringing survivors up. She made Ted and me stay at home with the neighbours and after a two-hour wait, which seemed everlasting, a police car drove up. She had a beaming smile, father looked very tired but was without a scratch, and we were all hugging, laughing and crying at the same time.

Thankfully, no one was killed. A fall had cut off their escape and they could only sit there and wait to be rescued. Within 24 hours he was back down the pit and life returned to normal. It was just one of the hazards of being a miner.

At this time my uncle Mat was at his peak as a sprinter, and I often accompanied my grandfather and father when they went to race meetings to see him run. He practised every day and raced about once a month. He was at a meeting at Horden and running in the 100 yards sprint. There were huge crowds by the time we got to the meeting and Mat left us to find out what his handicap was. Depending on his last race, or how many races he'd won, determined his starting place (at the back or given a few yards start). Sometimes runners deliberately didn't try to win in order to get a better handicap at the next race meeting. Alongside the track were dozens of bookies. The runners weren't allowed to gamble, but the public were pouring money on every race. As usual my father and my grandfather made a bee-line for the beer tent, and I wandered around the field watching the races (high jump and other sports), all the time watching the time coming up for Mat's race—I always liked to be near the finishing line. I knew that today Mat was trying to win, but he was up against the favourite. Mat had lost his last four races and had a few yards start on the favourite so fancied his chance in today's race.

Uncle Mat was a runner, 1938

The time for the 100 yards race was getting near so I made my way to where Mat was changing. The runners all knew each other—they raced against each other regularly—and as I got near, Mat beckoned me over and whispered: 'David, neither the favourite nor anyone else is trying today. Get to your father quick as you can, tell him I can't lose and put every penny he's got on me.' I ran to the beer tent, but it was absolutely packed. I pushed in and out of people, it took ages to find them in a corner. I blurted our Mat's message. Beer was ignored, they both pushed their way through the crowd, ran to the line of bookies—just as the starter's gun cracked. Mat won the race easily. They'd had a small bet before going into the beer tent, but it could have been one of life's certainties if I'd got to them sooner. Mat didn't do much more running, in fact I don't think he won another race.

The year 1939 began like many others but it was destined to be momentous in a small way for me and to a slightly bigger extent for the world.

My aunt Bella died from TB at Seaham sanatorium. She was only eighteen and mother was devastated for months. Both my grandfather and grandmother had died within months of each other. Ted was now stronger than ever, but was always looked on as a weakling and our daily ritual continued. Father would get out the huge bottle of cod liver oil, a tablespoon full for Ted, the same for me, and he drank out of the bottle. 'It'll do you good,' Mother always said, without finding the need for her to take some.

There were two chores we had to do at home: coals were delivered every three weeks, Ted and I had to shovel them into the coalhouse. It was a heavy and dirty job. The clean job was doing fifty times with the poss stick on washing day in a tub of soapy water. (A poss stick was a heavy wooden stick used to beat the washing as it soaked in a wooden wash tub.)

The war was only three months old. Apart from having a gas mask and being aware of rationing, it had no effect on my life. I was a working man with the world at my feet. I actually received pocket money from my mother (6d). No longer would we need to depend solely on my father as provider. I was a wage earner: at fourteen years of age I left school on the Friday and became a wage earner on the following Monday morning. I was a butcher boy earning 7s 6d for a 45-hour week. It was absolutely awful. The job lasted three months in atrocious weather: it was bitter cold, the meat was frozen solid, and I hated delivery time (everyone wanted meat delivered to the door). The delivery bike was far too big for my short legs, the snow was deep that winter, and I pushed the bike for miles. On return to the shop, I was only too pleased to get my hands into hot water to wash down blood soaked benches and to make innumerable cups of tea for the boss and his two side-kicks. It was hard work, cold, but a happy shop. No matter how you felt, it was demanded that immediately a customer entered we were happy. If you wanted to be miserable, you were told: 'Go to the toilet'. Being outside, the toilet was like a trip to Siberia, so it paid to be happy. I hated making black pudding, washing tripe, and trying to clean windows covered with frost every morning. However, a free parcel of meat on pay-day—Saturday—made it a joy to see a smile on my mother's face.

March 1940 was the month that set the pattern for my life, although I didn't know it at the time. The two main employers throughout the North East in the 1940s were the pit (where the work was dirty, hard and exempt from call-up to the armed forces) or, if you were very lucky, the Co-op, where the work was clean with various perks, and considered to be a job for life.

The Co-op was a huge organisation with shops in every area. Each town had its own Co-op Society and almost every street had a Co-op shop. The majority of people were Co-op members and all could remember their Co-op number. The Co-op supplied everything from the cradle to the grave, gave credit, paid dividend, and had a virtual monopoly.

Supermarkets, self-service shops, dairy cabinets, frozen foods and check-outs weren't even in existence. A man on the moon was only for comic books and mass communication depended on the wireless and newspapers.

Little did I know I would be responsible for some changes in retailing that would ultimately develop into the ultra-modern supermarkets of the 1990s.

The Murton Colliery Society, 1939

2

JOB AT THE CO-OP

'There's a vacancy at the Co-op'

The news spread through Murton like wildfire, and my mother submitted my application almost immediately, then asked if I'd like to work at the Co-op. Of course I would, it couldn't be worse than the butcher's, but I'd be lucky to get the job as a grocery apprentice—there would be dozens of applicants. The Co-op manager had no say in the appointment of staff in the 1940s. A committee of men (elected by the Co-op members) were all-powerful, and even a junior grocery boy had to be interrogated by all ten committee men. At 4p.m. on the Friday afternoon, I stood midway in a queue of about 30 boys my own age, dressed in our Sunday best, all mentally rehearsing answers to possible questions, and apprehensive about the ordeal facing us behind the panelled door of the committee room.

'What's it like?'

'What questions did they ask?'

'Have you got the job?'

Questions were shouted to each boy as he came out of his interview, but rarely was a response other than 'Sod off!' or 'Get lost!' offered.

Step by slow step, the heavy oak panelled door got nearer and my apprehension more acute. Only the fear of facing my mother stopped me leaving the queue. Eventually—my turn. The committee room was enormous. I could only see through a haze of smoke. A long oak table was the parking place for the committee men, who all looked in my direction as I obeyed an instruction to sit on a high backed chair placed at one end of the table. I faced ten pairs of eyes, below which was a pipe or cigarette emitting clouds of smoke. I was terrified.

A fat man with a huge nose sat directly opposite and was the main questioner. I learned he was chairman, a very powerful gentleman. Taking his pipe from below a shaggy moustache he said:

'Is your father Ned Hughes?'

'Yes sir,' I replied in a voice I hardly recognised.

'Would you like to work at the Co-op?' A squeaky voice on my left enquired. What a stupid question, but I simply replied:

'Yes sir.' For more than ten minutes the questions were about my family and what schools I'd attended. No questions on my scholastic ability or achievements—thank God—and before I was aware, I was on my way out refusing to answer questions by the remaining applicants.

'Well, what happened?' My mother wasn't satisfied until I'd described every detail and explained that I'd get a letter next week.

'Don't worry I'll go down to the club and see if you've got the job.' My father was standing at the mirror brushing his hair, already dressed in his 'drinking' suit and preparing to go to the Workman's Club. This was the first time I'd known him go out on a Friday night—he must have had some contact with the Co-op. The clock chimed 11p.m. It was way past my bedtime but my mother and I sat in apprehension waiting for my father to deliver the verdict that would determine my future. Ted had gone to bed ages ago, he couldn't have cared less.

The door opened and, with a beaming smile and a very rare hug, my father announced: 'You've got the job, son.' He even gave my mother a hug and kiss. I'd never seen such a public display of affection in our house except on New Year's Eve. Apparently the majority of the committee were either workmates or drinking pals of my father. God knows how many pints of beer my first job at the Co-op cost, but my first lesson on success was learned that night—it's not what you know, it's who you know that counts.

I'd been at the Co-op three days and hadn't even seen the general manager. Some people had worked there for years and hadn't even exchanged a word with him. Unless he spoke to you, on no account did you speak to him. The Co-op general manager was God so far as staff and even customers were concerned. He had the power over jobs and credit—that was almost life and death in the early 1940s. The general manager wasn't my problem, I had enough learning the ropes and getting to know people.

'Allan will explain what to do,' were the first words Mr Lightfoot, the grocery manager said on my first morning. He looked very smart in his dark suit with a gold watch chain draped over the front of his waistcoat and a spotless white apron protecting his trousers. Although quiet-spoken, his voice had authority and no one questioned his word. A reply of 'Yes, Mr Lightfoot' was automatic.

Allan was a different kettle of fish. He had ginger hair, a spotty face, was two years older than me and too cocky for his own good. He made my life hell for the first few weeks. I was to do his job so he could move up to the provision counter (a very important promotion). He made every job seem like life or death: I was at the beck and call of every one of the twenty-odd grocery staff. Their position in the hierarchy was determined by the number of people they could dominate and I was bottom of the heap.

First job in the morning was to sweep the bare wooden floor and cover it with fresh sawdust from the funeral department. It made the shop smell lovely and fresh before the first customer entered. Meanwhile, the provision staff were cutting bacon, cooked ham and other meats for the display on marble slabs. Grocery counter staff were grinding coffee, filling fixtures and preparing for the inevitable queue. The aroma was lovely. Not that I saw many customers. According to Allan I was back-shop staff, 'the lowest of the low'.

Helping to load horse-drawn mobile shops, unload huge lorries and generally keep the place tidy were my main duties. I was shown how to wash sides of bacon in vinegar to keep them free of maggots and turn rounds of cheese, but the most tedious job was tea-making. Every day I made gallons of tea, remembering who took sugar, milk or neither. Every time I caught his eye, the grocery manager demanded a cup of tea (no milk, two sugars).

I only began to enjoy being a grocer when I was allowed to do 'skilled' jobs. Prepacked goods didn't exist, so everything had to be weighed and packed. Currants were a joy to do, soapflakes were awful, but I was learning to weigh and pack. I began to feel like a Grocer.

The committee of Murton Co-op, where I had my first Co-op job

Typical grocery, 1939

Typical grocery, 1939

Friday afternoon was special. Pay packets were distributed (I was now earning 15s a week). All staff put on clean white starched overalls. It was also pay-day for customers, who formed long queues at every counter to pay for the previous week's credit and start off a new week 'in the book'. It was the social occasion of the week. Everyone dressed in their best to have a good gossip at the Co-op, and even the general manager made his rare excursion from his office to mingle with customers for a chat.

After six months I felt part of the staff, no longer dominated by Allan, and on good terms with everyone. I knew staff in the butchers', greengrocers' and other departments and was happy to go to work every morning.

'David, put a clean overall on and go to the General Manager's Office.' The grocery manager stunned me with this instruction. No one ever entered 'The Man's' office, I'd never even seen the door open. 'You're not in trouble, he won't bite,' a smiling grocery manager tried to allay my fear.

'Sit down David.' Mr Deans was standing looking out of his office window. (I hadn't realised he knew my name). He was a huge man, well over 6 feet tall, very broad and dressed in an immaculate dark suit, spotless white shirt, with cuffs clearly showing. I sat on a hard chair opposite his enormous desk, hardly daring to speak. I felt tiny near this mountain of a man, and could only assume I'd done something wrong. Sitting down, he fixed his eyes on me.

'Do you like working at the Co-op?' he asked.

'I love it, sir,' I answered with truthful enthusiasm.

'Have you any plans for your future?' With my school record, lack of opportunity in the area and lack of finance at home I could only reply:

'No sir.' He was silent for a few moments then he stunned me by saying:

'How would you like a life at the Co-op and being a manager one day?' To ask a 14-year-old grocer boy such a mind-blowing question left me speechless. I was waiting for him to laugh and say it was a joke. 'I've watched you since you started, I've checked your school, and if you're prepared to work hard and spend many years studying, I believe you can make it.'

I could only sit there trying to absorb what he'd said, I was too overwhelmed to know what to say. Realising my confusion he smiled, rose from his chair, handed me a bag full of books and leaflets and said:

'Read these, talk to your parents, and one week today I'd like to see them and you to hear your answer.'

I told no one of our conversation, but a week later I was full of it. By studying at home I could qualify to be a manager eventually (little did I know that it would take *twenty years* to fulfil an ambition that had grown in one week).

'I believe David has the potential to be a future Co-op manager', Mr Deans told my father and mother as we sat in front of him. They were dressed in their Sunday best and were bursting with pride.

'I don't think we can afford the cost of books and things,' my father said. (A few less pints and cigarettes would help, I silently thought).

'With your income David can qualify for a Co-op grant to cover the cost. All that is required is your consent and David's enthusiasm and hard work from now on.'

My parents returned home more happy than I'd ever seen them, I went back to tea-making with one thought—Why me? I never had an answer but assumed Mr and Mrs Deans had never had a family and he saw in me the potential of a son he had never had—but I could be miles wrong.

That brief meeting set a pattern for the whole of my working life with repercussions far beyond anyone's imagination at the time. My second lesson on success was learned—if your face fits and you're in the right place at the right time, you get opportunities.

Mr Deans wasted no time. I was soon studying by correspondence with the Co-op Education Department at Manchester (my first step to qualify as a manager). Inevitably the news got out and I had my first experience of jealousy, usually from people I least expected. I suppose you couldn't blame people—why should I get preferential treatment? (Even I didn't know the answer to that.) Within a few weeks it was arranged that I'd work in every department for two weeks at a time to gain experience. The greengrocery I enjoyed, ladies' underwear was embarrassing, and the funeral section was depressing. Out on a mobile shop was interesting but I didn't enjoy grooming the horse at the end of the day. I still hadn't reached 15 years of age, but so much was happening. Life was exciting and I was totally unprepared for the shock in store for me.

My father had been born in the Times Inn at Dalton-le-Dale on 4 April 1904. With his parents and three sisters he had had a happy and prosperous childhood. Sadly his father (my grandfather) died when my father was in his early teens, debts were high, and the family had to leave the pub. When he married my mother in 1924 he was a poorly-paid coal miner with a desire to get back to pub life one day. My mother had no love of drink, but shared his ambition, and every week tried to save (sometimes only a few coppers) for the necessary bond money required by the brewery to take over a pub. I knew of their desire but never believed they'd ever save the £300 bond money.

'David, we have a pub and we'll be moving to Hetton Lyons in four weeks time.' Ted and I were stunned by my father's excited announcement. No discussion. We had no say. It had taken my mother over 15 years to save the bond money and the Golden Lion pub at Hetton Lyons would be our home.

'What about my job and studies?'

'You can travel, it's only twenty minutes on the bus,' my mother said with some annoyance at my lack of enthusiasm. Ted, as usual, shrugged his shoulders and let me take the flak.

The Golden Lion, 1941

The Golden Lion pub was tiny, probably all they could get for a small bond. Every pint required walking three steps down to a cellar and was drawn direct from the barrel. The bar and lounge were very small. The kitchen was the main room: it was large, dominated by a square table almost the size of the room and surrounded by forms to sit on. A huge open fire had the room as warm as toast. The living quarters were upstairs and awful. Only two small bedrooms, a so-called lounge, and a kitchen too small for two people. The place was so dark and dingy I hated it on sight—the pub was overshadowed by a huge railway shed.

'My God,' I thought. 'They are desperate to get a pub.'

The pub was too small to provide an adequate income so my father continued to work at Murton pit for six months until they had built up a good business. My mother looked after the pub until 11p.m. every day. Home life ceased the day we moved into that pub.

I travelled to the Co-op every day in all weathers and noticed a change in the general manager's attitude to me. No less encouraging, he always checked on the progress of my studies but was very critical if a job wasn't done perfectly. He seemed to check on everything I did, while ignoring other staff. One day in early 1941 the snow was deep, buses were stopped and I walked to work. I didn't get told off for being late nor was I praised for walking through deep snow, but Mr Deans was highly annoyed when he saw me without a tie (I'd put a scarf on for the cold).

'Go to the drapery, David,' he instructed. 'Get a tie, and never come to work without one.' For the next 45 years I never was at work without a tie.

To be sacked at the Co-op was unheard of, but one day Mr Deans sacked three staff for stealing. This was a major shock to staff, customers and the community. It gave me my first experience of the effect on staff. Morale dropped to rock bottom but it did wonders for discipline and awareness of doing things correctly. Many years later I was to recall that occasion when I was in the same position as Mr Deans.

About one year later a vacancy arose three miles away at Hetton Downs Co-op for a grocery assistant. I told Mr Deans I'd like to apply, I was tired of the long travel every day, but my enthusiasm for the Co-op had not diminished. With a promise to continue my studies by correspondence, and keep him informed of my progress, Mr Deans made a phone call, wished me well and arranged for me to be transferred to Hetton Downs Co-op. This move was my first step to the most incredible career imaginable.

Hetton Downs Co-op, 1942

3

HETTON DOWNS CO-OP

Now almost 16 years of age, I began my new job with the confidence of youth. I was out to prove I could do any job in the grocery department, but the grocery manager (a huge red-faced man) was equally determined to show me who was the boss, and this cocky foreigner from Murton would do as he was told. I washed sides of bacon, packed soda and soapflakes and helped to clean out the stables. It would be a long time before I was allowed to stand behind the long counter, a spotless clean apron round my waist, and say: 'Good Morning, Madam.'

It was 1941. My contribution to the war effort was to join the ATC (Air Training Corps) with ambition to be a pilot when I was eighteen years old, and I took my turn with other male staff as Air Raid Wardens to guard the Co-op in the event of a bomb falling. I never became a pilot and the nearest bomb was five miles away.

My ambition to be a Co-op manager never diminished. I succeeded in the elementary exams and was gaining some grudging respect for my dedication, but my teenage activities were not neglected. I played cricket and football, met girls, one of whom was a lovely girl with long hair, a beautiful smile, and a fabulous personality. She also worked as a grocer in one of the Co-op branches. One year younger, May Robson would marry me six years later and we would have 52 years of blissful married life—but I'm getting ahead of my story.

The grocery department produced more than 50 per cent of the total turnover of Hetton Downs Co-op and tradition dictated that the grocery manager was automatically promoted to general manager (the Co-op was strong on many traditions). Over the next two years I became accepted, learned my trade, passed more exams, and fell hopelessly in love with May Robson. We spent every spare minute together.

I was offered, and accepted, a grant to attend as a full-time student at the Co-op Union College in Manchester, boarding at a beautiful, large detached house in Wilmslow. There were only six students, we had almost one-to-one intensive tuition, and I loved every minute. I was away from home, a completely new life, independence and involvement in studying accountancy, commercial law and a host of other subjects. The only downside was being away from May—we wrote to each other every day. Nine months later students moved to a new mansion in Loughborough, the home of an ex-millionaire. The new college was established and I was one of its first six students. I didn't know such luxury existed and we had the time of our lives.

However, I was quickly brought back to reality whenever I returned home for a brief holiday. May and I were blissfully happy, my father and mother were delighted to see me, but the deal with my Co-op grant demanded I return to work every college holiday.

'College education is no bloody good here, son,' the fat, foul-mouthed grocery manager greeted me as his less-than-favourite son. 'I've got just the job for you, David,' he continued, without waiting for my response. 'Yoke a horse and deliver those grocery orders.' After the first time I learned to expect animosity from him and everyone else. No one from Hetton Co-op had ever been a full-time student. In their eyes I was a waste of space, a scrounging, skiving college student who returned every so often to do a bit of graft, then return to a life of luxury.

'One day I'll show them!!!' If I'd known then that it would be another fourteen years before I 'saw my day', I'd probably have packed the whole thing in there and then. But I continued at college and progressed until . . .

Early in 1946 I was called up for the army direct from college. May was distraught: I was to be in the army two long years. But since the war had ended, at least I wouldn't be in danger, or so I thought. Four weeks' holiday would see me in the RAOC, Private Hughes D., No 14113685.

May in 1947

May and me in 1947

4

TWO YEARS' ARMY SERVICE

I was on a train travelling south. It was March 1946, and I was all alone, even though the compartment was crammed full of people. I was utterly miserable, every mile taking me further away from my girlfriend, family, friends and work. I would be away at least two years. I had already travelled further than I had ever been before and I could do nothing about it. If I didn't go, the alternative was six months in prison. I'd been 'called up' for the army and was heading for Budbrook Barracks in Warwick to join the Royal Army Ordinance Corps.

I was twenty years old and should have been called up earlier, but as a full-time student at the Co-op College in Loughborough, my call-up had been delayed for two years. Thank goodness I had been deferred, otherwise I'd have been in the D-Day landings in France where thousands were killed in the first two days—but this didn't make me feel any happier.

A few hours before, I had said goodbye to my girlfriend, May Robson, at Durham Station. Looking out of the train window, all I could see was her tearful face as I waved goodbye. I hoped she'd wait another two years, having already waited more than a year while I was at college, qualifying to be a manager. We'd been going out together three years, and I couldn't imagine marrying anyone else, even though we weren't even engaged. I was going to miss her so much.

After a long, tedious journey, the train pulled into a station, and a voice boomed 'Warwick Station' over a loudspeaker. With a feeling of anxiety and anticipation, I collected my case, squeezed past the crowded corridor and stepped on to the platform.

My life would never be the same from this moment on.

'Budbrook Barracks,' a voice boomed along the platform. The source was a thin, weedy looking corporal who was trying to improve his authoritative image by sporting a moustache—it failed miserably!

I joined a queue of ten others, all with call-up papers at the ready. With a flourish of importance, the corporal ticked my name off his clip-board list, and directed me to an army lorry parked outside the station with its engine running. The driver, smoking a cigarette, nodded his head to indicate that I jump into the back of the lorry. By the time we headed for our destination, there were fifteen others seated on wooden benches down each side of the lorry.

We were all males, quietly minding our own business, anticipating our future—all except a ginger-haired, obnoxious, young cockney. The journey lasted only twenty minutes, but long enough to loathe 'Ginger' and his loud mouth. He made certain we were all aware he was a hard man, a 'boy soldier' from the age of fourteen, before which he had survived a youth detention camp. To reinforce the image, he used language that was a shock to my inexperienced ears. He was a know-all, knew all the dodges, and was going to enjoy the army. I just looked at him and said nothing.

The lorry shuddered to a stop at the same time as a voice yelled:

'All out at the double, line up, come on, look sharp.' We all stood in a line facing a sergeant major, or so he said. He looked a bit overweight, but full of his own importance.

'Welcome to Budbrook,' he said. 'You're not allowed out for eight weeks—by then you'll look like soldiers.' He turned to 'the moustache' and instructed: 'Corporal, take this lot to the canteen, then report with them to the stores.'

As we were taken to the canteen, I looked at the coldest, most unfriendly set of buildings I'd ever seen in my life. Huge, six-storey, grey stone barracks, built in a square to surround a drill area the size of two football pitches. Someone screaming their head off was already drilling two squads of soldiers. A less friendly place would be hard to find.

I was so hungry, anything would have been enjoyable. The spam covered in batter, powdered egg and chips, washed down with hot, sweet tea was gorgeous. We then joined a queue at the quartermaster's stores. At the other side of a long smooth counter were six soldiers spaced out in front of shelves full of uniforms. I reached the first soldier, he looked me up and down, then handed me a khaki blouse and trousers—no measurements. When I reached the end of the line, I was loaded with underwear, boots, PT kit, greatcoat and a cap stuck on my head (no slippers or dressing gown!). All the time, someone was shouting:

'Come on, hurry up, it isn't Butlins.' We didn't know if we were coming or going.

We were then directed to the sleeping quarters—a long bare Nissen Hut, made of corrugated steel (the barracks must be for real soldiers). A metal stove with a pipe leading out of the roof dominated the centre of the floor and beds lined the walls.

'Put your gear on a bed, and stand at the side of the bed and keep quiet,' the corporal shouted. The door opened with a crash. We all jumped two feet in the air, and in walked a mountain of a man.

Well over six feet tall, the crease in his trousers could have sliced bread, his shoes dazzled, and his handlebar moustache seemed to quiver every time he blinked. What an entrance! He toured the hut, silently looking at each one of us for what seemed like an eternity. In my civvy clothes, I felt a complete scruff when faced with such an immaculate, ramrod of a man. If his aim was to intimidate, he succeeded. With a quiet voice he said:

'You are now in the army, and by six o'clock you will all look like soldiers.' He quickly turned to face the cockney boy soldier who had made some comment.

'Well?' he enquired.

'Sorry, Sir.' I thought the officer was going to explode.

'You don't call me "Sir". I am a Sergeant Major. Don't you dare speak until I say you can.' His quiet voice had gone, his voice boomed round the hut. No one moved an eyelid. We stood silently as he marched out, leaving it to the corporal to explain that six o'clock meant in the morning.

We had twelve hours to look like soldiers, as the man said! That meant polishing shoes, cleaning brasses, pressing uniforms and feeling scared to face that sergeant major ever again. It was two o'clock in the morning when I crawled into bed, less that 24 hours since I had said goodbye to May, and my life was now completely changed. I was tired, demoralised and utterly miserable.

The next morning wasn't as bad as we expected. We had a parade, but it was a formality without hassle. My first full day in the army was very busy, but I now know it was the calm before the storm.

It was a day of queuing: for a haircut, medical, dentist, and individual interviews to assess to which part of the army we would eventually go. My first day ended at five o'clock and I had time to write my first letter to May. I also had a chance to get to know others in the squad.

George Sinclair had a bed next to me. He was quite friendly, a couple of years younger, and didn't have the foul mouth of most in our hut. He was from Cardiff and destined to spend his entire army career with me. We would be good friends, up until a point. He was the only black person in the whole of the barracks.

Brian Ferris, in the bed opposite, worked for the BBC Radio. Eighteen years old, tall and fat, every other word was an oath. He followed the same posting as George and me. The others in the hut were a mixture of big-heads, rogues, timid, and shy. We all changed over the next eight weeks.

The biggest shock for me was the perpetual filthy language used by almost everyone in the hut. I must have led a very sheltered life. The biggest lesson learned quickly was to leave nothing lying around—it would disappear in seconds!

I learned to stand up for myself. At least four in the group were out to dominate, if given the chance. They had already set up mini-rackets, like polishing boots (for money), offering to get drink into the hut (for money) etc., etc.

It was a relief to crawl into bed at the end of my first full day. I was no longer a person: I was number 14113685 Private Hughes D., RAOC, and I was stuck in Budbrook Barracks for eight weeks or even more.

Eight weeks' initial army training was divided into:

PHYSICAL TRAINING—DRILL—FATIGUES—MANOEUVRES.

For eight weeks we never walked, everything was 'at the double' and, unless off duty, we didn't talk without being instructed to.

PHYSICAL TRAINING was absolute torture. The PT sergeant, who was fit as a fiddle, went prancing around like a ballet dancer but was an absolute sadist. Only the 'boy soldier' was fit, the rest of us went through agony. Exercise never stopped and the screaming of the sergeant made us all feel like doing murder. I was having pain on top of pain.

Boxing was the favourite of the hard lads. They tried to beat everyone. One punch and I was out. A hero I was not! We endured four hours every day of this relentless agony until strangely, after four weeks, I actually began to enjoy it!

DRILL (Square Bashing): Until now I had always been able to put one foot in front of the other without difficulty. I could easily count one, two, three, four, and, like any child, knew left from right. On a parade ground with nineteen other soldiers and a sergeant major who scares the daylights out of you just looking at him, we had problems! Everything you've seen on comic films of soldiers turning right instead of left, half the squad halting when the rest kept on marching: all of this we did, and more—much more!

Hour after hour, day after day, we missed so many meals due to being kept on the parade ground. The NAAFI did a roaring trade—we had to pay.

'You're the worst squad I've ever seen,' the sergeant major was always shouting. I had a feeling that this time he was telling the truth.

After two or three hours each day, I was shattered and my feet were killing me. It didn't help knowing that the afternoon required our reporting for yet another session of physical training.

After about six weeks, we got the hang of the army drill and, unbelievably, I thoroughly enjoyed the last two weeks of parade-ground drill.

It's a great feeling of pride when twenty soldiers can do every drill at precisely the same second without a mistake. The sound of every boot hitting the ground as if it were one was now a challenge to all of us not to let the squad down. We now looked like soldiers, paraded like soldiers, and felt as fit as soldiers. Was I becoming a soldier?

FATIGUES: Not satisfied with breaking our bodies and spirit, the slightest excuse for anyone with authority resulted in being given fatigues. This consisted of cookhouse, cleaning toilets, sweeping roads and painting stones and fences white.

Luckily, only once in eight weeks was I caught without a hat, and told to report to the cookhouse. It took me and two others three hours to peel a mountain of potatoes. My fingers were raw and numb when I had finished, but it was still better than cleaning toilets!

MANOEUVRES: It was essential we were fit and disciplined to carry out manoeuvres. Up to a ten-mile hike with full pack was boring and soul-destroying. Sleeping out in tents in all weathers, eating cold food, was miserable. Rifle training, live ammunition and bayonet practice was not a pleasant experience, but I suppose this is what soldiering was all about.

I was one of the few who didn't enjoy being a soldier, but the first eight weeks in the army completely changed me. I was fitter than I had ever been in my whole life. I had changed into a hard, less trusting person in order to survive among thieves, bullies and con-men. George Sinclair, Brian Ferris and I became close friends, watched out for each other, helped and encouraged, and generally made the first eight weeks bearable.

I kept my promise to write a letter every day to May, but some days it was after midnight and it was difficult not to put my misery in the writing. I missed her, and her daily letters confirmed that she felt the same way.

Eight long weeks came to an end. We were considered to be disciplined soldiers and fit to be seen in public. We were allowed out of the barracks on the Sunday, but only after being inspected by the sergeant major. Sunday in Warwick is not the fun place I would select. It was late April but we were out—now I knew what it was to get out of jail. We could actually walk where we liked and do what we liked, but after two or three hours we drifted back to the camp—so much for freedom!

At eight o'clock the next day, we lined up to receive a 72-hour pass, a train voucher, and news of our posting to Bicester to be trained as storekeepers. George, Brian and I had been posted to the same place with only two others from the squad.

I was going home, and couldn't get to the station fast enough. I had to change at York, but in about five hours I would see May.

'Are we anywhere near York?' I asked the elderly man sitting next to me. I had dozed off after the train left Warwick.

'York?' he said with surprise, 'I'm afraid the next stop is Carlisle!' It couldn't be, I had only had a nap, and my pass was only 72 hours. I could have cried—but I had to be a brave soldier! I got home via Newcastle, and had only one full day before travelling all the way back to the RAOC depot at Bicester.

The short time at home, spent mainly with May, was bliss. I was back in reality, in the real life. To me, the army was only an interlude I would have to endure—for two whole years.

Of my entire army career, Bicester was the best period. In my three months' stay, I don't remember one day of hassle.

The billet George, Brian and I shared was a wooden hut that housed ten soldiers, so there was ample space. We had a cupboard of our own and even a lock! Discipline was almost non-existent. Of course we had to dress properly, salute every officer in sight, and do guard duty, but the rest of the time was spent sitting in a classroom.

We were being trained to control army stores, from rifles, clothing, tanks, to boots and even socks. Day after day, we were at school. We were able to talk to a sergeant or corporal on normal terms without being shouted at. Brian and I found training fairly easy, the systems were elementary. George had more difficulty, but we spent time at night helping him to keep up. There were no tests or exams, and one or two were sent to other duties. Those remaining were destined to be army storekeepers somewhere in the world.

The enjoyable part of each day was after duty. The NAAFI was a huge brick building full of small tables surrounding two table-tennis tables, a couple of dart boards on one wall, and a piano in the corner. A huge counter stretched down one side of the building, with staff serving everything from tea, beer, cakes and sandwiches to hot meals. Anyone with the rank of sergeant or above was not allowed in the NAAFI under any circumstances.

Constant competitions were organised for darts and table tennis. With a regular 200 or so in the NAAFI every night, competition was fierce. I never liked darts, I enjoyed table tennis, but never won anything. George Sinclair was a natural table-tennis player. He was fast and aggressive and often won the money, which meant we had funds to buy a meal. We didn't need money for drink—that came free of charge.

I played the piano and most nights I was asked to accompany lads who fancied themselves as singers. After the song I was always rewarded with a free drink from the singer or his pals. I didn't drink very much, but George and Brian did their best to keep the stock of drinks down.

The army had a military band and a dance band. I was asked to join the dance band, which would have guaranteed I would stay at Bicester for the two years of military service. I declined—I hoped I would be posted nearer to home (Catterick or Brancepeth). What a mistake I made!

Part of the way through the course, I was told to report to a huge mansion situated about five miles away. My friends couldn't believe their eyes when I returned some days later with white epaulets on my shoulder, indicating I was suddenly an officer cadet. I couldn't comprehend that the army should consider me as a possible officer, but being an ex-student opened doors. I was still very much a private, took a lot of stick, but found it didn't affect friendships yet.

For a couple of weeks, back and forth I went for tests, lectures and assessments. Things were going well. I could see myself cutting the dash as an officer, hoping May would approve! During one interview I was instructed to sign a form, agreeing to stay in the army for six years' minimum.

'No thank you, Sir,' I said to the captain sitting opposite.

'It's the rule if you want to be an officer,' he replied. It was all over. White flashes were off, I took more stick than ever from the lads, and dreams of 'Jack the Lad' in officer's uniform were gone. No way did I want six years army service.

I took every opportunity to get a few days leave to see May. Never again did I go to sleep on the train. Our partings were becoming more and more sad.

I had been a soldier six months. We knew the time had arrived to be posted somewhere else. I hoped I would be sent north, George wanted Wales, and Brian naturally wanted to go to London. It would be the end of our friendship. The day before the posting lists were put up, the three of us were surprised to be instructed to have four inoculations. No one gave a reason.

It was a sad journey home on the train next day. I was going home to tell May the good news: I would be home for ten whole days. The bad news: I had to report back to Liverpool to board a ship for an unknown destination. If only I'd joined that army dance band!

That brief leave was bliss. May and I spent almost every moment together. Although we knew we'd be parted for a long time, we made certain it would be a happy holiday. To our great surprise, both our parents agreed to our going to Blackpool for a week. Nothing strange in that, you may think, but this was the 1940s, and we weren't even engaged! It was the happiest week of our lives.

Travelling home by train still didn't diminish our joy, even though we were silently counting the days. Sitting in front was a woman wearing a huge hat. Our bags in the rack above contained some cherries and juice was dripping relentlessly and staining her hat. We didn't dare own up to her! This incident helped to maintain our happiness for a little longer. We could only see the funny side, and it stopped us thinking of our parting.

Nevertheless, parting was inevitable. Having said goodbye to May's family and to my family, she and I had to part once again. Her tearful face, as we said goodbye at Durham station was the saddest sight I'd ever seen. We were too emotional to speak. Once this army service was over, we'd never part again.

5

POSTED ABROAD

I had never been to Liverpool and saw very little on this occasion. Stepping from the train, I saw a sign with instructions to report to a building at the end of the platform. On reporting to a warrant officer, I found myself on a lorry with other unhappy souls heading for the docks. We were directed to a huge building the size of an aircraft hanger. Once in, we weren't allowed out. Hundreds of camp beds were lined up, a canteen of sorts was provided, and here we were confined until 6a.m. the next morning.

The biggest ship I had ever seen loomed in front of me as I slowly shuffled in a very long queue, heading to the steps that would take us on board. I was loaded down with kitbag, full pack, and a rifle (no ammunition). There were hundreds of us boarding without a clue as to our destination. Officers were strutting around with their little sticks as if we were going to war. Did they know something we didn't? NCOs were yelling instructions to keep in line, keep quiet, and anything else to justify their rank. I kept my head down, followed the man in front, and kept quiet. Once up the steps and on deck, we weren't allowed to stop. We were directed down metal steps to a lower deck, then another, and another, and another until we were at the very bottom of the ship. If this ship sinks, we haven't a hope, I thought.

'David—over here!' A voice I recognised was yelling from somewhere on the deck. George and Brian had seen me in the queue behind them, and had kept me a hammock—yes, a hammock! Stretched end to end, virtually touching each other, this was to be our sleeping quarters for the next goodness-knows-how-long. The place was chaos, there was no air, the lighting was poor, and we were instructed to stay put until we sailed. Trying to climb into a hammock suspended from the ceiling would have been hilarious if it hadn't been so serious. This was to be my bed, and I couldn't even get into it!

As time went by, everyone became restless, arguments were erupting all over the deck, and clothing was discarded as the place became hotter. Like many on the deck, George, Brian and I joined a card school, and played pontoon for what seemed like hours. Suddenly a voice over the tannoy instructed us to form groups of four. Two stayed behind to watch the kit, and two went on to Deck 3 to have a meal. No one was allowed on the top deck—and fresh air. By the time we had all eaten and washed, it was well into the afternoon. We were all tired of being stuck on the lower deck when, without warning, engines started, the ship moved and in a short time we could feel we were at sea by the up and down motion of the ship.

I never saw Liverpool fade into the distance—that pleasure was for NCOs and officers. When we were well out to sea, we could move anywhere on the ship, except the engine room and crew quarters. This was no ferry; it was a massive ship with hundreds of troops on board. My first view of the sea was a shaker: we towered so high above the water, the ship was so big, the sea was so vast, and we were going up and down with such regularity, I already had a queer feeling in my stomach.

The canteen was huge, and all I could smell was boiled fish. The ship was ploughing through the water and I hadn't a clue whether we were going north, south, east or west. The hammock didn't have the pleasure of my body that night or the next! After a tea of boiled fish, peas and potatoes, I immediately felt sick. I had the choice of going down below with the crowd and a warm atmosphere, or up on deck with clean, fresh air, but bitterly cold, and so very near to that heaving water.

I opted for the deck. George brought me my greatcoat and blanket from my kitbag, and the deck was my bed for two nights. Even in early August, an open deck at sea is not very warm, but I was not alone. All over the deck bodies were lying, then suddenly rushing to the rail to be sick. Thank God I hadn't joined the navy!

'Make sure you eat something son,' an old navy man said the next morning as he went round the deck checking to see if we had survived the night. I couldn't face the cook house, but thankfully had two good friends who kept me supplied with bread and tea. George's description of the lovely kippers he had had for breakfast, nearly ended our friendship there and then.

The ship docked at Gibraltar on the morning of the third day, to take off a soldier with severe seasickness. I thought I was bad! We stopped moving for six hours—it was bliss. I actually felt much better, the stop must have rested my stomach, and I even began to feel hungry, and that night climbed into a hammock and slept like a baby!

The next three days were boring to the extreme. We had no information, nothing to do, but eat, sleep, play cards and go on to the deck to look over the side. If this was cruising, you could keep it. If only I had known what was to come, I would have enjoyed the ride when I had the chance.

After breakfast on days six and seven, we went almost all day standing in long queues on the top deck preparing for land. We were kitted out with tropical uniform, thin khaki shorts, shirts, trousers, etc. This time, great care was taken to ensure they fitted. Thank goodness we could wear some lightweight uniform, because the temperature was rising rapidly the further east we travelled.

An officer who queried our family background, education, and 100 other things, interviewed us individually. He particularly queried my reason for turning down officer training.

We were told we were heading for Egypt to join the MELF (Middle East Land Force). We would land at Port Said, then proceed to Tel-el-Kabir, which was a transit camp situated ten miles into the desert. After three or four weeks we would be posted to Aden, Palestine (now called Israel), Cyprus, or remain in Egypt. As a parting shot, the officer handed us badges to stitch on to our uniform to indicate we were part of a major land force. The badges had the picture of a camel with the letters MELF underneath. Very impressive. Until that point, my few months in the army hadn't been taken too seriously. Training had been tough, but after that it was almost like an extension to college. Now I was a member of a land force with an army brigade badge for instant identification. This was too much like wartime to me. I wasn't alone in my apprehension. Back on our deck everyone discussed where our posting was likely to be.

CAIRO, in Egypt, seemed to be the best posting. Although hot, there was no trouble.

ADEN was considered to be a hellhole, with temperatures over 120 degrees and a lot of trouble with terrorists.

PALESTINE—no one wanted Palestine. It was all-out war with terrorist gangs killing army personnel at every opportunity. They were fighting to get the British Army out, and declare Palestine a country exclusively for the Jewish people of the world.

CYPRUS—everyone wanted this posting to a so-called beautiful island off Palestine with no troubles and nothing to do, so everyone said!

You can't beat the army rumour machinery to know everything about everything, and usually miles wrong! I was still feeling anxious as to what was ahead when we docked in Port Said in Egypt, and were told to be ready for disembarkation in four hours.

Port Said was just like Liverpool, with high cranes and stacks of cargo everywhere, except that everyone was wearing long sheets, sandals and fez hats. Not a grain of sand to be seen. The noise was terrific. Little boats surrounded our ship; people were trying to sell rugs, trinkets and all manner of things, one shouting above the other. The most fascinating was small boys as young as ten years old diving into the water to retrieve a coin thrown from the ship. How they remained under the water for so long I don't know, but they always emerged holding the coin high to produce a round of applause from everyone watching.

Soon we were winding down the steps of the ship to a long line of lorries waiting to take us to the next stage of our journey. Rifle and kitbag by my side, I was driven with the rest of the draft in open-sided lorries through the maze of docks, past white-walled buildings, and in no time we were on an open road with nothing to see in every direction, but sand, sand and more sand! The heat was terrific; already we were soaked with sweat, and to our right, saw our first camel train in the distance. Occasionally an Arab rode past on a bicycle, but for a long time we trundled along in convoy over miles of sand.

Suddenly, from nowhere, a huge camp appeared. A high barbed wire perimeter fence enclosed 'Army Camp—Tel-el-Kabir'. Our lorry swept into the gate guarded by armed soldiers and we were instructed to jump out and line up on a parade ground marked in the sand by stones painted white. By the time every lorry had emptied and NCOs had checked their lists, we were thirsty, weary, and so very hot in the glaring sun. The heat was like an oven. Suddenly a command rang out:

'Attention!' A colonel stepped out on to a raised platform, and slowly swept his eyes over the whole parade, then nodded to the sergeant major who commanded:

'Stand easy.'

'Welcome to Tel-el-Kabir.' he spoke with a deep authoritative voice, then went on with a long, rehearsed speech, which basically said we would not be allowed out of the camp. We were here to get acclimatised to the heat before being posted elsewhere. There would be no square bashing, but we would get physical training, and take our turn at guard duty and cookhouse fatigues. It seemed we just had to sit out the next three or four weeks, then move on.

We came to attention as the colonel left the parade. The sergeant major told us to select a tent, dump our gear, hand our rifle into the armoury for safety, and go to the cookhouse for a meal.

'Before you go, the following will report to the company office immediately.' The sergeant major read out about twenty names and, to my utter amazement, mine was included. It could only be trouble. No one goes to a company office for good news, but I hadn't put a foot wrong since leaving England. George took my kit, promised to keep a space in his tent, and off I went to the 'office'. I later found George in the cookhouse, eating a plate of egg and chips.

'Well?' They both stared, waiting for an explanation. I didn't speak, but simply opened my hands to show the stripes of a lance corporal. Incredibly, I had been promoted. From now on I would be officially addressed as 'Lance Corporal'. Of course the comments and remarks of my friends were unprintable, because a 'Lance Jack', as he is known, is the least respected rank in the army. He is a dogsbody. Orders from officers are passed down from rank to rank, until the 'Lance Jack' carries it out. He has little authority, and soldiers take the mickey as often as they can get away with it.

I didn't care, I was quietly chuffed. It meant a few extra shillings in my wages and, you never knew, one stripe could lead to two, and I wouldn't be in the army long enough to get three, or so I thought. Being an ex-college student and my brief stay at an officer selection must have qualified me for promotion.

Tel-el-Kabir consisted of a cookhouse, NAAFI, armoury, company office, and rows of tents, with six people to a tent. No streets, paths or roads, just deep, soft sand that was so hot it was essential we always wore heavy army boots. It was an offence to allow your feet to become sunburnt in the desert. It was utterly boring and the heat was overpowering, but this was nothing compared to the flies—not the normal British housefly, but tiny pinhead-size midges. They got everywhere. There was no escape; you just had to learn to live with them. A close look at the sand revealed millions of these tiny insects. For the first few days, we were constantly shaking our clothing, hair and boots; eating was a chore: it took so long looking for flies. Slowly we became acclimatised to the heat, insects and boredom. We even developed energy to kick a ball around.

A number of authorised Arabs were allowed to roam the camp, picking up litter and doing odd jobs. For a couple of coins, they would do your washing. Free of charge, they would relieve you of anything if you were stupid enough to leave it lying around! Of course there was always someone bullying or shouting at these Arab labourers. One in particular made their lives miserable. He was a bully, racist, and a thug, but they got their own back in a horrendous way.

For toilets, we had to walk 200 yards to the far end of the camp. Occasionally, we ran! Flush toilets didn't exist. A hole the size of a room had been excavated out of the desert and cubicles created. Nothing could have been more primitive, and the smell of disinfectant took your breath away.

About midnight, a few days before our posting from Tel-el-Kabir, a piercing scream woke the whole camp. The Arabs had waited patiently for their worst tormentor to go to the toilet on his own, in the dark. How he was pulled out of that deep hole, what happened to him, and if he survived the horror, I don't know, but thinking about it makes me shudder. From then on, every Arab was treated with the greatest respect.

Four weeks to the day of arriving, news spread through the camp: 'Postings are on the notice board.' I was being posted to Palestine. Nearly everyone was posted to the place we all dreaded most. Some were instructed to report to Hebron, some to Jerusalem. Incredibly, George, Brian and I were in the group to report to Mount Carmel and Haifa.

We would travel by train from Egypt through the Sinai Desert to Haifa, and would depart by lorry to the nearest railhead at 8a.m. the next morning. A pack of food would be provided, rifle issued, with three clips of ammunition (18 bullets). We weren't allowed to tell anyone our destination, so my letters to May simply said we were moving to a new depot and I would write again when I could. Thankfully, her letters kept arriving regularly.

PALESTINE was a country controlled and occupied by British forces, and in the middle of an all-out war with two gangs of terrorists who were fighting for independence. One gang was called the Irgun, the other Haganah. If rumour was only half-right, they were utterly ruthless. Their aim was simple: to drive out all British troops and declare a state exclusively for Jewish people, and call it Israel. This was where I was heading, equipped with live ammunition for the first time in my life.

To reach the train, we had to cross the ferry over the Suez Canal. While disembarking, a voice behind me yelled:

'Stop that wog, he's pinched my rifle.' A young Arab was out of sight in a second. He had sliced through the rifle strap and was never seen again. The soldier was eventually court-marshalled—it is a very serious offence to lose a rifle in the army.

Eventually we boarded the train; it had wooden seats, wooden tables, wooden window shutters and no air conditioning. The heat was stifling, and every carriage was full of bodies and kit.

As a lance corporal, I was responsible for one carriage, so claimed a seat with my back to the engine. We had 24-hour rations, and a crate of oranges between fifteen. George, Brian and I had been split up, so everyone in the carriage was a stranger to me. By the end of this journey, we certainly knew each other! At the beginning, we played cards, looked at the landscape and were pleased we had no glass in the windows. The draught kept the temperature down—not that we were travelling very fast. It was an old steam engine that chugged along at about 20m.p.h.

After about three hours, we had passed through Egypt and began the journey through the Sinai Desert. The heat got worse, the seats got hard and everyone was getting bored. The only thing to see was sand and, occasionally, a camel train in the distance, who had no more interest in us than we had in them.

Travelling all day was bad enough, but at night-time things didn't improve because it turned very cold, and pulling the shutters down to stop the draught simply put us in total darkness. The breaking of dawn was the most beautiful sight I had ever seen: as the sun rose on the distant horizon the colour was breathtaking. By now our rations and oranges had all been devoured, water was getting low, and suddenly, out of nowhere, a town came into view: white-walled, ramshackle houses, crowds of Arabs and pandemonium as children ran alongside the train. Some tried to jump on and one or two even managed to climb on to the roof. The train shuddered to a halt at a so-called station, which consisted only of a raised platform. We had arrived at Gaza, our first stop. We had been in that travelling wooden box for almost 24 hours.

All NCOs were ordered off the train for instructions. I jumped out, and joined the circle round the company sergeant major.

'We leave here in two hours.' The CSM. wasn't one to waste time on long explanations! 'Half of each carriage out at one time,' he continued. 'Wash, shave, breakfast, collect rations, and NCOs will eat last'.

After my wash and shave on a makeshift bench that held bowls of cold water, I enjoyed the most delicious breakfast of bacon, eggs and beans provided by cooks from a field kitchen. How they organised such food in such a God-forsaken place, I will never know.

Throughout the stop at Gaza, the train was surrounded by hundreds of Arabs, some trying to sell, others to steal anything they could get their hands on. Most just stood and stared. There were women in long black robes behind their black veils—a detachment of military police kept them well away from the train. Even so, we all kept our eyes open. Surprisingly I never saw George or Brian during our stop, but with luck we would meet again at Haifa. Precisely two hours, and the train pulled out. We all felt clean, well-fed and in better spirits.

Another day and night was endured. With anticipation of another hot meal, we pulled into Lydda early next morning, to a repeat performance of the previous day, except that before we pulled out we were all paraded and addressed by the commanding officer. He informed us that within a few hours we would enter Palestine, next stop Haifa, and everyone would be on full alert because the terrorists would be well aware of our existence. Ominously, he said that if the train stopped and a whistle blew everyone would load a clip of ammunition into their rifles, and get under the train. To say we were no longer bored was a major understatement. We were convinced we were heading for World War Three, and feeling rather anxious! Soon the landscape changed from sand to lush green trees, orange groves, and a slightly cooler temperature.

The train now stopped at frequent intervals. The anticipated whistle never came, but we were all on full alert, and no mistake. Apparently a reinforced train had been placed in front of our train in case of a bomb on the line, and as we came into any village a platoon was sent ahead to check out a possible attack by terrorists. So it was with a lot of relief we pulled into a large station, Haifa, our final destination.

The first one I saw as we lined up was George Sinclair, but we couldn't speak on parade.

'There are lorries to take you to your depot,' the CSM shouted. I was going to Mount Carmel, others to Jerusalem, Tel Aviv and Nazareth.

'If you hear rifle fire, get down on the floor of your lorry.' At that moment a terrific bang went off. We all jumped two feet in the air. The CSM didn't bat an eyelid. 'Don't worry, that bomb's half a mile away.'

I was suddenly rather scared, and not looking forward to my stay in Palestine.

'By the way,' the CSM concluded, 'keep away from any black huts. There's an epidemic of cholera and people bring their dead each morning.' On the way to Mount Carmel, we heard rifle fire, but it seemed a long way away. No one said very much, we were almost in a state of shock, and far from happy. I'm sure I'd read something in the Bible about Mount Carmel when I went to Sunday school, but I guess the place had changed slightly.

The sheer joy of being in a hut with electric light, a bed and cupboard, bath with hot water, even chairs to sit on, was luxury beyond dreams. Since leaving England nearly two months ago, I had slept in a hammock, in a tent, or on a train.

Mount Carmel was a strict regimental depot on 24-hour alert. No slouching around in this place. You marched, saluted every officer in sight, and under no conditions were you allowed past the armed guard at the gate. Everything was painted white, even the stones lining the main entry road. The cookhouse was huge and clean, with a great menu. The NAAFI was like a club, and the view over Haifa harbour was magnificent. We new arrivals were easily identified. We jumped with alarm at every explosion (about twice every hour). The regulars ignored them and gave us a supercilious smirk.

New arrivals were ordered to parade at 0900 hours the next morning. To our great surprise, twenty of us were dismissed from the parade ground and ordered to report to a nearby lecture hall. Our party consisted of a sergeant, corporal, seventeen privates, and myself. Amazingly George and Brian were in the same group. We were all apprehensive—was this some special job we were going to, would we be sent somewhere else, and would it be dangerous?

All these thoughts were in our minds, when suddenly the door swept open and a colonel marched in. We all jumped to attention until ordered to sit down.

'Gentlemen, you are going to Cyprus in a few weeks' time.' The colonel's opening comment was like getting all our Christmases in one day! Everyone wanted to go to Cyprus. No trouble, no terrorists, a real cushy posting!

'You are all going to a high-profile job that is bound to attract a great deal of world attention. You have a lot to learn in a short time. The task ahead is of vital importance.' The staff sergeant, a pleasant and relaxed man of about 30 years old, put us at our ease but heightened our curiosity beyond all bounds. His explanation began during World War Two that had ended a few months earlier.

Throughout the war, the Germans had ruthlessly imprisoned hundreds of thousands of Jewish families in concentration camps at Auschwitz, Dachau and other sites in Europe, then systematically eliminated them in what became known as the 'holocaust'. The war ended, and survivors of these camps, who had seen unspeakable horrors, now found themselves free, with no food, no clothing, and no home—absolutely nothing. They made their way to the south of France, boarded any ship that would take them slowly across the Mediterranean to Palestine—their 'Promised Land'. It would take many weeks for these vessels to make the journey. Little did they know that a decision had already been made by Ernest Bevin, the British Foreign Secretary, that the boats would be diverted to Cyprus and the survivors would be held there until the terrorists in Palestine had been defeated. (This was very heavy stuff—way above my head. Where would I fit into this scenario?)

'You will be employed in stores, supplying clothing, etc. to the Jewish survivors after they have been put into camps.' The staff sergeant had answered my silent question. Now we realised that all our training in England had been for a specific job: to supply Jewish concentration camp survivors with supplies of every kind. The staff sergeant went on to explain that these camps had already been built, stores were already in operation, and in fact a few Jews had already trickled into the island, but a huge influx was expected within weeks.

Already newspapers were taking up the story, and terrorists in Palestine were increasing their dire threats against British troops. Our joy at being sent to Cyprus was dampened by the explanation for our being there. Before going to Cyprus we were given more detailed training on specific stores, for example, shoe sizes, types of dresses to issue to young girls and older ladies, clothing for babies, and many other details.

In addition, we had to go out on mobile patrol in Palestine to become 'acclimatised'. These were not pleasant excursions. Day and night patrols toured Haifa, Jerusalem, Nazareth, and all areas of Palestine looking for Jewish terrorists. Each jeep carried a driver and three soldiers all armed with live ammunition. I did the tour three times with very experienced soldiers who had done the same job for months. To my intense relief we had no trouble, and no incidents, returning to Mount Carmel barracks in one piece. Mentally I was a bundle of nerves, but considered myself lucky. Both George and Brian were involved in minor incidents, with guns being fired but no one hurt. They were both in a much worse state than I was on their return. We couldn't wait to leave for Cyprus. Each day we became more accustomed to gunfire and the crunch of explosions, yet not once did I feel in real danger. It always seemed far away down below in the town of Haifa.

At last the order came to report with full kit to Haifa harbour, then go by boat to the port of Famagusta on the east coast of Cyprus. I was pleased to see Haifa fade in the distance, with its atmosphere of tension and violence. I hoped I would never see the place again (but I did—twice!).

The boat was small, nothing more than a ferry that bobbed up and down in a rough Mediterranean Sea. I wasn't seasick, and almost enjoyed the cooling breeze, looking ahead expectantly for the sight of an island. We were all animated and so pleased to be moving further and further from Palestine. Cyprus could only be better—so we thought! Finally someone shouted: 'I can see land,' and sure enough, Cyprus came into view. Within a short time we were tied up on the quayside. Famagusta was to be my home until March 1948. All the training, all the travelling had been for one purpose: I was to do my army service here on a small island in the Mediterranean Sea.

George Sinclair, Brian Ferris and me, 1946

Lt. Lambert, Sgt. Tasker and me, 1946

Depot football team, 1946

Famagusta, 1946

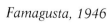

6

CYPRUS – HOLOCAUST SURVIVORS

My first impression of Famagusta was very favourable. The heat was intense, but the sea breeze made it bearable. The whiteness of the buildings, the masses of palm trees, and the friendliness of the people struck me. An air of calm tranquillity was in direct contrast to the country I had just left. As months went by, I saw acres of orange groves, lemons, grapes, pomegranates and melons. The island was a paradise of beauty, with ancient ruins dating back long before the birth of Jesus. How sad that my most vivid memory in future years would be not of beauty and tranquillity, but of misery, violence and hatred.

I'm getting way ahead of my story! I had just landed and was heading by lorry to the RAOC depot, Famagusta—my home for the rest of my army service. The depot was about two miles outside the town on the main Salamas Road. It covered about six acres of land and was surrounded by a 10-feet-high fence, topped with barbed wire. There was only one entrance, permanently guarded by armed soldiers. In addition, every inch of the perimeter fence was patrolled day and night by more armed guards. Tranquillity there might be, but no chances were being taken!

Inside the depot were two distinct areas—the military zone where civilian labourers were forbidden to enter on penalty of immediate dismissal. The other zone was free for civilians to work. This area comprised six huge aircraft-hangar-type buildings full of stores of every description, and a sewing area where about 50 women sat all day long making tents, mosquito nets and a variety of civilian clothes. A total of 200 civilian labourers were recruited from Famagusta and nearby villages.

The military zone was concentrated under the shade of masses of trees. It was never under the full glare of the sun, and approximately 100 troops were housed in tents set out in four long rows, four to a tent. There were four sergeants housed in the quietest corner of the depot. No one below the rank of sergeant was allowed anywhere near. The commanding officer and his second in command were billeted in a house outside the depot, near Famagusta. An armoury, vehicle section, cookhouse, NAAFI and admin offices completed the military zone.

We drove past an armed guard on the main gate and jumped out of the lorry as it halted at the guardhouse. After our identity was checked by the guard commander, we were ordered to take over the vacant tents, so George, Brian and I made sure we were together and were joined by a pleasant West Countryman called Tony Adamson. There was ample room, the camp beds were clean and comfortable, and a tall locker with a key was a reassuring piece of furniture. The floor was of wood and—surprise, surprise—we had an electric light, and even a plug with an electric iron: luxury indeed!

We were shaded from the sun and only a few yards from the wash-house, cookhouse and NAAFI. After storing our kit and getting cleaned up, we strolled around the camp before our main meal. 'I think I might like it here,' George Sinclair said as we looked inside the NAAFI to see table tennis, darts and an old upright piano in the corner! We were amazed at the lack of military pomp about the place. We saw neither officers nor sergeants and soldiers walked casually with open neck shirts, some even with their hands in their pockets. Every day began at 8a.m. with a parade of all personnel, except those on guard duty. We had already washed, dressed and had breakfast. After parade we began our particular duties, which continued until 5p.m., with breaks for tea and lunch. It was virtually a 9-to-5 job, with Saturday and Sunday off.

Our first morning parade was to be pure formality, like every parade that followed throughout my stay in Cyprus. We all lined up, sergeants at the front and corporals at the rear. The duty sergeant shouted 'Attention', at which precise time the commanding officer, Captain Anderson, followed by his second in command, 2nd Lieutenant Lambert, came out of the company office, accepted the duty sergeant's confirmation: 'All present and correct, Sir,' slowly walked down each rank without comment, then spoke four words:

'Dismiss the men, Sergeant'.

'Parade dismiss!' It was over in minutes.

My first job was responsibility for the armoury. I was replacing a corporal who had been transferred to HQ Nicosia. I had three days to learn the job, with the help of four private soldiers. Civilians weren't allowed in the armoury. It was a very simple job, issuing arms to the duty guard three times a day, collecting them back, and oiling and cleaning every item. In addition to rifles, there were mortars, sten guns, grenades and a couple of field guns with thousands of rounds of ammunition. The biggest problem was the need to report daily to the duty sergeant that everything was correct, which required a daily stock check. If anything was missing I could be court-marshalled. Was one stripe worth such a responsibility? So long as I ensured checking in and out was done correctly, there was no problem. If the stock check wasn't properly done, I nearly had a heart attack, and we all worked late until the error was rectified!

Brian had been allocated a job in the company office, possibly because he could type. He was very happy! George was sent to the motor pool. He couldn't drive, hadn't a clue about engines and, being the only black man in the depot, needed a thick skin to ride the abuse. However, at the end of each day, we had plenty of time for relaxation. A good wash, change of uniform, an evening meal, then most nights in the NAAFI. We hadn't much money, but I spent hours at the piano, and George taught me to a high standard of table tennis. Every night part of my time was taken up writing to May, much to the ribbing of friends. She wrote to me every day, and every one of our letters seemed to be bringing us closer together. She seemed so far away.

The depot had a football team that played against other army and civilian teams throughout the island. After a few weeks, George and I worked our way into the team, which was great for filling in our Saturday afternoons. We were allowed out of the depot on a Saturday night, dressed in a clean uniform with very little money, but pleased to get out.

'Famagusta, here we come!' It was a small town with one cinema, two nightclubs and dozens of small cafes with different Greek music blaring out of each one, but it was lively, and we were out! The cinema was an outdoor screen, Greek film with English sub-titles, so we soon lost interest. The nightclubs were way out of our price range, and it was obvious we were not welcome with our meagre earnings. So it was a walk out and a meal in one of the cafes. George and Brian would try any foreign dish; my favourite was pork chop and egg omelette! Cyprus was very religious. Women walked behind the men, girls never ever walked out on their own and soldiers were forbidden to fraternise. Even so we found it a friendly town and it was our regular Saturday night out.

There is one word to describe Sunday: boring. Nothing to do and nowhere to go. I wrote back to college in England and did some correspondence courses on Sunday. The lads thought I was mad!

Tension was beginning to mount on the island, press stories indicated that an armada of small boats was nearing Cyprus. Two destroyers stationed outside Haifa would divert the boats to Famagusta; everyone was expecting terrorist activity to spread to Cyprus.

'Have you seen today's orders?' one of the lads said on my way to breakfast. I quickly walked down to the office to see the notice board. Maybe I had been posted back to England. No such luck, but surprise, surprise, I had been promoted to full corporal and transferred to civilian stores that would supply the camps. There was no mention of George or Brian being promoted, but I would get more money, more responsibility and, although I would still billet and eat with the lads, army discipline demanded that from now on I would always be addressed as Corporal when on duty. Thank goodness it didn't effect my friendship with George or Brian.

The next day I reported to Sergeant Tasker, in charge of civilian stores. With ten privates and 50 civilian labourers, we were responsible for six huge stores that had blankets, towels, clothing of every description, footwear of every type and size, plus hundreds of other items that destitute people would require.

As a full corporal I was much more responsible, so was more involved in the depot activities and really enjoying it. Ships were arriving every day with more and more stores—they must have been expecting a lot of Jews. You could feel the tension rising as the day drew near for the first ship to arrive. Even the Cypriots seemed less friendly, and every day a civilian was dismissed for stealing from the stores.

A couple of days before the ship carrying survivors was due, Sergeant Tasker and I went by jeep to the camps to plan deliveries.

'My God, fancy being put in here after surviving the concentration camps,' the sergeant whispered to me as we were stopped by an armed soldier of the King's Regiment who checked our identity cards. The place was like a fortress, armed troops were everywhere, and barbed wire topped a huge perimeter fence with observation towers erected at strategic points. It was just like the prisoner of war camps we saw in old war films. Inside the fence was a long Nissen hut near the gate where new arrivals would be searched. A cookhouse, toilets and wash-house were the only wooden buildings; the remaining space was covered with hundreds and hundreds of tents.

If all these tents were to be full, I could see nothing but chaos, unless a full regiment of armed soldiers was to be kept busy. The whole place had the atmosphere of depression, yet it was still empty.

Having established with the camp quartermaster the procedures for delivery, the sergeant and I were pleased to travel the four miles down the coast back to the relative comfort of our own depot and prepare our own procedures. When the first ship had docked we would need to go on board, quickly calculate the number of men, women and children, then return to the stores where civilian labourers would load the lorries without delay and get the required stores to the camps.

Army top brass were constantly visiting the depot to see if we were prepared, every news bulletin was listened to intently, and it was almost with relief that I was ordered to accompany a sergeant and lieutenant at 7a.m. the next morning to the dockside.

I was amazed to see soldiers patrolling the road long before we reached Famagusta Harbour. We passed through at least three checkpoints and drove to the quayside to see an armed fortress. The whole King's Regiment and dozens of military police were on duty with enough military power to start World War Three!

'I don't like the look of this,' I said.

'Let's hope we can dive for cover if anything blows up with the terrorists,' the sergeant replied. Everyone was on full alert. It seemed incredible that we were all waiting for destitute Jewish survivors, although the armed troops were prepared for Jewish terrorists.

'We have an hour to wait,' the officer informed us as he slumped down on the back seat of the jeep. 'After the boat has docked, it will be checked for security before we are allowed on board,' he continued.

'I don't think only three of us can get accurate lists in a short time,' the sergeant said, turning his head.

'Don't worry,' he answered. 'Make sure you are on the high side of counting, because they reckon there could be 50 boats heading our way.' As a lowly corporal, I kept out of the conversation, but I was conscious that some major incident was happening, and I was a tiny part of it. This might be a day to remember, and I hadn't a clue what to expect.

Nothing and no one could have prepared us for the scene that has stayed with me forever. Even writing about it more than 50 years later has my heart pounding.

It was a rusty, broken down ferryboat, not fit to cross the River Wear, never mind hundreds of miles across the Mediterranean. Half a dozen soldiers had spent ages checking every nook and cranny for arms and we couldn't understand why they were shaking their heads as they came off and declared the boat clear for us to do a head-count. I don't know why I expected it, but I thought we would see people pleased to reach land after weeks at sea, and happy to meet people who would clothe, feed and care for them after years of horror in concentration camps.

How stupid and naïve I was! My first shock was to see children, boys and girls of various ages. For some reason I had expected to see only adults, even though we had a section of stores exclusive to children. My second shock was the sight before my eyes. Nothing had prepared me for the image of poverty, starvation and sheer misery. Every single person was covered in rags; one or two still wore the striped uniform of the concentration camps. Their clothes were simply covering skin and bone. The faces were all long, gaunt, and oh so miserable. I had never seen so much misery in my life. No one smiled, spoke or moved. There was total silence. Moving about the boat, it seemed as if we were intruding on the collective misery.

My third shock was the overpowering and all-pervasive smell. A strong horrible scent of dirt and death. (I had only ever seen one dead person: my Aunt Hilda died when I was a teenager.) On this boat about ten people had died on the journey, but had still been brought to the 'Promised Land'. To the people on board, poverty, starvation and death was part of their existence. Incredibly, they were used to it. Their anger and disappointment at being refused entry to Palestine had now subsided to utter dejection at being forced to yet another camp, armed soldiers, and barbed wire.

To me this was utter cruelty. We had fought a war to rid the world of camps, yet Britain was putting these poor souls back into captivity. It was beyond my understanding. In almost a daze, we made our way, stepping over people, counting as best we could and estimating the numbers of men, women and children. Occasionally a head would lift, and eyes showing pure hatred silently stared. We reached the end, turning to meet the lieutenant, and were shocked to see him bending over a man and holding his hand. Tears were streaming down the lieutenant's face. The man had just died; no one near him had moved a muscle. The journey back to the depot was in total silence. It was very difficult to absorb what we had just seen.

However, we did our job, requisitioned the stores, organised loading and delivery. I then had the longest, hottest bath I had ever had, changed into clean clothes, but could never get rid of that smell or scene of misery that will stay with me forever. The next few weeks saw the arrival of boats of all shapes and sizes. In all, about 30,000 Jews eventually arrived, but the atmosphere in the camps changed dramatically in weeks to come.

Although I was fully occupied, I was able to get the occasional game of football on a Saturday with George Sinclair. We had a reasonable team: I played on the left wing and usually got hacked to bits! On the island was a German prisoner-of-war camp, with about 1,000 prisoners waiting to be repatriated. Every so often, we played against them. It was usually a good afternoon out, although the crowd watching were all Germans shouting for us to get beaten! For obvious reasons, the game was played inside the camp; the German team never had an away-game!

Tom Cunningham, our left full-back, was the oldest man in the team. A regular soldier, he had already spent years in the army and had fought throughout the war in Europe. To see a German was like a red rag to a bull! He was a hard man who tackled the players with venom. To him, the war was still on, and he tackled the German players as if it was a battle zone. We lost count of the times he was sent off. After the game, the Germans provided a good tea (they seemed to eat better than we did), but Tom absolutely refused their hospitality and sat in the lorry. He hated Germans so much, and only played in order to get a crack at them!

Throughout my army service, May and I wrote to each other every day. No matter how busy, I made time to write a letter to tell her of the day's news. We never actually mentioned getting married, but I think we both assumed that one day we would. In one of my letters, I was writing about how I longed for my first leave, even though it was still a long way off. I said it would be lovely to get married, and to my utter delight she agreed. We would be married sometime in September 1947 if I got leave on time. That night George, Brian and I went to the NAAFI to celebrate. The party got bigger and bigger as the night wore on, until twenty of us were thrown out near midnight by the duty sergeant, although he was quite understanding when told the reason for the celebration.· He even wished me good luck and I was absolutely broke for the next fortnight.

My other celebration was on 19 December 1946 when I was 21 years old. The three of us had saved up to treat ourselves to a visit to one of the nightclubs in Famagusta. We had a great night, a terrific meal that cost a bomb, and a good cabaret with plenty of plate-smashing completed the evening. To help the celebration, many of the Cypriots sent us drinks when they learned I was 21 years old and consequently this was one of the few occasions in my life I was drunk.

When I had been overseas for six months, one particular morning started as usual. There were no ships that day, we mainly did stock checking. I had my usual mid-morning cup of tea, and at lunchtime I decided to read the orders of the day on my way to the cookhouse.

I don't remember eating lunch that day. I don't very much remember anything of the remainder of the day. I do know that I read that notice with disbelief. My life would never be the same again. An army friend would ignore me, and I would be subjected to violence as a consequence of seeing my name on company orders: 14113685 Sgt. Hughes D—I had been promoted from the following morning.

To say I was surprised is a major understatement. I had arrived in Egypt as a private soldier and in only six months I was now a sergeant. In our depot, there were only four sergeants and they were top dogs: one in charge of stores, another transport, then security, and, finally, external liaison.

The two officers in the depot handled administration; consequently a sergeant in charge of, say, stores, had authority over everything and everyone in his section, and demanded absolute acceptance of his instructions. It put the sergeant in an incredible position of authority; even the officers were dependent on the four sergeants for the smooth and efficient control of the depot. Every fourth day a different sergeant took over as depot duty sergeant: he took morning parade, inspected the guard three times a day and was responsible for camp discipline. I was replacing the sergeant in charge of external liaison who was due for demob, and had one week to show me the ropes before leaving Cyprus for good.

Brian was very pleased, and congratulated me on my promotion. George simply said: 'Well done, Sergeant', and emphasised the word 'Sergeant'. The three of us had spent almost a year together, but no longer would we billet together in a tent, eat together in the cookhouse or socialise on a Saturday night. Sergeants and other ranks did not get together in the army. George knew this, and seemed to have an immediate animosity towards me and would never again show a hint of our close friendship, but I felt it was his problem—not mine.

The extra pay would be a godsend seeing May and I would soon be married. The extra perks of being a sergeant would be beyond my wildest dreams. I hardly slept that night. The atmosphere in our tent with George was not good. I still couldn't believe that tomorrow I would have the highest NCO rank in the depot. I had always looked at sergeants as unapproachable, as men who issued orders for others to carry out. Tomorrow I would be one of them!

Next morning, I collected the sets of sergeant's stripes for my uniform, shirts, etc., and carried all my gear to the sergeants' quarters, a large white-walled house set in a quiet corner of the depot surrounded by a garden full of flowers, and one wall completely covered by a grapevine. Four steps up to the front door, a big entrance hall, and a smiling Sergeant Tasker with outstretched hand welcomed me and invited me to join them for breakfast.

Having worked together, I knew Sergeant Tasker. We got on well. The other faces were familiar, but almost unknown. I was made incredibly welcome. They were all seated at a large table, and a place was already set for me. I couldn't believe what I was seeing. A spotless white tablecloth, linen serviettes, and a Cypriot waiter enquiring if I wanted a full English breakfast or continental. I requested an English breakfast, because I didn't know what a continental breakfast was! He brought me the best-cooked breakfast I had ever seen. Orange juice, fresh fruit and all the tea I could drink, and I didn't lift a finger. It was like being in a four-star hotel—and this was just breakfast. Already my regret at leaving George and Brian was fading. It was hard to believe we were in the same depot.

The four sergeants had a cook, a waiter who did our washing and ironing, and a cleaner who kept the whole house clean and tended the garden. To say sergeants were pampered was an understatement, and other ranks in the depot hadn't a clue.

After breakfast, I was shown to my own room, which had a bed, cupboard, huge armchair and a desk in one corner, and even curtains at the window. This was luxury I didn't know existed in the army. My meals would always be on time, well cooked, with a wide menu. My uniform would be fresh, clean and immaculately ironed every day. My room would always be clean and every request provided. The army provided all of this free of charge in return for my acceptance of huge responsibility for men, army property and security. I was only 21 years old and hoped I would be able to do the job.

'Sergeant in charge of external liaison' was a job I knew nothing about. In fact very few in the depot knew of its existence. I had an office, ten staff and a jeep with a driver. The Signals Regiment was based on the Troodos Mountains, German POWs were guarded by the King's Regiment at Dhekelia, the island HQ was at Nicosia, and about 20 other units were scattered about the island. They all required stores of every description. My job was to liaise between every unit and our depot, establish their requirements and arrange delivery.

The phones rang constantly. The staff I had were terrific. They knew exactly what to do and hardly needed me, but the army system required a sergeant in charge, and I wasn't complaining! It was necessary the commanding officer of each unit knew the liaison sergeant, consequently about once a month I made a tour. This was long before tourists visited the island, and I saw Cyprus as it had been for centuries. Very primitive villages, all with the inevitable coffee shop, where men sat for hours drinking harsh black coffee, smoking vile smelling cigarettes and endlessly gossiping, but always friendly. Acres of orange groves, lemons, melons, pomegranates, sweet seedless grapes and old ruins scattered throughout the island. It was beautiful. I had a jeep and was being driven around almost at my leisure. I didn't like the army, I didn't like being away from May, but I'd landed a job in a million, and hoped it would last until my demob. However, the other part of the job was less enjoyable (there's always a snag). A separate section arranged routine supplies to the Jewish camps, but supplies to the King's Regiment (who guarded the Jews) was my responsibility which required me to visit the camps on a regular basis.

Jews were still arriving by the boatload, and I was now seeing them in a different light. Once behind the high barbed-wire gate no Jews were allowed out. Armed guards toured the perimeter fence day and night, and huge lights ensured darkness never descended on the camp. Each camp housed hundreds of Jews, many of whom had now been there several weeks, and were well fed, well dressed, and no longer the cowed, depressed, and miserable people I had seen on their arrival on the island.

Now they were organised behind barbed wire. Children sat in groups being taught lessons. Keep-fit classes, sewing sections, and a host of well-organised activities kept everyone busy and apparently happy. More sinister was the matching and training, constantly going on between the young male Jews. These were terrorists in the making and the army didn't interfere. There was now a growing confidence, a continued hostility, and a feeling that they were watching us as much as we watched them. Although their activity created a contented image, the atmosphere was tense and hostile. I never enjoyed going to the camps. It had been agreed to supply the women with rolls of material to make their own dresses. As I was already going to the camp, I was asked to arrange hand-over of six sewing machines being delivered on a lorry.

Our lorry had backed into one of the camps, the machines were being unloaded, everyone was happy, quite friendly, and they seemed to be pleased to be getting the machines. Suddenly a horrendous scream rang out, followed by two rifle shots. Yells and screams were followed by deathly silence, and in seconds the two soldiers and I were bundled out of the camp by armed soldiers and the guard round the camp was immediately trebled.

I was stunned and shaken. Everything had happened so quickly, but this was routine to the King's Regiment: they had to deal with regular incidents, and hostility was just below the surface. However, this incident was more serious. One of the guards had gone too near the fence and a Jew stabbed him with a steel tent peg, and disappeared back into the crowd.

One other task I had to perform was in the camp's arrival hut. New arrivals had to pass down a long table where their meagre belongings were examined, their clothing searched, and a sergeant of the King's Regiment had to decide if they had anything to be confiscated. One day when I was due to visit the arrival hut to process another boatload of Jews, tension on the island was high, because terrorism on the mainland of Palestine had escalated. The King David Hotel had been blown up, two sergeants had been hanged from lampposts in Tel Aviv, and terrorists were fully expected to try to land in Cyprus.

After the four-mile ride to Salamis Camp, the slow procession of new arrivals was going through the search when one of the military police was handed a crude tin cigarette case, with a map of Cyprus scratched on the back, indicating the main towns and ports. Without hesitation, he said: 'Confiscate it.' I knew no more until I opened my eyes, lying on my stomach on a bed in Nicosia Hospital.

On being deprived of his cigarette case, the Jew, in anger, had dived for a rifle leaning at the side of the hut. He swung it in an arc, and I was exactly in the way, and was knocked out cold with the butt-end of the rifle. A bruise the size of a dinner plate had my back very sore. Nothing was broken, and I was soon back at the depot, sadder and wiser.

I knew May would have enough to worry about reading about the bombing and killing, so my next letter simply said I had a bad back—only too true!

Civilian foreman and me, outside camp

7

MARRIED

My leave was now only weeks away; all letters from May were full of plans for our wedding—she seemed pleased to be doing all the arranging. The only thing we couldn't plan was the actual date, but September seemed a certainty. Suddenly, I caught dysentery and was ill for almost a month. I became very weak and lost a lot of weight. It's a miserable complaint, and only time seems to clear up the problem. I was beginning to worry in case I was too ill to travel. However, by the time my leave was due, I was able to plan my departure.

I was surprised that no new sergeant had been promoted to replace me. I only had six months left to do and there was no way the army would send me all the way back to Cyprus. Still, my replacement wasn't my problem, and I was quite happy to say goodbye to everyone, board the ferry back to Palestine and begin that unbearable journey across the Sinai Desert. I felt a great deal happier going home, because now special food and accommodation were provided for officers and senior NCOs. I even shared a cabin on the ship with a sergeant travelling from India. It was luxury compared to my journey out as a private soldier.

The ship docked at Liverpool at dawn on a lovely August morning. I received my travel warrant and reporting instructions and was surprised to see I had to report back to Liverpool in four weeks' time. I didn't query this as I just wanted to get back home. So I collected my kit bag and on the way to the train took time to send May a telegram to say I was on my way home. The train to Durham was packed, and I spent the whole journey sitting on my kit bag in the corridor. There was no buffet or refreshments, the train seemed to be crawling and stopping at every station, but I didn't care. I was too excited. Every minute took me nearer to May.

It was a lovely summer's day, but I felt cold, compared to the heat of the Middle East. The English countryside flashing past was beautiful, then the best sight in the world loomed out of the window—I could see Durham Cathedral! It was late at night, no buses, and too far to walk, so I shared a taxi with a soldier who lived at Fence Houses, and in no time I was home.

May and I spent almost every moment together. I had missed her so much and it seemed I had been away a long, long time. The wedding was arranged for the following week and we weren't even engaged, so we went to Sunderland and bought engagement and wedding rings at the same time. We took a bus to Seaburn, walked along the seafront, and I asked her to marry me. She said yes, and slipped on the engagement ring. It was the happiest day of my life (and now, 50 years later we still enjoy our walk along Seaburn seafront).

I know my father and mother had been as worried as May with news from the Middle East, and I'm sure they were shocked at my loss of weight but this was all forgotten at 3p.m. on Wednesday, 3 September 1947—our wedding day.

It was an unforgettable day. Clothing coupons and food rationing were still in operation, yet May was beautiful in her wedding dress with lovely bridesmaids. Her mother provided a fabulous meal. My brother Ted was best man and the whole family turned out to help make it a fabulous wedding day.

My Aunt Nora and family who lived in Taunton in Somerset invited us there for our honeymoon. It was delightful. We were young, very much in love, and dreading it to end, knowing we must part once again. The four weeks' leave seemed to fly over. I could easily have deserted the army and stayed at home with May but, inevitably, May and I once again had a tearful goodbye at Durham Station. One consolation was the almost certainty that I would be stationed in England and, with luck, May could live in married quarters (a perk of being a sergeant).

I returned my travel warrant to the transport officer as soon as I arrived in Liverpool and enquired as to my next destination.

'Sir, I've only six months to do,' I responded to his instruction to board a ship and return to Cyprus.

'Take it up with your depot commander when you return,' he replied. 'The ship leaves at midnight. Be on it, Sergeant,' he ended my interview.

I was devastated. With only six months' army service remaining, I couldn't believe I was going all that way back.

I had arranged to phone May in a phone box at 9p.m. to tell her my destination. I didn't know how to break the news that it would be another six months before we'd see each other again. The call was more tears than conversation, promises to continue writing to each other was little consolation—I hated the army.

Our wedding day: 3 September 1947

8

BACK TO CYPRUS

Three weeks later, I reported back for duty at the depot in Famagusta. Everyone was surprised to see me return, except the depot commander. He had known all along that I was returning and hadn't said a word. I could have killed him.

Nothing had changed. Some new recruits had replaced people on demob. Jews were still landing at regular intervals. George Sinclair and Brian Ferris were still privates, and kept their distance because of my three stripes. My duties now concentrated on the camps; someone else travelled the island, supplying army depots. About 30,000 Jews filled the camps and an overflow camp was being built at Larnaca. The main camp stretched for miles on the road between Famagusta and the ruins of Salamis.

The Jews had segregated themselves into camps of different nationalities (Poles, French, Italians etc.) Many attempts at breakout were being made, and it was a daily routine for an alert to sound. These were all survivors of the holocaust, but my sympathy, like everyone else's, was wearing thin. We were doing all we could, but the hostility was overbearing, hatred was everywhere, we could do nothing right.

Thankfully, we still had time for weekend football. Rank didn't matter: if you were good enough, you played! We had one officer in the team, two corporals, myself, and the rest of the team were privates (including George Sinclair). There were only three army teams on the island, and dozens of civilian teams that played in a league. The army top brass thought it would be a good idea for an army team to play a representative civilian team to help public relations. I was one of four from our depot instructed to play for the army. We travelled by jeep to Nicosia assuming it was just another game of football. There seemed to be lots of people making their way to the stadium, and we didn't think much about it until we arrived to see queues actually paying money to get in. Maybe there was some big match on and we were the warm-up entertainment?

We *were* the big match!

Apparently the Cypriots had been advertising the game throughout Nicosia as an England v. Cyprus representative match. We had never played together, we didn't even know each other's names, and in that stadium were hundreds of spectators who had paid money to see us get hammered. I had a feeling they wouldn't be disappointed!

Before the kick-off, the island commanding officer came to wish us well—the clown! It had been his idea and he hadn't a clue as to how we were all feeling. I played at outside-left, hardly got a kick of the ball and I was clattered to the ground by a half-back twice my size every time the ball came my way. We were hammered and went into the dressing room with a score of 4—0 at half-time. It could easily have been 40, we were like lambs to the slaughter and ended the game 7—1 simply because we got a penalty. I had never been so pleased to leave a football ground. I was black and blue, and sick as a parrot!

However, the crowd was happy—they had just beaten England. We never saw the commanding officer and I hope he was feeling stupid for arranging such a farce. The four of us were only too pleased to get back to our depot in Famagusta.

I was now counting the days to demob. Every job was a chore, every Jew a nuisance, and every problem a potential delay to my demob. The United Nations was now involved trying to solve the Jewish problem. Tension was reducing, because a monthly quota of 1,500 Jews were now allowed to leave the camp and enter Palestine. I was simply going through the motions of being a soldier when, out of the blue, my whole cosy plan collapsed.

I had just returned from Larnaca camp, making my way up the steps into the sergeants' mess, when I sank to my knees with the most excruciating pain in my back. A soldier, seeing me in trouble, sent for the doctor who had me in an ambulance and on my way to Nicosia hospital. The pain got no less, and the doctor's prodding and probing did not help. However, he considered a lumbar puncture was required. I hadn't a clue what he was talking about, and was exhausted with the continuous pain.

Within half an hour, a medical orderly came breezing in with the comment: 'Get on your side, mate, this will cure your bad back.' He then proceeded to insert a huge needle into the base of my spine. I don't think I made a sound, but I felt my whole body scream with the agony of that needle. I had never known such pain. I was in a daze with shock, and could only lie there exhausted, demoralised, and feeling very sorry for myself. To my relief the pain subsided within a few days, and I returned to duty feeling fragile, but pleased to be told: 'It's only a bad back.'

Little did I know that 'just a bad back' would later be diagnosed as spondylitis and would trouble me for the rest of my life. For now, I was happy: the pain had gone, I was back on duty, and counting the days.

A dramatic development caused major concern. By now, many Jews had been repatriated to Palestine and some had inevitably joined the terrorists and were fighting against the British troops. A month prior to my demob, the terrorists had issued a warning that anyone with the rank of sergeant or above who had been involved with Jewish camps would be a special target if they ever set foot in Palestine. In other words, my life was in danger if I followed the route home that I had taken to get married. Unless the army found an alternative way, I could be stuck in Cyprus for a very long time.

George Sinclair, Brian Ferris and others due for demob had already left on the long journey through Palestine. We had said goodbye and I never saw or heard from them again. Two officers, a staff sergeant, and three sergeants, including me, were kicking our heels waiting for transport home. Every day seemed like a month. Eventually, there it was, bold letters on the notice board: 'Sgt Hughes D. will proceed to Famagusta harbour, board the troop ship Durban Castle and proceed to Liverpool, United Kingdom, for demobilisation.'

The sweetest words I had ever read. I had 48 hours to pack, say goodbyes, collect travel documents, and write to May with the good news. I had never seen a ship so big: it was a massive liner, too big to enter Famagusta harbour. We had to go out to it in a small boat, so I was going home direct from Cyprus, never to see Palestine again. As the ship pulled away, I looked back at Cyprus and didn't have one regret at leaving. Without doubt it had been an experience I would never forget. I had been a tiny part of an historic incident, and I had no doubt the experience would make me more worldly wise than if I had never joined the army, but I had too many bad memories to look back on Cyprus with affection.

Eventually, I was back in Liverpool, walking down the gangway of the ship, little knowing that years later the same ship would make headline news when a crew member murdered a passenger and pushed her through a porthole.

No such drama today, this was the end of being a soldier. After checking with the transport officer, I was sent to the demob centre, handed in my rifle and army gear, and was issued with a civilian demob suit. The officer who handed me my ticket home and demob papers shook my hand and said: 'Good luck, Mr Hughes,' putting emphasis on 'Mr' Hughes. I could have kissed him. I was out of uniform, out of the army—free at last!

May and I were on cloud nine. Our first home together was in two rooms behind the Three Tuns Inn at Hetton. I discarded my uniform, never to wear it again. My army service was over. For May and me, the rest of our lives could now begin.

9

DEMOB—HOME

I was now just over 22 years old, but I'd returned to Hetton Downs Co-op in a state of utter and absolute frustration. The same idiot of a man was still in charge and most of the same staff were doing the same jobs. Nothing had changed and it was driving me crazy. All I could see was inefficiency, tradition, and complacency, and I was now one of them with no chance of being even a junior branch manager for at least twenty years. I'd studied all those years, nurtured an ambition, but no one cared. The impatience of youth was driving me crazy. I was offered a branch Manager's job in South Wales, but there was no way May would live so far away from her mother and friends. I was simply too young for the Co-op and its damned tradition.

One night over tea I said:

'May, I'd like to pack my job in!' Only she would know the shock I'd given her. She was aware of my frustration, but to pack in a secure job when we had no money and wanted our first child! She didn't say I was mad, but she had every right to think it, looking back. I took a huge risk. Her response was brief:

'Let's talk it over,' she said, probably hoping I'd forget the idea. I had studied business, I thought I knew about business, and if the Co-op wouldn't give me a chance I'd open my own business. Without money and with no practical management my options were limited, to say the least. With May's full agreement, I found an empty shop in Toward Road, Sunderland, next door to a prosperous butcher and grocery shop, gave in my notice to the Co-op and left. I opened a greengrocery because I'd worked in the greengrocery shop at Hetton Co-op and only one week's stock was required. My mother gave the bank her guarantee for my credit, and I opened up.

For the first two months I lost no money but made none. May and I lived on fruit and veg until slowly but surely we began to succeed. My theory was becoming practical and produced profit. Trade to hotels and organisations boosted turnover and soon I employed two boys to deliver orders and the purchase of a small three-wheeler van was a major asset. May and I were blissfully happy, our income was now much higher than the Co-op wage, and prospects looked good, but I worked extremely hard and very long hours. Then another set-back: one day, while lifting a sack of potatoes, I sank to my knees with an excruciating pain in my back—the same pain I'd experienced years ago in Cyprus in the army after I was hit by a Jewish partisan.

Memories came flooding back: the attack, a hospital lumbar puncture, and constant pain. I was now a married man with a business and responsibilities. In the following weeks and months the pain was constant. When the blink of an eye was agony, I tried everything, but my only solace was a hot-water bottle made ready by May as soon as I walked through the door after a hard day at the shop. Over the next four years my doctor sent me to anyone who might have helped:

A blind masseur who was charming, expensive, and a waste of time.

An ex-Marine osteopath who was brutal, inexpensive, and damaging.

A coal board spine consultant who was immaculate, costly, and no help.

A faith-healer who was embarrassing and free, but I didn't have the faith.

During all this time I continued creating a successful greengrocery but without the help and support of May I'd have failed completely. A new treatment called deep X-ray was suggested. It was painless and gave some relief, but after each session I was violently sick and came to dread treatment day. It also meant that May looked after the shop while I had treatment at Newcastle. Eventually the treatment was stopped due to a risk of leukaemia. I was told I had severe spondylitis that could only get worse, unless I kept active. If I gave in to pain then I would eventually need a wheel chair. May didn't cry or get emotional. She simply said: 'Thank God it's not a killer.' (I suspect she had difficulty hiding her true feelings.)

The fear of a wheelchair kept me active and I studied positive thinking to keep my mind as active as my body. May and I were so happy: the work was hard but we worked as a team, we were so in love, and had a son David, followed a few years later by a beautiful daughter, Sheila. We felt complete: a profitable business, a new car, even one of the first 9-inch TVs—but, more important, two of the most lovely children who had ever been born.

During this time my brother Ted was in London as a professional musician. My father and mother had moved into the nearby Three Tuns Inn and May's parents lived nearby and all were well. Life was good, happy, and contented until suddenly our world changed completely. One night, while handing me a hot water bottle, May said:

'I see they're advertising for a general manager at Hetton Co-op.'

'So Jack must be retiring,' I replied, without any real interest. She stunned me by saying:

'Why don't you apply for his job?' I thought she was kidding, so answered:

'I'm only 34 years old, no one gets the top job in the Co-op under 60 years old, and anyway Ernie Harrison is next in line for the job.' May persisted, saying:

'It would be much easier than lifting sacks of potatoes, it's good money and it's what you studied for all those years.' It would be easier on my back, no cold mornings to the market, and boy, would I not love it!

'May there's no way I'd even be considered,' I replied. 'But if it'll please you I'll apply just for some experience at an interview, though there's no way they would take me back as a branch manager, never mind the top job of general manager.'

I took care with my application, but had no expectations. However, I asked Mr Deans (my mentor at Murton and now a director at CWS Manchester) to provide a reference which he did with delight.

May's mother and grandmother were on cloud nine. To have a son-in-law who was a Co-op manager was as good as royalty. I tried to convince them, my father and mother, and even May that I had no chance, but in their eyes I was a certainty. I knew different.

I didn't feel nervous waiting for my turn to be interviewed, maybe because I didn't expect to be successful. After all, I was only 34 years old, which was at least 25 years younger than anyone had ever been in a similar job. My only experience in management was the control of my own

REGISTERED OFFICE: I, BALLOON STREET, MANCHESTER, 4

TELEGRAPHIC ADDRESS: "WHOLESALE, NEWCASTLE-ON-TYNE"   TELEPHONE: NEWCASTLE-ON-TYNE 2-6040

CO-OPERATIVE WHOLESALE SOCIETY LIMITED

BOARDROOM.

RD/JW

WEST BLANDFORD STREET,

NEWCASTLE-ON-TYNE

20th August, 1959.

<u>To the President and Members of Committee
of the Hetton Downs Co-operative Society Limited</u>.

Gentlemen,

David Hughes has informed me that he is making application for the position of General Manager with your Society.

I feel that the applicant will not be unknown to you, and am sure that he is a comparatively young man possessing both ability and initiative. I am, of course, not familiar with the more recent years of Mr. Hughes' career, but I do know that he has always taken a very keen interest in the Co-operative Movement. He was for some years under me as an apprentice during my service with the Murton Colliery Society, and he evinced a keen interest both in his work and in study. He will no doubt advise you as to the reasons why he commenced business on his own account and the success he has achieved.

I believe Mr. Hughes to be worthy of your consideration on two counts. First, he recognises that no man can hold his position without justifying it by the results achieved and, secondly, I believe him to have a keen interest in the Movement from the angle of its ideals and social purpose, and there are not many men these days who are so convinced as he that their career lies in that direction.

I understand that even despite the fact that he has been in his own business for some years he has continued his Co-operative studies, and you will be familiar with the period he was at the Co-operative College and also the studies he has undertaken since then.

I trust that you will find Mr. Hughes' application sufficiently worthy to grant him an interview when, no doubt, he can explain more fully his achievements and desires.

Yours faithfully,

R Deans.

Mr Deans' reference letter

business with two boys. I'd served my apprenticeship as a grocer, but even that experience had been obtained here, at Hetton Co-op, the same company to which I was now applying to be the general manager and food buyer. In my favour were qualifications and an intense desire to change the old-fashioned image of the Co-op, but I didn't expect to succeed over the other five who had been short-listed. They all had more practical experience and were older than me, which had always been a dominating factor in top Co-op jobs. Nevertheless, this would give me good experience for future interviews.

At last my name was called and I was directed to a lone chair placed at one end of a huge, highly-polished, board-room table. The air was dense with smoke and, between constant puffs on his pipe, the chairman, sitting at the opposite end of the table, congratulated me on being short-listed and reminded me of the terms of the job. This was followed by questions that pierced the haze from other smokers sitting around the table. It was obvious the questions had been pre-planned and my answers justified my pre-empting of them. The atmosphere was cordial until, suddenly, a voice said:

'Why should we give you such an important job?' The question quietly reached my ears from a small man sitting next to the chairman. He was Jack Walls, my ex-boss, now retiring, and the tone of his voice didn't indicate any enthusiasm for my candidature. I looked round at the faces who were scrutinising me and waiting for my response. Every face was familiar: as an employee in 1942 I'd known many of these men intimately, and although they were now older, little had changed.

I'd anticipated the question and prepared a radical response.

'You have a greengrocery department losing money,' I said. 'I can resolve the problem.' I could see eyebrows lift, yet no one interrupted to ask how I intended such an instant miracle. 'Competition is going to be very fierce in the 1960s,' I continued. 'I can prepare your business to meet any modern competitor.' No one spoke, they either thought I was crazy or were waiting for more revelations. I assumed the latter and continued with my proposals.

'The Co-op needs modernising, the staff and systems need to be more efficient, and I have no doubt that I can do the job.'

Incredibly, no one asked how I would achieve such promises. The only question posed was by a board member on my immediate right.

'You own a shop. If you're offered the job what will you do with it?'

'I'll sell it immediately,' I replied. I could see this was received favourably from everyone, so I continued before anyone else could ask a question. 'Of course in order to achieve changes, I'd need some freedom to manage.' I had said the wrong thing, I could feel an immediate change of atmosphere.

'What do you mean by that?' the chairman asked very abruptly. There was no retracting. Anyway, I wouldn't get the job, so why not be bold?

'The board is the ultimate authority,' I said, looking directly at him. 'I'd bring proposals for your approval, but then I'd need complete freedom to carry them out.' The chairman responded immediately:

'I think that's only fair,' he said, looking round the table soliciting nods of approval.

'There's another item I'd like to discuss!' Everyone looked in my direction. 'I would want to be responsible for hiring and firing staff.' The silence was embarrassing. I knew I'd blown it, but what the hell, I still had my own business, they could keep the job. My ex-boss was the first to speak, and I could see the delight on his face at my dilemma.

'It's tradition in the Co-op for the board to employ and dismiss all staff,' he said looking at each board member. 'You can't take over such a responsibility.'

'I wouldn't be against it.' I looked with surprise in the direction of the youngest board member and silently thanked Billy for his support. We'd worked together years ago and he was on my side just at the right time.

'As manager, I would be responsible,' I said, 'so I believe I should have full control.'

The chairman brought the interview to an end by thanking me for a stimulating discussion. I, in turn, offered my thanks for their time and then made my way home. If they were looking for a manager to continue for another decade or two in Traditional Co-operative Business Methods, then I wouldn't be offered the job.

May and I were having a cup of tea, discussing the interview.

'Well, the meeting will be over by now,' she said, looking at the clock. Almost as she said the words there was a knock at the door. It was Billy, who had called directly from the meeting to tell me I'd been successful. I'd got the job! The voting had been unanimous. I couldn't believe it.

'Everyone was impressed at your interview,' Billy said, 'You'll get official confirmation in a couple of days.'

May and I discussed the job until early hours. It had hardly sunk in when I opened our greengrocery shop the next morning. However, it was confirmed. I quickly sold the business and May, Sheila, David and I had a few days holiday before I was ready to begin a career that was to be more eventful and exciting than I could ever have imagined possible.

I was taking over a position steeped in great tradition. Since Hetton Co-op's formation in 1863, I was now only the seventh manager to take control—not only the youngest manager to control Hetton Co-op, but the youngest Co-op general manager throughout Britain. In the late 1950s the Co-op dominated all business. Some crumbs of business were picked up by Walter Willson's, but other major operators hadn't yet arrived on the northern scene. Television was still in its infancy and words such as microchip, word processor and video weren't even in the dictionary. The Co-op hadn't changed its image for decades. So long as the dividend was no less than the neighbouring Co-op, members would accept almost anything.

Hetton Co-op had a turnover of almost £1 million per year, which was quite considerable in 1959. It paid a high dividend and was considered above average, but to my eyes it was incredibly old-fashioned and I couldn't wait to do something about it. The food shops had long wooden counters, with ample seating facilities for the elderly. Every customer was given personal attention and very little was pre-packed. Frozen foods were slowly developing, dairy cabinets were non-existent, marble slabs were everywhere, and brass balance scales were on every level surface. Clean sawdust was sprinkled on the floor every morning and single electric bulbs hung from a dark-painted ceiling. The smells of ground coffee, soap powder and boiled ham intermingled. Cash was whisked to the cashier by high speed suction tubes. Heating consisted of a coal fire in the centre of the back-shop floor. In winter the staff made any excuse to go near, in windy weather the clouds of smoke made everyone curse. A fleet of horse-drawn carts delivered meat, greengrocery, flour and orders. This was a modern food operation of the 1950s.

Ernie Harrison had held the position of buyer for over a decade. He fixed prices and controlled the branch activities. His power and influence were considerable. Ernie was more than 25 years my senior, I'd worked under him as an apprentice. He'd been short-listed for the general manager's job and failed. Not only had I arrived to be the general manager, I was also taking over his power of buyer and controller of the food group. Our first meeting would be very interesting.

In addition to food, the business activity covered footwear, drapery, fashions, chemist, funerals, and hardware. A huge order and credit business was covered by a team of canvassers, a warehouse supplied all branches, and a central administration operated without the luxury of computers or calculators (they hadn't yet been commercially developed). A hierarchy of managers controlled this complex business. They were all much older than me, had a wealth of experience, and were all steeped in traditional Co-op methods. Most of them had been in the same position when I worked in the company as a junior. I had never managed people, I had never been a food buyer, I had no experience in financial control, and a balance sheet was a document I'd studied at college, yet never actually compiled. In addition, the all-important dividend had to be calculated and allotted.

The responsibility of general manager had been given to me by a fifteen-man board and, at my insistence, they had agreed to allow me more freedom and power than any Co-op manager had ever known. I hadn't a clue where to begin, yet I couldn't wait to get started.

Hetton Downs Co-op committee, 1960

10

THE FIRST DAY AS MANAGER

I travelled to my office feeling quite confident. It was my first day and I was replacing a man who had promised to return this morning to introduce me to various managers and departments. He would show me all the confidential information about the business and generally help the day to proceed smoothly. I was aware he hadn't endorsed my appointment, but nevertheless I appreciated his offer of help on my first day.

Walking up the stairs I was aware that I was the new boy. I carried a brief case with very little contents, my suit was new and I felt conspicuous. I tapped on the door, entered, and found the manager's office completely empty. The dark wooden filing cabinets and roll-top desk were still in place, but the whole office had been tidied with hardly a piece of paper in sight. It was quiet, with not a soul about. I patiently waited and waited, then realised my predecessor wouldn't appear. He was leaving me high and dry. Well, if I was to be the boss I may as well make a move. I walked into the general office where a mass of female faces turned in my direction. I had a feeling my presence had been known all along and they'd just been waiting for my entrance.

'Good morning,' I said in a voice I hoped sounded more confident than I felt. To the young girl nearest, I said: 'Will you ask Mr Shenton to come into the office?' Ernie Shenton was the chief clerk and cashier. He'd held the job for many years and was a good friend of the retiring manager. He'd always considered himself far more essential to the company than anyone else, and I wasn't expecting an overwhelming welcome. I wasn't disappointed.

'Can I be of help, Mr Hughes?' he said, as if we were total strangers. I knew this opening encounter would set the pattern of our business relationship. At our previous meeting, years ago, I'd been very much his junior. I would need his help, but it was essential I established my position as manager.

'Hello Ernie,' I said, aware that I'd always addressed him as Mr Shenton in the past. 'I'd like to see all the latest trading and financial accounts, and the confidential documents from the safe.'

'But Mr Walls will get them,' he began. I cut him short.

'Mr Walls is now retired, Ernie. I need to be aware of the position of the society, so please get them.' He didn't argue and, as he left the office, I said: 'Organise me a cup of tea, please.' Ernie would ensure everyone was made aware of our brief encounter.

I soon realised that rarely would anyone come to a general manager's office uninvited unless there was an emergency. By lunchtime I'd seen no one, nor had any phone calls, so I concentrated my time studying the figures. After lunch, I visited each departmental manager and became reacquainted. The reception was friendly and at the end of the tour I felt quite satisfied.

The food group was over 70 per cent of the total business. Its success or failure determined the future of the entire company. I deliberately left the food until last, and decided to invite Ernie Harrison to my office. Our meeting would be on my ground. As senior food manager, Ernie would be affected more than anyone else. Although he wouldn't suffer financially, the blow to his ego would be tremendous. After all, he was losing a great amount of power and influence and, as an ex-junior employee, I was now his boss. My greeting produced no more than a weak smile and a handshake. I tried to soften the blow and tell him I needed his experience, but the atmosphere was icy, so I quietly abandoned that approach and simply explained his new responsibility. He would control day-to-day operations; I would determine price, buying, and marketing policy.

'Does that mean I do no more buying?' he said in a very surly voice.

'Believe me, you won't have time,' I said without enlarging on the subject. It was obvious it wasn't to be a fruitful meeting, so I concluded by saying: 'I'm aware it's a big change after so many years, Ernie. I'll be altering many things in the future and I expect your support.'

'Will that be all then Mr. Hughes?' was his only response.

'Not quite,' I replied. 'I'd like a list of all your current problems and any recommendations—by tomorrow.' He looked, said nothing, and left the office. I hadn't enjoyed that meeting. I'd hoped for better but, after all, Ernie had very little to thank me for—except maybe his future employment.

I was just ready to go home, when a knock at the door produced a small man, about 50 years old, with a neatly trimmed moustache. A rolled umbrella and bowler hat complemented an elegant dark suit and white shirt.

'I've been sent up by Mr Harrison,' he explained 'He tells me you're now the buyer. I'm from Procter and Gamble and my name's Bill Hinkley.'

'You're my first rep and I haven't a clue what our order should be,' I answered. He smiled and immediately I felt that I could trust him.

'You'll know better than me our requirements, so you order our usual,' I said. 'But if you pull a fast one, you'll never get another order.' He and I became friends from that moment and never once did we have a disagreement.

So ended the first day. It seemed to have been uneventful, but little did I realise the traumas and excitements that would develop over the next quarter of a century.

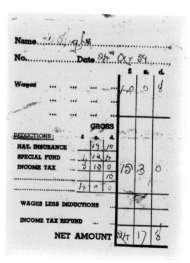

My first pay packet as general manager, 1959

General manager, 1959

The Grocer, *1959*

The Man At The Helm

AT 3½ years old, Mr David Hughes, the general manager of the Hetton Downs Co-operative Society, is one of the youngest chief executives in the movement.

He is the fourth general manager since the appointment was first made in 1903.

Mr Hughes, whose ideas for future shopping at the Co-op have brought many varied reactions, began his career with the Murton Society as a 14-year-old grocery assistant. He joined the Hetton Downs Society as a grocery assistant following his Army service, and then began studies at the Co-operative College and took a correspondence course.

ONE AIM

For ten years Mr Hughes went into business on his own but took over as general manager in 1959. Since his appointment, Mr Hughes has worked with one aim in mind — the creation of a new image for the Co-op. shop. He felt that the Co-operative at Hetton could continue to trade along the old lines and possibly slide out of existence, or it could adopt new progressive methods of modern cut-price shopping and become a force to be reckoned with in the County Durham business world.

Mr Hughes commented: "I don't want to put any local businessmen out of a job by price-cutting but, after all, as a Society our duty is to provide members with top-quality goods at the lowest possible price."

NEW IMAGE

Mr Hughes, who is married, with two children, took over from Mr John Walls, who retired in 1959 after 20 years in the general manager's chair.

During the past year the Hetton Downs Co-op, has been building up its new image.

Following the modernization of its headquarters in Market Street and its various branches, the Co-op, stepped into the public eye in March this year when it cut the price of whisky and other spirits by five shillings a bottle.

CHEAPER TYRES

It followed up ten days later by slashing the price of tyres by 10s and later started selling cars.

On April 15 the price of beer at the Co-op was cut by 2d. and on April 27 the half-yearly meeting of the Society agreed to continue the price-cutting policy.

What comes next? said Mr Hughes. "I have one or two ideas up my sleeve which should really make people sit up and take notice of the Co-op, with the enthusiasm they had when the movement first began."

During the first six months, I had a problem convincing people that the Co-op needed to change.

Although competition wasn't yet very intensive, it was obvious to me that times were changing, the greatest factor being television. It would bring aggressive advertising, but so many people considered the Co-op could withstand anything.

Every month a meeting was held at the Three Tuns Hotel in Durham, attended by all Co-op general managers in the county. I felt like a schoolboy among teachers: the age gap was so wide, and there was an almighty chasm of difference in our philosophy towards the Co-op. I attended the first three meetings and only listened. It was like an Old Boys' Club, where nothing of substance was discussed, no decisions were made, and disagreement was unthinkable. When the agenda for my fourth meeting arrived, I couldn't believe my eyes. The secretary of Newbottle Co-op was proposing that all staff pension funds should be withdrawn from the current gilt-edged investment and used by each society to boost profits. I studied the pension rules and prepared my maiden speech. The proposal would need 100 per cent support from every Society; I wouldn't support it, because the risk to staff pensions would be too great.

David Jones, the general manager of Brandon Co-op, was the permanent chairman of the group. Before the meeting started, I indicated I would like to speak on the proposal and some other items. I realise now that he must have had an idea that my comments wouldn't follow the general opinions. The meeting went on and on, time was passing by and David didn't even look in my direction until the talk was exhausted and no one had yet spoken against the proposal.

'I think our new colleague has something to say,' David said to the meeting, looking in my direction. I noticed many looked at their watches and were ready to visit the bar. By the time I got to my feet I was angry and broke all the rules of diplomacy and tact. I criticised Co-op complacency, inefficiency and lack of forward planning. I indicated that we were the people responsible to change and secure the future.

'Finally, Mr Chairman,' I concluded, 'I am totally against the proposal on staff pensions until we have a better and more efficient organisation.'

I sat down to total silence. David slowly stood up, looked directly at me, and said: 'Gentlemen, we've got to allow for the impetuosity of youth.' He then closed the meeting without further discussion.

The Co-op grapevine was swift and efficient. News of my outburst quickly spread. My buying visit to the CWS Newcastle the next Tuesday confirmed my opinion that I was very much in the minority. Senior Co-op managers from the whole of the north east congregated for the weekly ritual, but very few acknowledged me as a colleague. In fact some adverse comments were loudly spoken to reach my ears. If this was the attitude following a few words spoken in the heat of the moment, God knows what their reaction would be if they knew my future plans.

I couldn't allow myself to be diverted by other opinions, my priority was to create a modern and efficient business at Hetton. This required changing attitudes and outmoded practices. The major weakness in the Society was the greengrocery department: it was losing money every day. It didn't take long to identify the problem. The manager was too weak for the job, he'd been promoted simply because it was his turn for promotion, and he was very popular with every member of the board. Ability had never been a consideration. Controls within the department were *non-existent*—nothing and no one was ever checked. This would be my first move since my appointment. I'd been given freedom to manage, but decided to acquaint the board of my intentions.

First on the agenda was—*Greengrocery Reorganisation*. The board had always taken every decision. No manager could move in any direction without their agreement—their power and influence had always been absolute. This meeting would be my first move to dilute their power.

They'd been elected by members and were a cross section of miners, teachers and retired men. I'd been employed as the professional manager. The meeting had all the signs of being very interesting. I gave them a document with some statistics identifying the amount of losses, plus my forecast of profits after reorganisation.

'You really believe this turn-round in the greengrocery is possible?' the chairman queried after a few moments' examination of the figures.

'I'll never give you figures I won't stand by,' I replied 'But it can only be achieved by some changes. First, the manager will be demoted. Second, every item will be checked daily. Third, a young branch manager will take over. Fourth,the buying will be taken over by myself.'

Almost every man sitting round the table tried to get in with a question or a comment.

'You suggest demoting a man we promoted?'

'You want to promote a man out of turn?'

'Staff won't tolerate such checking!'

I sat quietly until comments were exhausted, then took a deep breath, knowing that the next few minutes would determine my future.

'Mr Chairman, Gentlemen,' I began in a quiet and controlled voice. 'You appointed me with complete freedom to manage. If anything goes wrong I will be held accountable.'

'We're not discussing policy, this is a management re-organisation.'

'I didn't bring this for your approval, but to notify you of my intentions. I know I'm going against tradition, but you appointed me with freedom to manage.'

No one spoke, all looked for a lead from the chairman.

Bill Lowery had been a union man, staff representative, and now chairman. His next few words set the stage for everything that was to follow in future years, for which I'll be forever grateful.

'Gentlemen, our manager is quite right. We discarded traditional applicants for someone who would take our society into the 1960s. We agreed to his freedom to manage.' He paused for a second. 'Now we know exactly what that means.' He concluded by moving to the next item on the agenda without further discussion.

The reorganisation took place without delay. Tom Hauxwell took over with tremendous enthusiasm. High profits from the greengrocery department soon gave the answer to critics and forecasters of doom. This was followed by every section, department and activity in the company being examined, weaknesses strengthened, systems streamlined, and employees analysed. It wasn't an easy exercise: there was concern about jobs, suspicion about motives and, in some cases, direct opposition to the efficiency and honesty I was insisting upon. The most dramatic example came from a board member.

It had always been the custom to call at the local pub after a board meeting on Friday evenings. Although not a drinker, I continued the custom, and every Friday joined them for a beer. On this occasion I talked mainly to the employees' representative, local union organiser, and a mobile-shop salesman for the society. Like other salesmen, he hadn't been enthusiastic about the control systems. The next morning he was caught stealing cigarettes.

'This is a serious charge. Is it true?' I asked, as he stood at my desk.

'I'm afraid it is,' he admitted in a voice that surprised me by its lack of concern. I turned to the warehouse manager.

'There is no doubt or mistake?'

'No sir,' he replied.

'Have you any comment?' I turned back to the salesman.

'Well, I can only say it won't happen again.' From his attitude I could feel he was challenging me to take action. He was in a strong position and was the first to be caught. I was aware that every employee would be watching the outcome.

'Of all employees, you're aware of what I'm trying to do,' I said. 'You're in a position that should be showing a good example. I have no alternative but to dismiss you.' He looked at me as if I was mad.

'You can't do that—I'm on the board!' he almost shouted. 'How can you drink with me one night and sack me the next morning?'

'The two aren't related,' I answered. 'In any case, I won't alter my decision. You're dismissed.'

I never again socialised with the board after each meeting. Everyone was now aware I wouldn't accept dishonesty. A number of other staff were caught stealing. The overall standards improved considerably. We were operating as an efficient business, I could feel the enthusiasm among staff improving. Time was drawing near for some real changes.

Hetton Downs Co-op mobile shops, 1960

Hetton-le-Hole becomes...

The mouse that roared

HETTON-LE-HOLE in Co. Durham is a mining community with 17,500 inhabitants and a co-operative society with nine shops. Hardly the setting for a success story. And yet the transformation which has taken place within Hetton Downs Amicable Industrial Society is exactly that. Six years ago their image was symbolised by the brown oak counters of their five shops. Today they have nine stores, all on self-service, and they are doing 20 per cent more business than six years ago despite a shrinking population.

The present healthy state of this tiny society, which celebrated its centenary last year, is entirely due to the far-sightedness and determination of two men. One is Mr. David Hughes, who started work with the society at 15, left to run his own grocery business and returned at the age of 34 to become general manager; the other is Mr. Fred Hall, who has spent all his life in the co-operative movement and became secretary at Hetton at 32.

When the two men took up their appointments in 1959 this was the situation they found. Hetton overlapped with five other societies and the duplication was so bad that at times mobile vans from rival societies were competing for trade in the same street! All of the societies were "divi conscious". The dividend was the yardstick by which the merit of each society was measured.

Hetton's five shops catered almost entirely for loyal dyed-in-the-wool co-op members. This inevitably meant most of its customers were old. The society gave dividend, credit, delivery, and life insurance. The policy was to pay a high dividend and plough back as much as possible into reserves. Development had low priority.

Overcoming resistance

Self-service was an essential part of Mr. Hughes' plans to modernise the

The two responsible for the transformation: Mr. David Hughes, general manager (left), and Mr. Fred Hall, secretary.

society and new thinking was called for on dividend and the other co-op facilities. But he also realised that he was dealing with people who had never seen self-service before; he had to overcome resistance to change; and he had to have the support of the board of nine laymen at each stage. He could not rush things. His plan was to introduce each innovation at the right psychological moment

continued overleaf

Self-Service
magazine, 1961

*Hetton Downs Co-op
senior managers, 1962*

11

THE FIRST SELF-SERVICE

About eighteen months after taking over I considered it was time to bring Hetton Co-op into the 1960s. Each department was operating efficiently and profitably, the management had been reorganised, a dishonest butchery departmental manager had been replaced by a live-wire, and many old-fashioned practices had been discarded.

Fred Hall, the Society secretary, shared my enthusiasm and agreed to analyse the financial position to determine our capability for capital expenditure. We could afford three moves to improve our image. First, we discarded the horses and replaced them with a modern fleet of mobile shops. Sales doubled on these vehicles almost overnight. The board, customers, and staff were delighted with the end of the horse era. Second, I consulted a number of shop-fitters for ideas and costs for modernising the whole Society. John Anderson of Sunderland was awarded the contract and one Friday night he gave an impressive presentation to the board. The footwear department would be ultra-modern, and the shop fronts of a higher standard than any local competitor. I could see by the board members' expressions they would be proud of 'their' Co-op.

The controversial change would be left till last. The food stores would be converted to self-service. Everyone considered that the north, and particularly the Co-op, was decades away from such modern innovations. However, I convinced the board that they could lead the way in bringing the Co-op into the 1960s.

Ernie Harrison, the grocery manager, hadn't put a foot wrong since I'd taken over his buying duties, nor had he shown any enthusiasm or initiative. Consequently, I decided to personally oversee the conversion to self-service, mainly because I knew exactly how I wanted the fixtures, layout and merchandising to be completed, and I didn't trust Ernie to organise or motivate the staff on such a tight schedule. The change to modernisation would be completed in 36 hours.

'I'll never go in there from now on.'

'You're going to lose a lot of customers!'

'The Co-op will never be the same!'

The news that self-service was coming to Hetton split the community in two. Many of the older members were opposed and didn't hesitate to let me know. I had phone calls and letters, and was often stopped in the street. I was convinced the anti-self-service customers would change their views when they saw the outcome.

It was essential the conversion be completed correctly. Many hours were spent on explaining and training Ernie and his staff on the specialities of self-service. After the old-fashioned counter service we were now asking customers to pick up a basket, actually serve themselves, then queue at a little desk called a check-out and pay cash. No delivery, and no credit.

It was as traumatic a change for staff as for the customers. By the time I went home at 5a.m. on the Monday morning for a couple of hours' sleep before the shop opened, I was delighted. The conversion was perfect: new self-service fixtures, modern strip-lighting, bright colours, and a new floor. Gone was the open fire, replaced by an electric heating system. The younger staff had always been enthusiastic and even Ernie was now showing reluctant pleasure at 'his' modern store. The staff had worked a shift system over the weekend; I had missed two nights' sleep.

When the alarm rang at 8 o'clock I quickly jumped out of bed then fell flat on my face. I didn't see the opening of the First Self-Service Co-op Food Store in the north east, I was exhausted and fast asleep.

From the beginning self-service was a total success. Sales trebled, staff were happy, the board was delighted. Personal satisfaction came when general managers from neighbouring Co-ops asked to visit. They hadn't liked my ideas but were now keen to see the outcome.

The third capital expenditure was exclusively for staff. New overalls and uniforms were provided and a bonus system based on profit was introduced. We were slowly shedding the old Co-op image, and preparing for even bigger changes.

MR. DAVID HUGHES does not mind 21-year-old Robert Morris trying his chair for size.

For on Monday morning Mr. Morris also takes over his job as general manager of Hetton Downs Co-op... into top jobs with the society, which employs more than 100 and has a £690,000-a-year turnover.

Alan Brown, 15, will take charge of the drapery department only two months after leaving school.

Frank Robinson, also 15, will head the grocery section, and Brian Smales, 19, will become manager of the central supermarket with 16-year-old new head of provisions sections and Keith Robinson, also 19, will be a branch manager.

Notices went out to the staff yesterday telling them of the changes and demanding proper respect for the new bosses.

But the moves are only temporary. After three days the youngsters will return to their normal jobs as apprentices and assistants.

part of his long-term training scheme.

By giving youngsters practical experience of the jobs he hopes to assess their capabilities and potential as future managers.

From opening on Monday to closing on Wednesday, a youngsters will take complete charge of the society, its ten branches, and five mobile shops.

Mr. Hughes said: "The whole thing has been planned to wait to see how the rest o... the staff react.

"During their three days a... charge the boys will be com... pletely responsible for the running of the society. The... will deal with representatives... customers' questions, and even... price changes if need be.

One or two deliberate prob... lems have been set up by outside... manufacturers, but the boss...

Management trainee takes over for a day, 1965

12

A BANKRUPT CO-OP

'May, will you provide a meal if I organise an important meeting here?'

'You mean in the house?' she responded with some surprise.

'Yes, what we have to discuss will best be done very privately.' Only three people with myself would be at the meeting: the Co-op Bank manager from Newcastle, a CWS director and the CWS accountant, both from Manchester. Very high-powered stuff!

None of them wanted to be seen to be involved in a major Co-op move being quietly planned. May persuaded her cousin June to help, and together they produced a magnificent dinner. We would have a cup of coffee, then get down to business.

I was talking to the bank manager when suddenly there was pandemonium. While serving, May slipped and a full cup of hot coffee fell on the lap of the CWS director. I thought she would faint—God knows how he felt. He was charming, put May at her ease, got cleaned up and carried on as if nothing had happened.

The meeting was concerning a neighbouring Co-op called Moorsley. Although it was in direct competition with Hetton it was less than half the size and extremely old-fashioned. Unfortunately it was bankrupt! In the past any Co-op in difficulty had been quietly supported or integrated into another Co-op without any publicity. But the ball game was about to change.

The bank believed that a number of Co-ops in the North East were facing similar problems and support on a multi-million-pound scale wasn't feasible. Moorsley wouldn't be supported or subsidised. I had already examined their accounts, studied every branch and discussed, confidentially, with my chairman the possibility of controlling Moorsley—in addition to Hetton Co-op.

'Well David,' Hedley Whitehead, the CWS director, opened the meeting. 'Have you considered our proposals?'

'Two questions I'd like answered first,' I replied. 'Will there be any financial help at all?'

'No,' the bank manager broke in with some haste.

'CWS can't help either.' Roy Harrison, the accountant, spoke quietly.

'What happens to Moorsley Committee?' I enquired. No one answered immediately, then Hedley said:

'Let's come back to that subject.' A lame duck like Moorsley was the last thing Hetton Co-op wanted, yet it would eliminate a competitor. I sat silent for a few moments, absorbing the fact that I could be taking on an impossible task without help.

'I've given this a great deal of thought over the past two weeks,' I said as our three guests listened intently. 'I have a feeling you intend this to be an example to other Co-ops.' Hedley smiled but didn't speak. 'Well I have a proposal, I don't expect you to accept, but it's the only way I'd consider taking over.' I now had their full attention.

'I'll recommend to my board that we absorb Moorsley into Hetton Co-op,'—the bank manager was just about to say something when I saw Hedley touch his arm: he'd guessed there was more to come—'but only on the following conditions,' I continued:

'1. Moorsley committee to be disbanded;

'2. The general manager to be dismissed;

'3. *Non-profit* branches to be closed;

'4. Members' share capital to be *devalued* by 50 per cent.'

Roy Harrison spoke first.

'There'll be hell on throughout the movement,' he exclaimed. After a few moments consideration, Hedley said:

'It means you will only be taking over the profitable branches and members' share capital will be paying the debts.' I nodded, then said:

'It wouldn't be fair to expect members of Hetton Co-op to pay for the inefficiency of Moorsley. The bank manager looked very thoughtful, when he said:

'It will certainly make other societies take notice.' My proposals were accepted and a timetable set up, but little did I realise the bitterness I would face in the next few weeks.

Hetton Board also accepted the proposals and on the following Monday I attended the Moorsley Board with Hedley. The chairman, a man in his late sixties, thin with balding head, looked devastated. He seemed to be lost in the huge chair at the head of the board room table. Their manager hadn't acquainted them with the problems; the shock of bankruptcy and the proposed action provoked a mixed reaction. One or two, with the chairman, were drained of emotion; others were vicious in their criticism—of their own manager, the CWS, and the bank for lack of support. A tremendous amount of anger was directed at me, claiming I'd taken trade away from them and was now only taking over the best parts of their business.

Moorsley Co-op. Take-over

THE 4,700 - member Hetton Downs Amicable Industrial Society, Ltd., has been asked by its board of management of the 900-member Moorsley Co-operative Society to take over full managerial control of the Moorsley concern.

Negotiations for the amalgamation of the two societies fell through 18 months ago after Moorsley members had opposed the merger.

At a recent meeting the Moorsley board decided to ask Mr David Hughes, general manager of the Hetton Downs society to undertake full managerial control.

The Hetton Downs society has a share capital of £292,000. The Moorsley Society has a share capital of £12,000.

Mr Hughes said today the Hetton Downs board of management felt it could not take over any liabilities of the Moorsley Society which could be detrimental to the strong financial position of the Hetton Downs Society and added: "We are merely taking over fixed assets and goods stock at Moorsley."

TEN REDUNDANT

Mr Hughes said that in the interest of economy it had been necessary to declare ten members of the Moorsley staff redundant and that they would receive redundancy pay. He added that the complete take-over could not be effected until the share-holders of the Moorsley Society met within the next two weeks to discuss the position.

Sunderland Echo, 1963

I was near to walking out—I had been invited into this mess—but Hedley whispered a plea to stay. He slowly rose to his feet:

'Gentlemen I understand your shock and anger, but you have a decision to make—tonight'. You could have heard a pin drop. 'The CWS cannot extend your credit, the Co-op Bank will not increase your overdraft. Unless you accept these proposals to save *part* of your business, you will be declared bankrupt. You and your members could lose everything.'

He sat down, I could feel my heart pounding, I had never experienced such a tense situation in my life. A long silence was broken by a board member asking me if I would ensure his brother (the butchery manager) would keep his job. I didn't answer; the looks of disgust from his colleagues made my response unnecessary.

I was amazed at the lack of concern by the general manager (although the next few days would provide a better understanding). The chairman went through the formality of a vote. One of the oldest Co-op societies in Britain ceased to exist from that moment. I went through the technicalities of takeover with the manager and arranged to be in attendance when he and *all* members of his board would meet their staff on Monday morning, explain the position, announce shop closures and staff redundancies. The press soon got hold of the story and focussed their attention on the 50 per cent devaluation of share capital and the hardships being created. When asked for comment, I pledged to restore shares to full value as soon as possible, but this didn't abate the anger generated during the following weeks.

I arrived at Moorsley a few minutes before the staff meeting. The room was packed full. The chairman came over to me in a state of absolute panic, pulled me to one side, and said:

'The manager's gone and I'm the only one here from the board.'

'So who's going to speak to the staff?' I whispered.

'I can't,' he whimpered. 'It's up to you.' He pushed some papers into my hand, which were details of shop closures and the names of staff redundancies. I couldn't believe it. I'd been left to hold the baby.

I had never met any of these staff before, yet I was being asked to give them such devastating news. The manager had actually moved away overnight and not one board member had turned up except the chairman, and he was too emotional to be of any use. I'd never known such a cowardly group of men in my life. I was in a dilemma. From today I was responsible for their business, pressmen were outside, but—more important—these staff were waiting to be told if they had a job or not. I was tempted to cancel the meeting. My God, I had plenty of excuse, but it would only delay the inevitable.

The room went silent as I rose to my feet, I looked round for the chairman, but he was nowhere in sight.

'Ladies and Gentlemen, this is not a happy occasion for anyone.' I then slowly and simply explained the events leading up to the meeting. Although they had heard rumours over the weekend, to be told they were bankrupt and abandoned by the people supposed to lead them was too much. Shouts of bitterness and anger came from the back of the room, many of the female staff were sobbing, everyone was in a state of shock. A man in his late twenties came forward and said:

'I'm Peter Clenell, the union branch secretary. Do you mind if I say a few words?'

'Depends what you plan to say,' I answered.

'Don't worry, I won't make things worse.' It took a few minutes to get order, then he spoke in a quiet and caring voice. 'If we were honest we all knew things weren't right. It's no good shouting at the man,'—looking in my direction—'it's the manager and committee who've let us down. Now I suggest we let Mr Hughes tell us the worst, and we'll know where we stand.'

I offered a silent prayer. Thank God one man showed some courage among this chaos. I thanked him, then proceeded with the most difficult job I'd ever performed in my life. First I read out the shops for closure, followed by the names of those staff to be redundant. It produced a mixture of relief and dejection, smiles and tears. Someone should be made to pay for this, I thought, as I completed the list. Finally the meeting ended, staff dispersed and I was left all alone. Even the chairman had gone.

Organising the closures and integrating the business with Hetton Co-op was relatively easy. The heart-breaking problem was dealing with hundreds of people who suddenly found that their savings had halved in value overnight. The majority were persuaded to sit tight until the value improved. (In fact within 18 months all shares were back to full value.)

I never saw or heard from the runaway manager. He left a trail of debts and chaos. Integration took three months to complete.

13

NO CO-OP DIVIDEND!

Early 1960, competition arrived in the form of a Fine Fare supermarket at nearby Houghton. Now we'd find out if Co-op members preferred credit and dividend or immediate price cuts. Tyne Tees Television was bombarding us with advertising, unknown a few years before. The 1960s showed signs of being very interesting. One of the branches we'd taken over from Moorsley Co-op was a small counter-service shop in the centre of Hetton called Church Villa. It sold food, drapery and hardware. Sales were only £300 per week and half of that was credit. It was a tatty and neglected shop, not profitable, but an ideal site. A shop next door was to be opened by a food retailer with a reputation for aggressive price cutting. The board had gone along with everything I'd proposed up to now, but my next idea would require a fantastic act of faith.

Friday evening was late-night shopping and the highlight of the week. Staff had a tea break and changed into clean overalls. It had a unique atmosphere, every shop in Market Street was busy, women stood in groups gossiping, the Co-op was the focal point.

Our meeting started at 7 o'clock and board members began to circulate an hour before and made sure they talked to as many members as possible. I always enjoyed the atmosphere as a prelude to the weekly meeting. Tonight would create a revolution in the Co-op, if I was successful. It would all depend on these men, pleasantly chatting with members, oblivious to the decision I would ask them to take.

'Have you forgotten the agenda?' the chairman enquired as everyone settled down.

'The manager asked me to ignore an agenda tonight, he has an important item to discuss,' the secretary replied. This immediately ensured I had everyone's attention.

'Mr Chairman, Gentlemen, no one could have had better support than me,' I began. 'Tonight I'm going to ask you to make a decision that no other Co-op has ever made. If my idea works it could change our whole philosophy to dividend.' The mention of dividend was like speaking of the Holy Grail. Everyone was looking, wondering what was coming next. 'Fine Fare is opening at Houghton, a cut-price retailer will open soon in Hetton, and more competition is on the way.' No one interrupted, so I continued.

'We can't give credit, delivery, dividend—and also compete on prices. I believe the customers, particularly young ones, prefer low prices.' Still no one spoke. 'I'd like to compete at one branch only: *No Credit, Delivery or Dividend*. Church Villa is the ideal site.'

I decided to stop speaking at that point. They were dumbfounded. I had asked them to abandon everything dear to their philosophy of the Co-op.

'Has this ever been tried before?' queried a board member.

'I don't think so,' Fred Hall interjected. The meeting continued for two hours longer than usual and no other subject was discussed. It wasn't an easy decision for them to make. Member reaction was the biggest concern and, to my surprise, they were worried about the feeling of other Co-op societies. Finally they had exhausted discussion and it was time to vote on my proposal.

Half an hour earlier Fred had passed a note on which he had written: 'I think you've won.' I wasn't so sure. They'd supported me up to now, but maybe I was expecting too much this time. The chairman summed up the arguments, then ended with a comment that made me feel optimistic.

'I never expected to see the day when a Co-op wouldn't pay dividend, particularly our Co-op,' he said. 'But we've done things in the past few months I never thought possible. The manager says this is an experiment, so I'm prepared to support the proposal.'

'Well done Bill,' I thought to myself. The board followed his lead, I got the go ahead. I stressed the need for secrecy, pointing out we didn't want member reaction prior to the shop opening, and we certainly didn't want to alert competitors.

To the outside world, including the manager and staff, we were simply modernising and converting to self-service. Staff couldn't understand why they hadn't been given new price lists, but I took the blame for the delay. I'd promoted Peter Clenell to manager (he was the union man who'd spoken up on that disastrous morning at Moorsley). He became one of the most successful managers I ever had.

A fantastic piece of luck came my way a few days before opening. I obtained a copy of the price list of the new competitor who was opening next door. He was opening on the Tuesday, I'd planned to open on the Thursday and Fine Fare issued a leaflet with their following week's prices (they weren't concerned about a new Co-op shop). From that moment it was all systems go.

I took Peter Clenell into my confidence, he was absolutely delighted. The opening was brought forward to Monday. A further review of our price list, and we would be all set to beat everyone. Posters and leaflets were distributed on the Sunday, press adverts booked for the Monday. I'll never forget the expression on the faces of the shop staff when I briefed them on the Sunday morning as they priced the products.

'You'll be creating history for the Co-op tomorrow,' I said. 'Many people will be watching how you handle the trade.'

'We won't let you down,' Peter said. I had never seen such enthusiasm among staff.

The response to the opening of the first non-dividend Co-op store was better than I ever imagined. The trade built up minute by minute, people were queuing to get into the shop, and buses stopped outside to produce customers from Murton, Easington, Houghton and other districts. In the first *three days* the sales were equal to the previous *three months*. I didn't realise that food could be sold so quickly. It needed quick reorganisation to ensure adequate supplies, extra staff and security. But we learned quickly and maintained the huge sales.

'What the hell are you trying to do to us?' the voice of the manager of Easington Lane Co-op shouted down the phone. 'Do you realise you're killing our trade?' his voice was quivering with emotion. 'You're not a Co-op man, you're taking trade from your colleagues,' he continued. (So now they were my colleagues!)

'Would you rather see Fine Fare take your trade?' I replied, but he wasn't in the mood for discussion. All my attempts to reason were wasted. I had made an enemy, and no mistake.

Unfortunately, the same attitude prevailed among all local Co-op managers. We were taking their trade, but they couldn't see that my concern was all the other competitors. I received enquiries from the Co-op union, CWS Manchester, and numerous societies throughout the country. I knew we were breaking with tradition, but the antagonism by the Co-op movement was much greater than I expected. David Carr, the manager of Crook Co-op, even put a proposal to the next Co-op Congress at Blackpool that Hetton Co-op be expelled from the movement. The proposal was narrowly defeated.

Three months later I called a meeting of all my senior managers.

'Gentlemen, I would like you to consider this meeting as very confidential. I'd welcome your opinions on a major policy change before I put it to the board.' The group of senior managers were silent with anticipation. We'd assembled in the board room. If my next move was to succeed it was essential I had their total support. I gave them an update of the success at Church Villa and the antagonism of other societies.

'The next move will affect the whole Society,' I said.

'You mean the non-food as well as food?' Arthur Belton, the drapery buyer exclaimed with surprise.

'I mean the whole business. Ernie,' I said turning to Ernie Harrison, 'would you give us your opinion about no dividend on food?' He was stunned at my direct question. He still had no love for me and hadn't expected to be consulted.

'I've always believed the Co-op should pay dividend, but the success at Church Villa, the new competition, and the constant demand by members for low prices has changed my mind, but I must say I'm very reluctant.'

His opinion impressed the whole meeting, so I asked for other opinions, all of which echoed that of Ernie.

'I'm concerned about the non-food,' Arthur Belton said. 'All the interest and activity on food makes me wonder what will happen to footwear, fashions and the rest,' he concluded.

'Well Gentlemen, I think I may have an idea you will accept,' I said. 'It's my intention to propose to the board that we stop paying dividend on food throughout the Society and the dividend on non-food be doubled to 2s in the pound. There was silence for a few moments then everyone spoke at once. They were all elated.

'There's always negatives to everything,' I continued. 'The policy will mean no credit or delivery on food, which will not please everyone.'

A centralised order department, hailed as ultra-modern only twelve months ago, would now be out of date. People who had always lived on Co-op credit would have to pay cash and dividend would end for food. Without exception, everyone in the Society was delighted at the idea of double dividend on non-food. The board accepted the proposal with equal enthusiasm. After careful planning and costing the policy was introduced. Sales soared to record heights, but not without criticism. Older members castigated me for eliminating credit, and the manager and staff of the redundant order department were very bitter.

We were now well-placed to compete against anyone in the food industry. Our non-food policy was a major attraction and customers came to Hetton from all parts of the county. Hetton was as good as any retailer: it was modern, efficient and very successful, but in the process, bringing the Society into the 1960s gave me the reputation of being a Co-op rebel by other Co-op managers.

First Co-op 'Non-Dividend Store' in Britain, Self Service *magazine*

14

I WON'T CHANGE!

By mid 1960 the new policy was established, criticism was less vocal, and many English Co-ops were now introducing similar tactics. Unfortunately, not one of the north-eastern Co-ops was interested in change. They continued with old-fashioned trading methods, lost sales, profit and prestige.

Around this time Procter & Gamble introduced a unique offer that was to create a new dimension in retailing. They produced a 'free' offer, in the form of a simple plastic flower with every packet of Daz. It was sensational. Customers given something 'free'—absolutely unheard of! The demand was incredible.

I quickly copied the idea and began creating our own 'free' offers. The most successful was a free packet of sugar with every sweeping brush bought—we sold *three years'* normal sales in *four weeks*. From then on free offers became an accepted promotional gimmick in food retailing.

During the war a control called Retail Price Maintenance was introduced, aimed at compelling retailers to sell products at a price recommended by the manufacturer. To sell below was to risk prosecution and no further supplies.

Now, 16 years after the end of the war, the control was still in operation. The profit on these products was exorbitant and completely alien to the 1960s new retailing philosophy.

Bread, spirits, cigarettes, tyres, and many other items were included in these controls. I carefully planned the timing, quietly organised supplies, and launched cut-price promotions of each item in turn, with national publicity. Press and television had a field day. Hetton Co-op was known nation-wide as the company forcing down prices. At first it was a novelty to see Hetton Co-op quoted on TV and national press. As time passed we were considered leaders in aggressive retailing. Threats of prosecution and stopping of supplies never materialised. Sales were so tremendous suppliers were queuing up to jump on the bandwagon.

One of the major items on price control was bread. Never before had anyone dared to sell bread below the recommended price. When I approached the Co-op bakery, I was amazed to find them enthusiastic and they promised continuous supplies. The launch of Britain's first cut-price bread was timed to coincide with a national price increase (this would ensure maximum free publicity).

It was like dropping a bomb into the retail industry. Everything else I'd done paled into insignificance compared to the reaction of customers, competitors, and the media. People queued to buy bread as if we were giving it away. The media descended on Hetton in force; the free publicity was worth a fortune.

Competitors were up in arms, yet incredibly no one followed suit and people came from miles away to buy cut-price bread—and, obviously, they bought other items including non-food. Membership increased in order to get the double dividend on fashions etc. Once again, the most fierce criticism came from other Co-op managers.

I had just arrived at work one morning when the phone rang. Harry Jennings was one of the most senior and well-respected Co-op managers in the north, a part-time CWS director and very much a Co-op traditionalist. With a very friendly voice he said:

'David would you meet a group of managers next Tuesday at Newcastle?' He didn't believe in small talk and he made the request sound like a Royal Command.

'What about?' I asked.

'Well, we're very concerned the way Co-op trade is going,' he answered. I knew that he was talking about my activities and said:

'Who are the managers you're talking about?'

'Well, you know, the managers with long experience.' That comment was intended to put me in my place. I was very tempted to give a similar response, but thought better of it and agreed to the meeting. This would be the first time I would face a concerted attack by other Co-op managers.

I didn't want to make small talk to men I suspected would be antagonistic, so I waited until I felt sure everyone had arrived at the meeting. I walked into the large, oak-panelled committee room and was dumbfounded to see it crowded with Co-op managers. The chatter of conversation subsided as I walked to a vacant chair in the front row.

'I was only expecting a few managers!' I said with some annoyance to Harry Jennings.

'Well there's a lot of interest, so we didn't stop those who wanted to attend,' he answered with a smile.

As everyone settled down I had a feeling that it had the makings of a kangaroo court—and I was the kangaroo.

'Gentlemen, the competition between societies has gone on long enough. It's doing our image a great deal of harm and I hope this meeting will produce a happy solution.' Harry spoke for twenty minutes, never mentioned my name or Hetton Co-op, but there was no doubt in anyone's mind who he was talking about. He sat down, and opened the meeting for anyone else to speak. Now the knives would be out!

After a deluge of criticism, I was in no doubt I'd created antagonism. Now I realised why there was this bitterness: they were under pressure from their committees because they were losing trade, and their members were demanding cut prices. Unfortunately their societies were too inefficient to embark on my policy. Cut-price bread had been the last straw.

'Do you realise you could jeopardise our society and my job?' shouted the manager of Murton Co-op (we had a branch in Murton).

'Are you wanting to take us over on the same terms as you took Moorsley?' the Sherburn Hill Co-op manager said with great bitterness. Similar speeches continued for over an hour. Harry Jennings asked if I wished to speak, but I declined, preferring to wait until the vitriolic comments were exhausted.

In fact, as people began repeating themselves, I began to feel some despair. Here was the so-called cream of experienced Co-op managers, in a state of absolute confusion because of me, and I'd only been a manager a couple of years. Maybe that was the real problem. I knew I had to respond. I had learned a lot since the jibe of David Jones when he had said: 'Allow for the impetuosity of youth.' This time tact and diplomacy were essential.

1,000 SHOP CONSORTIUM TO SLASH PRICES

ONE of the biggest cut-price plans in the north, involving a consortium of 60 societies, was announced last week and will cover a wide range of goods through a thousand shops.

Known as the North-East Co-operative Link Group, it spells an even bigger venture than the consortium of societies which cut bread prices so successfully recently.

The bread consortium, which grew from 14 to 23 societies to market loaves from the C.W.S. Bakery Division at Murton, has been integrated in the new group which covers over three-quarters of a million members.

The new group will probably concentrate on selling foodstuffs at cut rates.

"But it will not necessarily be only foodstuffs", Mr. David Hughes, spokesman for the group, told the "News".

"It could be dry goods as well", he said. "There is no set decision to exclude dry goods. But groceries will probably be more predominant.

"Every society that takes part will be under an obligation to sell the goods concerned at the agreed price, which will be advertised on television and in the press".

Mr. Hughes, who is general manager of Hetton Downs Society—which has featured in publicity for cut-price policies over a long period—said the bread consortium had proved very successful.

The societies in that had increased bread sales from 90,000 to almost 150,000 loaves per week.

He said the new group would be "a big thing", and would launch its publicity for the new cuts on March 12. But the range of goods could not be disclosed before then. A marketing committee would choose the goods and all the society shops involved would cut the price together.

"This is an innovation in group selling", pointed out Mr. Hughes. "The societies have gone in for aggressive selling. We intend to go after the housewife trade in a big way".

Sunderland Echo, *1966*

BREAD "PRICE WAR" IN N.E.

14 Co-ops To Cut Cost Of Loaf As Others Put 1d On

MR HUGHES

THREE - HUNDRED co-operative shops from the Tyne to the Tees are planning a "2d bread bonus" for North-East housewives. When an extra penny goes on a loaf nationally next week they will cut their price by 1d.

To make the cuts, 14 North-East societies have formed a group. They operate 300 shops—including more than 120 mobile shops—and it is the first time they have got together in the region to reduce the price of a basic comodity.

Spokesman for the group, Mr David Hughes, general manager of Hetton Downs Co-operative Society, which took the lead in price-cutting, told the Echo: "On Monday the price of a large loaf goes up throughout the country but North-East housewives can get a price reduction. Out of 25 societies in the region 14 have joined forces."

The Journal, *1964*

'David has listened to all your comments, now I think we should give him an opportunity to reply,' Harry said, indicating I join him at the table. Even as I moved to speak, I heard a voice say:

'I wish to hell he'd get out of the Co-op.' I stood for a few seconds looking at the faces of men all old enough to be my father, all in dark suits and white shirts, many with watch-chains dangling from waistcoat pockets.

Their image, business methods and attitudes hadn't changed for decades. No wonder Tesco and others weren't concerned about Co-op competition.

'Gentlemen, I don't accept your criticism, but I understand it,' I began. There was total silence as I continued. 'I couldn't reverse the policy now even if I wanted to—and I don't. The customers wouldn't accept it and I can tell you, the board wouldn't change.'

'But you're taking our trade,' someone shouted.

'If I don't Tesco or someone else will,' I responded. 'You have two choices, either continue as you are or join our policy.'

The manager of Ashington Co-op jumped to his feet and said:

'In spite of all this criticism, you won't stop price cutting?' I looked directly at him and said:

'No.' He stormed out of the meeting and a buzz of conversation continued until Harry brought the meeting to order and said:

'I think we should listen to what David has to say about joining his policy.' When the noise had subsided, I continued.

'I'm not your competitor, it's the multiples we should fight before they become established here. Unless you do something they'll take over. I'm not prepared to stick to tradition and go out of business.' No one interrupted, so I continued. 'Cut-price bread has been controversial, so why don't you do the same—sell at the same price, advertise as a group on television and in the press? One or two looked thoughtful, but then the room was filled with reasons why it *couldn't* be done.

'I'm not spending money on TV adverts.'

'We can't afford dividend *and* cut-price bread.'

'We can't group advertise—not everyone will join.'

'Why should we follow him?' It was a shambles until Harry, with typical compromise, said:

'Let's form a sub-committee to look at the idea.'

I returned to Hetton, not expecting to hear from them again.
With amazement, about two weeks later, I received an invitation to a meeting at the Roker Hotel at Seaburn. Every society had been surveyed, and out of 60 Co-ops fourteen had accepted my proposal. I couldn't believe it. What a turnaround: the meeting was friendly and positive.

I was asked to organise advertising and be spokesman to the media. Hetton wouldn't be fighting alone. Darlington, Gateshead, Stockton, Middlesbrough and other Co-ops now agreed to buy, sell and advertise as a group. The first TV commercial for cut-price bread was difficult to make, the seventeen societies insisted their name be shown. Nevertheless, it was a major success. Sales soared and soon the fourteen societies increased to 40 and then to 60.

The group activity soon embraced many products, and slowly even the critics began to join the group to receive the benefits. Little did any of us realise that this was the first move to the creation of the giant North Eastern Co-op. Nor did we anticipate that in less than ten years only six of those 60 Co-op managers would still work for the Co-op.

Sunderland Echo, *1965*

Hetton Co-op celebrates 100 years

15

100 YEARS OLD

In 1963 Hetton Co-op celebrated 100 years in business. We organised fashion shows, special promotions, and a host of special activities to mark the occasion. Staff and customers had an enjoyable time.

The Co-op had changed dramatically, the biggest changes occurring in the previous four years. In the early days of the Co-op, the manager was of equal standing in the community to the vicar and the pit manager and some of the older members still held me in the same esteem. People came for advice on a wide range of personal problems, assuming that as the Co-op manager I would surely have the answer. I was custodian and executor of innumerable wills and was always amazed how people would confide on topics far beyond my experience.

Co-op managers of the past had always been aloof and remote from staff, immaculately dressed, and always chauffeur-driven. I liked to be totally involved, I knew every employee by first name, and most of their families were as familiar. Some people thought I'd gone too far.

The society had survived 100 years, I was trying to ensure its continued survival, but I doubted whether small individual societies would survive a further ten years, let alone another century.

16

NO FIXTURES?

Nearby Houghton had been one of the best and most successful branches in the society, but population movement and creation of a modern shopping centre made the branch a candidate for closure. It was sited on the main road leaving Houghton to Sunderland at a spot called Houghton Cut. (The name was derived from an actual cut made in the rock by French prisoners of war during the Napoleonic wars).

From a contact on the local council, I learned that it was planned to widen 'the cut' to meet the demands of modern traffic. This would require the demolition of our shop after compulsory purchase. The amount of compensation would be based on turnover, which in our case would be very little—unless I could do something to increase sales. In business, as in life, a bit of luck is most acceptable and what followed was the most incredible sequence of lucky events I could have hoped for.

I needed to find a way to encourage more people to walk up a steep hill, away from a modern shopping precinct to an old shop in a derelict area. *Price*!! It had to be worth their while, *but how*? A few coppers cheaper wouldn't be sufficient—prices would need to be absolute rock bottom. I couldn't buy cheaper—it could only be done by cutting expenses.

The idea of *'Britain's First Economy Store'* was born. The first move was to eliminate fixtures (I couldn't afford staff to fill them). The bare walls were painted white to create a warehouse effect. The stock range was reduced to only 150 of the most popular product lines. Personal service was eliminated, everything was pre-packed. The shop would open for only 36 hours but staff would continue to be paid their 42-hour wage (they were delighted). Labour costs were minimal, stock was handled straight from the lorry, stacked against the wall and the front cut from the case.

The idea was to create the impression the customer was buying from a warehouse at warehouse prices. In the 1990s it is called 'cut-case display' and universally accepted, but in 1964 it hadn't been tried. I hoped it would succeed, but I wasn't too sure. We had nothing to lose—the shop would be demolished whatever the outcome.

But then emerged some lucky breaks that turned the idea from doubtful to a phenomenal success. 'Brand's soup' was a quality product but not the brand leader. A 'money off' coupon had been printed on the label to boost sales. When offered the deal I noticed the coupon had no restrictions. (A customer could redeem an unlimited quantity of labels). I offered to buy 10,000 cases, with an option for a further 10,000 cases—but only if I could redeem the coupons at the shop to save customers' postage. The order created a stir: no one had redeemed an unlimited offer at the shop before now, but the order was too big to refuse.

At last the marketing director phoned to agree to the order! Manufacturers normally expect a 5-per-cent coupon redemption and I was guaranteeing a 100-per-cent redemption. The soup arrived by the lorry load. Everyone thought I'd gone crazy—there was soup everywhere.

'David, I can't get you a spot for more price cuts,' Rod Griffiths had answered when I called Tyne Tees Television, hoping for a mention on local news. 'Unless you have another gimmick, there's no chance', he said.

'It's a shop without fixtures,' I answered hopefully. 'I'll see what I can do,' he replied, 'But I'm not very optimistic.'

The board members visited the shop on the afternoon before opening; their usual optimism was conspicuous by its absence. Just as they were leaving, an outside broadcast van arrived from Tyne Tees Television. The call to the TV studio had paid off.

The lights and cameras were set up. Brian Widlake, the presenter, was on camera and pointing out features of 'the shop without fixtures'. He stopped in front of a huge stack of Brand's soup, picked up a can and said:

'Four tins for sixpence? It's cheap enough to feed to the dogs.' That one sentence shown on TV that evening had incredible consequences. The normal price was sixpence a tin, the coupon was for four-and-a-half pence. By redeeming the coupon the customer would pay only one-and-a-half pence a can. 'Four cans for sixpence' (old money)!!

Within half an hour of the news broadcast, I had phone calls from almost every newspaper asking about the low prices in 'the shop without fixtures'. I couldn't believe my eyes the next morning. A queue of customers over 100 yards long was waiting for the shop opening and every minute saw more people join the queue. Although our prices were low, that comment about soup created an image of give-away prices. Even small shopkeepers were buying in bulk and—yes—dog owners bought soup by the case. Two hours after opening, the crowds were so big I requested a policeman to control traffic. I then phoned the TV studio, told them police were controlling the crowds and obtained another feature on the news that night.

The publicity was fantastic. People arrived every day by car and bus from every direction. Three days after opening I was confronted by an inspector from the Weights and Measures department.

'I've had a complaint from Walter Willsons, who claim you're selling soup without a label,' he said, 'for which you can be prosecuted.' Good God! I had never thought of that when I arranged to redeem the soup labels at the check out. The inspector and I travelled from my office to Houghton. I felt sick. I wished I'd never seen the damned soup. The shop was heaving with customers, the girls were almost knee-deep in soup labels, they just dropped them into the base of the check out. By the most incredible piece of luck the girls had got into a routine of taking payment *before* removing labels. Technically, the soup was sold *before* the labels were taken off. The inspector looked, smiled, and said:

'It's your lucky day.'

All retailers were convinced that Brands were subsidising our operation. They refused to stock the product with the consequence that the company was later taken over by Sutherland's and the Brand soup label was eventually eliminated.

The loophole of unrestricted coupon redemption was blocked and the Brand's soup exercise could never be repeated. When the shop eventually closed our compensation was ten times more than if we'd done nothing.

Stacking up the tins at Houghton Co-op branch.

AN experiment that could be a trend-setter for future shopping habits starts at Houghton-le-Spring tomorrow. The Co-operative Economy Store in Sunderland Street has no fixtures or fittings and will probably look like a glorified self-service warehouse.

But for the housewife on the look-out for a good buy, the "no frills" shop will mean rock-bottom prices.

It is the latest idea of 39-year-old Mr. David Hughes, the go-ahead general manager of the 8,500 member Hetton Downs Co-operative Society.

Yesterday Mr. Hughes explained: "Fixtures and fittings mean money. Our aim is to offer members and non-members foodstuffs at the ultimate in cut prices."

For example, sugar normally thought fairly competitive at 1s 4d for two pounds will be 1s, and a 1s 3½d loaf of bread will cost 1s 1d.

Less hours

Simplicity and peak period trading only seem to be the principles of the plan. Stock will be unloaded from a lorry and stacked straight on display in the shop.

And the three men and three girls who are to run it will be the envy of many. "They will work a 36-hour week—six hour less than other Society staff—bu

'No frills' Co-op revolutionises bargain shopping

Queue up at the Co-op

It was queues all day long at Britain's first Co-operative Economy Store at Houghton-le-Spring yesterday . . . Report : Page 9.

Money for soup as new Co-op opens

Bargain-hunters invade the cut-price Co-op.

THERE was a steady stream of customers when the Hetton Downs Co-operative Society's new "economy store," in Sunderland Street, Houghton, was officially opened yesterday.

Coun. Joseph Bartley, chairman of Houghton Urban Council, who was introduced by Mr. P. C. Richardson, president of the Society, formally opened the doors.

"The dividend has been 3d in the £1 I saved that much this morning for an outlay of only 2s 3d. for 2 lb. of sugar and a quarter pound of tea," said Mrs. Florence Smith, of Moore Crescent, Houghton, who was among the first in the queue which began to form shortly after 7.30 a.m. In all she spent 25s.

Our Houghton correspondent

Almost every customer took the opportunity to buy four tins soup for only sixpence.

One small shopkeeper, who said he went to purchase butter, to our reporter he normally went Sunderland to buy it wholesa at the same price.

Mr. Fred Hall, secretary of Society, said last night: "T response by the public has be fantastic It greatly exceeded e expectations

"The staff augmented for t opening day have been fu engaged. By mid-afternoon ta ings had actually exceeded t weekly total at the branch und the old system."

17

I WON'T BE BLACKMAILED!

Since taking over the greengrocery buying I had made many good contacts in the Newcastle fruit market. In 1965 I heard that a private greengrocery wholesale company was for sale. This could open the door to producers and importers that could be very profitable.

No local Co-op had ever owned a private company. It would be another first for Hetton. After a long and protracted negotiation, the company was ours. The two partners would be retained to operate the business.

There were six lorries with drivers, a turnover of £350,000 a year, and the company name would be retained to maintain the private trade. Business developed quite well, and although it was well known the company was now owned by the Co-op, it didn't stop private traders being customers and indeed some local Co-ops opened accounts. We were providing a good service and developing very satisfactorily until one day I became involved in the company to a far greater degree than I'd ever intended.

'Hello David,' Tom Lyon said as I indicated a chair. 'I think you have a problem.'

Tom was a fruit-broker in the market. We'd done a lot of business together and although I hadn't been in the market since buying the company, we had maintained regular contact. 'Your buyer's on the fiddle,' he continued.

'Can you prove it?' I asked.

'Well, you have a few friends in the market. We'd have no problem if you want him caught.'

'Of course I want him caught—the sooner the better.' I thanked him and made the necessary plans.

Tom phoned me each day with a list of market prices, and I checked the amount we were paying. A few days later the buyer was in my office, ashen-faced and ready to admit to anything, so long as I didn't prosecute. He'd been buying from well-known 'cowboy' fruit brokers and paying *above* the market price in return for a backhander. Tom Lyon and other 'legitimate' brokers had been losing business and didn't hesitate to 'shop' him. He admitted the offence with very little pressure from me. Half an hour after his dismissal, a knock on the door produced four of the six company lorry drivers.

'Are you serious?' I exclaimed on hearing their demand. 'Are you really prepared to lose your jobs?'

'Without us your company is finished. We know the customers and the journeys,' the spokesman driver said. The other three kept quiet. 'You'll have no buyer and only two drivers,' he concluded.

'Let's be in no doubt of your demand.' My quiet tone hid my seething anger. 'You're saying that unless I reinstate the buyer you four will walk out.'

'That's right,' each one answered in turn.

'Three of you have families,' I said 'So I suggest you think seriously of what you're saying, come back in one hour and if you're still of the same mind, I'll have your cards ready.'

They had all worked for the company long before I'd taken over. They had made a gesture, but I didn't think their loyalty would take them to the unemployment office. When they returned I had four cards on my desk and saw each one separately.

'Reinstate the buyer or I leave,' was demanded by each driver.

'I won't be blackmailed. He is sacked and will never work for me again,' I repeated four times. My desk was cleared of cards.

I had a problem. A driver from the society was diverted and the local milk depot produced other drivers (after their early milk round). For me, it was back to a 6a.m. start in the market, home for breakfast, then begin my job managing the Co-op. It would mean a long day, every day. We managed with a struggle. I later learned that the dismissed staff had waited two weeks, convinced I'd send for them. One of the replacements was milkman Allan Nicholson, who was worth any two other staff. His work rate was phenomenal. It didn't take long to teach him buying and I had no doubt about his honesty.

The business was beginning to boom again when an opportunity arose to buy Jaffa oranges direct off the boat at Hull docks. This would by-pass middlemen and be very profitable. Allan and I decided to travel to Hull. He was driving the car. I remember going through Stockton. The next thing I knew I was on the settee at home with a doctor bending over me. I'd collapsed with exhaustion. (We never did buy those Jaffas.) After a few days I returned, and delegated buying and day-to-day control to other people—the company would survive without my participation. I had enough to do managing the Co-op.

18

'CAN YOU HEAR ME MOTHER?'

For a long time Hetton Co-op was in the public eye. I was often interviewed on TV whenever a retailing topic was shown. Local and national newspapers continued to develop stories around our activities.

Two articles, 'The Mouse that Roared' and 'The Hetton Downs Story', created quite a stir in the retail industry and resulted in my being invited to speak on 'modern retailing' at functions throughout the country. Around this time, I had a phone call from a most unlikely source.

A man who claimed to be the agent of Sandy Powell was asking if I could involve the comedian in some form of publicity. In his day, Sandy Powell had been a top-class entertainer, a film star, and TV personality. Now he was appearing in a theatre at Gateshead and his popularity was disappearing. The only idea I could think of was for him to make a personal appearance at a small off-licence we'd recently modernised. I promised to contact the media. The agent would organise distribution of posters.

Half an hour before his arrival I went to the shop to see if the crowd of sightseers was under control (I had notified the police of the star's visit). The windows were covered with huge posters showing Sandy's famous grin, and proclaiming the personal appearance of this star of stage and screen. The only person in sight was the manageress, who smiled but didn't speak. There wasn't even a customer buying, and the press and TV who were constantly looking for a story must have found one—somewhere else. I suddenly felt sorry for the ex-mega star who couldn't attract one single fan throughout Hetton. We had to do something!

While the manageress went out knocking on doors of surrounding houses inviting the occupants for a free drink to meet Sandy Powell, I phoned every branch and 'invited' any two staff to the grand appearance. Some bottles of wine were opened, and the occupants of a huge car alighted to see some extremely happy 'fans' welcome the star who made a grand entrance with his fur-clad wife on his arm.

'Where the hell's the press boys?' the agent whispered.

'Be thankful, you're lucky to have these people here,' I replied. Sandy was oblivious to the arrangements for his visit, or the lack of enthusiasm of his fans. In fact he and his wife were charming and everyone enjoyed his visit.

As he left he pushed some tickets in my hand and said he'd be delighted for my family to see his show. Pressure from David and Sheila resulted in the whole family presenting itself for that Saturday matinee. There was no queue, we were shown to seats in the circle, where there were more seats empty than occupied. The show was tatty and the atmosphere embarrassing. At the interval, the theatre manager, dressed in evening suit and bow tie, said Mr Powell would be delighted to see us back stage. Sheila and David were thrilled, so we all followed in line down a winding metal staircase, along some narrow passages into the star's dressing room. It was no more than an extension of the passage with a door and a mirror on the wall. A half-full bottle of milk that had gone green-mouldy was on the floor and the costumes on a rail were very tatty—nothing like the elegance under stage lights.

Of course we perpetuated Sandy's illusion by praising the show and his performance, then said our goodbyes, never to meet again. Those who remember the star of 'Can you hear me mother' will have particular memories. Mine are clouded by mouldy milk and tatty costumes.

19

DEPARTURE UNDER FIRE

By 1966, my name was linked to almost every top Co-op job that became vacant. I was approached by London, Ipswich, Wolverhampton, CWS at Manchester and Harrogate.

Although it was flattering and good for my ego, there was no certainty I could repeat the Hetton success. You could only be first, once. Nor would I ever get a board as co-operative as Hetton. In addition, to uproot two children from school, and move the family away from friends and relations needed a great deal of thought. Any move from Hetton had to be right for everyone.

A few months earlier, the CWS at Manchester had appointed a new chief executive officer by the name of Philip Thomas. By all accounts, he was a brilliant man, an ex-director of Associated British Foods (the parent company of Fine Fare) and, as a barrister, he'd been one of the prosecutors at the War Crimes Tribunal in Japan. He'd been appointed by the CWS, with complete freedom to modernise and make efficient the whole Co-op movement. He'd begun his task in spectacular fashion. I was impressed by every news item published.

One day I was surprised to hear Philip Thomas on the phone, asking if I'd like to meet him to discuss a possible job with him. I was flattered, non-committal and indicated I'd need a great deal of information about the job. He said he would be in Newcastle in two weeks' time and could call at Hetton to discuss the job. I had nothing to lose, everything to gain, so agreed to meet.

The day of his visit began the same as most days. He wasn't expected until late afternoon. We'd had a few problems with some shop fittings and after John Anderson and I had discussed the problem in my office, we were walking to the footwear department when John looked up and said:

'There's smoke coming from the top of your drapery department.' Good God, so there was!

'I'll get the people out, you call the fire brigade,' I shouted, already running to the building. Inside, staff and customers were oblivious to the fire raging in the roof and had to be almost pushed out. Arthur Belton insisted on trying to save some expensive stock, but within minutes the smoke and heat were so intense, only the firemen could go near. A strong wind was blowing and in less than an hour the whole building was gutted.

Fred Hall and I were looking at the burning embers. I was absolutely filthy and we were discussing our insurance cover when a huge chauffeur-driven limousine glided up the street. The driver leaned out and asked:

'Where can I find Mr Hughes?' I stepped forward to see Philip Thomas in the back seat. I'd completely forgotten his visit.

He didn't even get out of the car, but simply said:

'I think you have enough to see to, I'll phone in a few days.' Then he was gone.

'Who was that?' Fred enquired.

'It's Philip Thomas from Manchester.' I said without explanation. Fred lifted his eyebrows but said nothing. The fire had been caused by an electrical fault, Fred negotiated the insurance payment and the drapery was re-sited in a vacated building.

I eventually had a meeting with Philip Thomas at Manchester. I couldn't believe the information he was giving while we were sitting in his palatial office on the top floor of New Century House. In addition to modernising factories and wholesale operations he was planning to create *only one retail Co-op Society throughout England.*

The first stage would be to take over those societies in financial difficulties and in debt to the CWS. He needed three people to literally take control of these societies and slowly integrate them into one society. He'd already appointed someone for the Midlands; I was being offered the north of England. I would operate as an advisory officer but, when taking over a society, I'd disband the committee, take the position of chief executive officer, and be responsible direct to Philip Thomas. Salary, car and conditions were no problem, they were far better than I'd have asked for. I said I'd think about it. We wouldn't need to move and, provided May agreed, I knew as I walked out of his office, I'd take the job.

The board didn't seem to be surprised when I announced my move. I'm sure they'd been expecting to lose my services for some time. An emotional presentation by the staff was organised for May and me (I hadn't realised I was so popular).

My years at Hetton Co-op had been the most interesting, traumatic and hard-working of my life. I now know they were no more than my apprenticeship in management.

The most eventful part of my career was just about to begin.

The gutted building after the blaze at Hetton Downs Co-op

BOOK 2

THE
WISDOM OF
MATURITY

'Selling for 14 Societies' EXPERIMENT
'No future in food divi'
Cut loaves at cut prices
CWS APPOINTS SECOND 'TROUBLE SHOOTER'

DAVID HUGHES, A CO-OPERATIVE TROUBLE-SHOOTER

by the Northern News Editor

THE man who raised the eyebrows of the Co-operative Movement by making his tiny 12-branch society front-page news throughout Britain starts a new job on Monday.

Instead of continuing his duties as chief executive officer of the tiny Hetton Downs Society near Durham City, 41-year-old Mr. David Hughes will, in future, be travelling a few extra miles North.

His destination?—Sunderland. His mission?—To begin work as the CWS second "troubleshooter"—part of a team of top executives whose job is to go to the aid of societies in difficulties.

Nine years ago Mr. Hughes was a retail greengrocer—a period in his life in which he admits he also sought the necessary know-how to enter retail society management.

He took over his first principal post about eight years ago—in charge of Hetton Downs Society, at Hetton-le-Hole, the 15,000-strong community between Durham City and the North Sea.

The day Mr. Hughes took over the new Hetton Downs story began.

Although very much a minnow in the retail society pool, the activities of Hetton Downs Society caused a stir in recent years and have sent ripples of comment all over the country.

Mr. Hughes's decision was a blunt one: "There is no future in giving a dividend on food."

From £300 a week to £2,700 in two days

With this in mind the society launched experimental, no-dividend, cut price policy in one of its stores. The result was that the unit which had previously taken £300 in one week, sold £2,700 worth of goods in its first two days.

Encouraged by this first success, the society introduced the policy into all its grocery branches with deep cuts on certain grocery lines.

Whisky was among the first lines to be cut, closely followed by bread—the latter happening at a time when there was talk of a bakers' strike in the area.

Sales soared and it was not long before the local Press and television were recording the aggressive selling tactics from Hetton-le-Hole.

Mr. Hughes told The Grocer last week: "The only way I could get people to shop with the society was to shout about the things we were doing."

Mr. Hughes's activities in the public relations field were successful. Turnover soared and a steady stream of executives from other parts of the country visited Hetton to study the operation.

The bread cutting campaign—along with 13 neighbouring societies—caused such a stir that Mr. Hughes said he was approached by a man claiming to represent "all supermarkets" and threatened "retaliatory action" if the price cutting did not cease.

The campaign continued despite this. Commenting on it last week, Mr. Hughes said: "I almost wish there had been some form of retaliation. Then we could really have had fun!"

The result of Mr. Hughes's efforts in the past eight years has been a 20% increase in the turnover of the 6,000-member group to the current figure with annual sales topping £750,000.

Commenting on his Hetton Downs activities last week, Mr. Hughes said: "I have been lucky in that my board of directors always listened sympathetically to my ideas.

"At the beginning, many of the more traditional co-operators seemed to frown on my activities. Even some of those societies which said the plan would never work are beginning to come around to our way of thinking.

"I have nothing against the principles of the Co-operative Movement as such. But I felt that some of those principles needed to be brought up to date.

"From the age of about 20 I could never accept the idea behind the overall dividend policy whereby a department which was not making enough net profit was giving a dividend."

When Mr. Hughes took over at Hetton, all grocery branches were counter service. More eyebrows were raised when, in an area where traditions die hard, he began conversions. Some customers said quite bluntly that they would never patronise the society's self-service stores—the rise in membership and turnover is a fair indication of their change of mind.

But this week David Hughes, ex-co-op apprentice, Co-op College student, retail greengrocer and chief executive officer, became an advisory officer (special services) with the CWS.

And the lively Hetton Downs story will go on as before. Taking over as general manager is Mr William Curry who has been one of Mr. Hughes's team in recent years and, more recently, food trades officer.

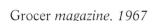

Grocer *magazine, 1967*

1

CO-OP TROUBLESHOOTER

I couldn't believe my eyes. The headline leapt out at me like an accusation:
'CO-OP TROUBLESHOOTER HEADING FOR SUNDERLAND!'

I was facing a tough enough job, but to be introduced by the press in this fashion would not be much help. The press story was out on the Friday, I was due to begin my new job on the following Monday. I had already contacted Bill Edmondson, the secretary of Sunderland Co-op Society, and informed him of my starting date—I didn't intend to arrive unexpected. I suppose I should have expected a news story because I was now nationally known in the retail industry, I'd acquired something of a reputation for aggressive retailing and as innovator of new ideas. I'd certainly matured as a manager during my years as general manager at Hetton Downs Co-op Society. Now I was going into a new ball game. In fact I was more apprehensive at my first assignment than I had been on my first day at Hetton Co-op.

Philip Thomas, the new chief executive officer of the CWS at Manchester, had been given a mandate to modernise and streamline the whole Co-op movement (including retail societies). His starting point when tackling the retail societies was the Co-ops in financial difficulties, indebted to the CWS, and on the verge of bankruptcy. I was one of the people to implement this part of the programme; my area was from the border at Scotland to a line south of Leeds. My job title was 'CWS Advisor (Special Services)'. I was to be responsible directly to Philip Thomas and any retail society in that vast area that was in financial difficulty would eventually be my personal responsibility. I had no illusions about the size of the job, nor had I any doubts about the terms on which I was to operate: at a meeting in Manchester, Philip Thomas had left me in no doubt.

When taking over an ailing society, I would automatically take over the position of chief executive officer, the society board members would lose all power and control, and operate only in an advisory capacity. Three CWS directors would sit on the board, but only as advisors. My authority would be absolute.

'You answer only to me and no one else,' Philip Thomas said at the end of the meeting. 'We'll meet once a month and I only want to know what you've done, not what you're going to do.' When I had started my Co-op management career at Hetton, I had asked for freedom to manage. This man was giving me a freedom that seemed frightening in its enormity and the consequences of failure to so many people (including myself) were equally frightening.

The head office of Sunderland Co-op was situated adjacent to Marks and Spencer's. It was a prime site, selling the usual merchandise of fashions, electricals, furniture, footwear, carpets, and a very small food department. The business was run-down, losses were enormous, and staff totally demoralised. In addition, there were a number of branches in an area of about twenty square miles around Sunderland, most were in a loss situation. Bankruptcy was being avoided only by the goodwill of the CWS and the Co-op Bank. My instructions were simple: 'Do what's necessary to bring Sunderland Co-op into profitability or, if it isn't possible, close down.'

'Good morning Mr. Hughes,' a mechanic stepped forward as I parked my car at the entrance to Sunderland Co-op garage. 'Give me your keys and I'll park it for you.' I thanked him, impressed that he knew my name, but concerned that an almost bankrupt company could afford such luxury for its management. I made my way into the store, which didn't open until 9a.m. so I didn't expect to see many staff around. I walked through a side door which was closed, but not locked, and arrived without challenge on the third floor where a shrill voice said:

'Reps aren't allowed in here till ten o'clock.' A very thin cleaner in a grubby overall and mobcap continued washing the floor without looking up.

'Good morning, my name is Hughes. Can you direct me to the

secretary's office please?' She looked up with a startled expression, dropped her mop with a clatter and said:

'He'll not be in for an hour, but I'll show you his office.'

'Just direct me, I'll not stop you working.' I replied.

I made my way to the top floor and waited, but after almost an hour the secretary still hadn't arrived. In fact, with ten minutes to store opening, I could see none of the bustle I expected in a departmental store preparing for another week's business. Staff stood in groups gossiping, covers were still on garment rails and no one seemed to be in control. As the clock chimed nine o'clock, four men I assumed to be senior management, strolled into the office in animated conversation as if they hadn't a care in the world. As if by some hidden signal, a girl arrived with a tray on which were four cups of tea and a plate of biscuits—such immaculate timing!!

'Good morning, Gentlemen,' I said without waiting for an introduction.

'Mr. Hughes?' A lean-faced, balding man, about forty years old, stepped forward with his hand outstretched.

'I'm Bill Edmondson. Would you like a cup of tea?' I hesitated only a second.

'No thank you, please show me to my office.' Turning to the others I said: 'No doubt I'll speak to you later.' They continued to drink their tea and I followed the secretary along a passage that I assumed would lead to an office from which I could control the business.

'We always have ten minutes together, every Monday morning to discuss the business,' he quickly explained as we walked along the passage. No doubt he was conscious of my silence as we proceeded. Inwardly I was fuming. They would have been well aware of my arrival—not only had they failed to produce a favourable impression, it seemed as if every effort had been made to create the opposite.

'What's the meaning of this?' I rounded on him angrily. We were standing in the middle of a completely empty room.

'On the phone you didn't mention furnishing an office,' Bill answered. 'I didn't know if you'd bring your own furniture.' His voice indicated neither concern nor apology. With great difficulty I controlled my temper.

'I'm going to visit every department in this store. It should take about two hours. When I return I expect a desk, chair, filing cabinet and a carpet on the floor.'

'Can I have a memo to authorise the carpet?' he replied. I didn't answer. I'm sure the look I gave him spoke volumes. I left my secretary, Rosemary Freeman, to supervise the setting up of a decent office and went to walk about the store.

My anticipated two-hour tour of the store actually took the whole day. I spent the time looking and listening. Some staff talked and talked, others were defensive, all were full of apathy. Store security was a farce. The quality of the merchandise in the fashion department was old, dusty and unsaleable. The number of customers could be counted on one hand. At the end of the day I'd introduced myself to everyone. Most of the staff were friendly (I suppose to them I was just another boss and unlikely to change their lives) but I could feel the animosity and the antagonism from section heads and departmental managers. This was our first meeting, but it was obvious from their comments and attitude I wasn't welcome and no one made any effort to hide the fact. That damned headline had done me no good at all.

I returned to see if I now had a workable office and found it properly furnished and even an extension telephone installed. I just sat for an hour, thinking of my first day and wondered: 'What the hell have I walked into?'

I had studied sufficient statistics to understand the financial and trading problems, but you don't get an understanding of people from balance sheets, and unless I could create a good team, there was no hope of success.

The next few days were occupied visiting branches, a coal depot, funeral department, and administration section. I was shocked at managers' apathy, and even some animosity, at a 'troubleshooter' moving into their cosy set-up. Only one manager showed any sign of co-operation and enthusiasm: John Love was the coal depot manager, one of the few sections that showed a regular profit.

By Friday I'd had enough. It seemed to be concerted action by the whole of the management to be non-co-operative and, in some instances, outright objectionable. I decided I wouldn't take this treatment one more day—it was either them or me, and I intended to succeed.

'Mr Edmondson, I want you to notify every manager to attend a meeting on Monday morning at 8 o'clock in the board room.'

'Who'll open the store and branches?' he asked.

'It won't be a long meeting and, by the way, I want everyone's P45 cards available at the meeting. The meeting doors will be closed at

8 o'clock. Anyone late won't be admitted.'

'How many managers are missing?' I asked as I entered the Monday morning meeting.

'Everyone's here,' Bill replied. The atmosphere in the packed room was electric, although a group at the rear seemed carefree from the sound of laughter.

'Give each person his cards,' I instructed. His mouth dropped open with shock, but I ignored him and turned to some notes I'd prepared. By the time everyone had been given their cards, the laughter at the back of the room had ceased. There was a low buzz of conversation that lapsed into total silence when I rose to my feet to speak to them.

For a few seconds, silence enveloped the room as I slowly and deliberately looked at every face. I wanted them to be well aware I was speaking to each individual manager sitting there.

'Sunderland Co-op is near to bankruptcy. Everyone in this room has some degree of responsibility for that situation. As managers you are responsible and accountable for such failure.' You could hear a pin drop as I continued. 'I'm here to try to save the society. I can't do it alone, I need a team of managers who want to help.' I still had their attention. 'During my first week here, I get the impression that some of you can't or don't wish to be part of my team. Well, I'm going to let you make the decision. You each have your cards. I'm giving you two choices: either return your cards to me personally before I go home today with the clear understanding that your attitude, co-operation and enthusiasm changes immediately, and that you wish to be a member of an honest, hard-working team—or keep your cards and go home now. I'll send on any outstanding money we owe you.'

I had planned to give them a shock. It seemed I'd succeeded. No one moved, spoke or even coughed, so I ended the meeting by concluding:

'Let's get back to work, I'll see each person separately in my office.'

Four section heads didn't return, and two branch managers decided (after their individual interviews) that my requirements were more demanding than they could accept (I suspected other reasons). The fashion buyer said yes to everything I said and promised full co-operation. The electrical buyer was too smarmy for words. I had little choice but to accept him—for the time being.

'There's my cards, boss.' John Love walked up to my desk with a confidence that was like a breath of fresh air.

'You're quite happy to work with me?' I asked, indicating he take a seat.

'I'm not a yes-man,' he said very forcefully, 'but I'm delighted we have someone who'll take control of this lot—there's been no control for years. I don't envy your job, but I'm ready to help in any way I can.' No doubt John would be quite an asset in future.

By the end of the day I'd lost six from a team of 35 managers. It could have been worse, but this was no way to build a team. All I'd achieved was to leave no one in any doubt as to who was the boss. At least we could start from a new base of discipline. I wasn't concerned about being popular, but I was determined to get their respect for my work-rate, fairness and achievement. At the end of my first week, I hadn't taken one step to improve the profitability of the company, but I now had an understanding with staff and, particularly, managers that changes would take place in their work-rate, performance, and attitude to the business. We had sufficient problems to avoid total bankruptcy, without carrying passengers among the staff.

2

I'VE SOLD THE STORE

My first action was to reorganise the 'new' management team into a workable structure and have only five people report directly to me. The individual responsibility would cover: finance, buying, marketing, personnel, and organisation. These senior managers and I virtually divorced ourselves from the business for two days. We discussed and analysed every aspect of the business and its problems. A lot was gained from the sessions: we got to know each other, everyone had an in-depth understanding of the situation and—most important—it gave a clear signal that this would not be a one man band. If we were to succeed it would only be as a team.

Sunderland Co-op had two major problems:

1. Desperate shortage of cash
2. Insufficient trade.

Philip Thomas had made it clear that no help could be expected from the CWS or the Co-op Bank. Any society I took over had to solve its own problems.

We needed new stock and aggressive promotion activity but, without cash, we could do neither. The bank overdraft was way over the top, suppliers were asking for payment before they would deliver the goods and we were having difficulty financing our credit trade. Obtaining a major cash injection into the company was my top priority.

'Bill, I want you to assume this is your business. Go through every single expense item and list everything that could be eliminated without harming the trade.' He was now enthusiastic and keen to get involved.

'Do you mean my department or the whole company?' he asked.

'Look everywhere and at everything,' I said. He left my office with a bounce I hadn't seen before.

'Allan, will you plan the biggest clearance sale ever seen in Sunderland, and I mean a REAL CLEARANCE. We're pulling out of fashions at the branches and I want all the rubbish stock cleared from this store.' The departmental store manager and assistant buyer were startled at my suggestion.

'But we'll almost need to give it away to get rid of some stock,' he replied. 'What happens then? We can't afford to re-stock.'

'Just prepare the plans. If my plan succeeds we'll have the money,' I replied.

I'm sure he thought I was crazy because I didn't give him an explanation. In fact I planned to tell very few people of my meeting with the Co-op Insurance Company at Manchester, whether I failed or succeeded.

'Good morning, David. Tea or coffee?' Philip Thomas was an enthusiast for breakfast-time meetings. My three-hour drive was of little concern to him. I had arrived fifteen minutes before our eight-thirty meeting. He didn't believe in small talk, which suited me fine. I didn't bother him with details of my problems or the small management problems I had had. Our talk over coffee and toast was about his long-term plans and intentions. Then suddenly he turned the conversation to my plan and reason for being in Manchester.

'Since you phoned me, I've had it valued and the best deal you can expect on the open market is £1.25 million.'

'You haven't spoken to the Co-op Insurance?' I interrupted.

'No, that's your job,' he answered. 'By the way,' he continued, 'you haven't asked my opinion on your plans.'

'I'm certain you will tell me if you think I'm doing the wrong thing,' I answered. He just smiled and wished me luck at my next meeting in an hour's time.

'Give me a ring and let me know the outcome,' he said as I shook his hand and left his office.

I had never handled such high financial negotiations in my life. Philip Thomas claimed he hadn't spoken to the Co-op Insurance, but throughout our long negotiations I had a feeling that he'd been involved, particularly when the deal was eventually for exactly £1.25 million.

'Well done David,' he replied to my phone call after the meeting. 'That should help the cash-flow problem, but your expenses will be high.' I smiled as I replaced the phone. He gave me the credit but I was convinced that he'd really done the business.

The next morning I called Bill Edmondson into my office as soon as I returned.

'You're kidding!' he said with surprise.

'No,' I replied. 'In six weeks time we'll have £1.25 million in the bank. The departmental store we were now sitting in no longer belonged to Sunderland Co-op. I'd sold it—and leased it back from the Co-op Insurance Society.

'I don't want the overdraft cleared, and still keep a tight control on paying bills,' I said. 'Tell no one of what I've done. We can use the money to save the business.'

'What about the local committee? There'll be hell on when they know you sold the store,' Bill said with concern in his voice.

'Don't worry,' I said. 'I'm not having a meeting for two months, we've plenty of time.'

While I had been away Bill had been doing his homework and produced a long list of expenses savings, including the garage. (My car parking mechanic would be going.) Three branches would close and a huge building in nearby Green Street would be sold. All in all we liquidated assets which added another £1.5 million to the cash I'd acquired from the sale of the store.

Cash was now available—everything depended on what we used it for.

3

THE SWINGING SIXTIES

Any plan to revitalise the trade had to be concentrated round the main departmental store in Sunderland. The whole image and future of Sunderland Co-op was dependent on the success of the store.

In 1966 there was very little competition in food retailing in Sunderland. Major multiples hadn't yet acquired sites, so I decided to allocate the whole of the ground floor to self-service. We would have the biggest supermarket for miles around, it would also be excellent to produce cash flow. We soon created some free publicity by giving a story to a local reporter that I was bringing the successful 'Hetton policy' to Sunderland.

'Mr Ibbitson would like to see you,' my secretary announced a couple of days after the press story was released. It was Herbert Ibbitson, owner of a very successful pork butchery business in the town. We'd never met, but we had an immediate rapport. He was a typical butcher, well made, fresh complexion, and very pleasant. He began by congratulating me on my success at Hetton and saying how pleased he was that my plans might create the same activity in Sunderland—he went way over the top with his compliments. I began to feel embarrassed, and was waiting to see what he was leading up to. Sure enough, the crunch came. He wanted to rent a site in the new food store. His enthusiasm was terrific. I could see he had visions of making a fortune and would give anything to get in. What he didn't know was I'd only budgeted to sell some 'pre-packed' meat. There were so many top-class butchers in Sunderland (including himself) that I didn't intend to risk a major butcher section. To Herbert I argued:

'Why should I let you come in when we could get all the profit ourselves?' This seemed to make him even more enthusiastic. He was absolutely convinced of success.

'I'll think about it,' I said as we parted. 'I'll give you an answer in a couple of days.'

I wanted time to think how far I could go. Of course I wanted the Ibbitson name in the store, but I wanted the best deal I could get. I still wasn't convinced of butcher success in the store, but Herbert was the butcher expert; his enthusiasm would cost him dearly.

I deliberately waited a week before I sent him my terms. He was required to provide fixtures and fittings and, in addition, provide all his own staff; a substantial rent to be paid one year in advance, and all terms to be renegotiated every year. To my delight, the deal was accepted, signed, and a cheque in the bank within the week. He was determined that no other butcher would get into the store (no one else was interested). The rent from Ibbitson was five times more than I'd expected to make in selling pre-packed meat—and I had the money a year in advance. I hoped Herbert would be as successful as he expected.

The next deal I made for the store was concerning the footwear section, which wasn't very successful. The stock range was old-fashioned and fixtures were very old. Shoefayre is a subsidiary of the CWS and I'd heard they were looking for a site in town, so I approached them, explained my plans for the store, and offered them a concession site on the first floor. They accepted, supplied their own modern fittings, well-trained staff, and a range of modern stock. We negotiated a five-year deal and I was very satisfied.

By leasing back the store from the Co-op Insurance, I'd created a heavy burden of rent in exchange for the cash we'd received. However, the deals with Ibbitson and Shoefayre offset a huge amount of the rent, which greatly reduced the pressure.

I was quite confident about the plans to create a supermarket: I had had sufficient experience at Hetton to feel sure it would succeed. But the non-food sections were a real concern. I'd been quietly checking invoices and stock sheets and found a number of discrepancies. I'd already recruited new security staff to cover the store and persuaded Linda Eggleston to join me from Hetton to control security. She was as dedicated to Co-op success as I was.

On the loading bay a man called Cyril Rochester was a loner who kept very much to himself, wasn't very popular because he was a stickler for procedures, and hinted he could be a help in solving problems of dishonesty. I briefed Linda on my concern about buying and stock recording, I indicated she could use Cyril if necessary—then waited to see if anything developed. For the next few weeks work progressed setting up the supermarket and getting Ibbitson installed, but the non-food sections continued to be depressed.

'There's the information you need.' Linda placed a folder on my desk. She had a look of triumph and I guessed it was to do with the non-food investigation I had instigated. Sure enough there was enough evidence to prove that some buyers were dishonest. They'd been buying exclusively from a wholesaler and between them could have robbed the Co-op of thousands of pounds. I thanked Linda for her work and told her to say nothing to anyone. I didn't want the bad publicity from a prosecution if it could be avoided. Everything would depend on their reaction when confronted with the evidence.

I invited the three to my office without giving a hint as to the reason. I could prove their dishonesty involving almost £2,000, but suspected much more. I'm sure they thought I'd invited them to discuss a major promotion to revive the non-food departments. One buyer was full of talk, the other two were more subdued, and talking business. When they realised I was ready to start the meeting, they went silent, waiting to hear my comments.

'I won't waste your time with trivialities,' I began. 'Since I arrived here three months ago I've been concerned about merchandise you two have been buying.' The wholesaler half rose to his feet.

'If this is a management discussion I'll wait outside,' he said.

'I'm sure you'll be interested in what I have to say,' I said. He slowly sat down without comment.

I now looked directly at the wholesaler as I spoke.

'These two have been buying from you at inflated prices and "seconds" have been delivered while "best" prices have been charged to the society.' He jumped to his feet and shouted:

'You can't speak to me like that, I could sue you for slander.' The other two didn't move or make a sound. I deliberately kept my voice quiet, put my hand on the telephone and said:

'I can prove it. Shall I phone the police or would you rather hear what

I've got to say?' The silence was deafening. I kept my hand on the phone, my eyes never left the face of the man standing in front of me. He looked sideways at the other two, they didn't respond. Then, after what seemed an age, he slowly returned to his seat. I then produced my evidence showing their signatures and delivery notes and bluffed that I was producing only a fraction of my total evidence.

No one spoke, they were all badly shaken and didn't attempt to make any excuse, although I'm sure the tone of my voice made them realise I was in no mood for excuses.

'From all this evidence I think we'll find that you've robbed this company of many thousands of pounds,' I said. 'By rights I should call the police, but before I do I've got a proposal.' I then took from my desk drawer an outstanding invoice for £9,000 that we owed the wholesaler. 'I assume you've robbed us of much more than this, but I'm prepared to accept it as settlement.' He looked at me long and hard, but I met his stare, then he slowly nodded his head, whereupon I deliberately tore the invoice into a number of pieces.

I then turned to the two staff and said:

'I assume you both agree to forfeit your holiday pay and outstanding money to clear your debt?' They both nodded, and left my office and a major drain on profits had been stopped. I made sure that Linda and Cyril had some extra money in their next pay packet—they'd done a good job for me. John Robertson was the replacement buyer. He had flair, expertise and contacts.

At last we were getting some decent stock to sell—but still the public stayed away. People had got out of the habit of shopping at Sunderland Co-op. Somehow I had to create a stir and remind people we were in the High Street. I decided to invest in radio and TV celebrities to make personal appearances at the store. I had never been involved in this type of promotional activity and hadn't a clue what to expect. I got an agent to provide me with a list of possible celebrities and their fees, and decided we could afford Alan Freeman, the TV and radio star. In 1966 he was at the height of his fame and might just do the job I wanted—to get the store away from its old fashioned Co-op image, and bring it into the swinging sixties. We planned promotions, leaflets and press advertising, all based on the star's first ever-appearance in Sunderland.

A huge crowd was building up outside the store more than two hours before he was due to arrive. I'd organised a car to meet him, but a phone call notified me that he was an hour late due to fans at Newcastle airport mobbing him for autographs. By the time he arrived, the store was solid with people of all ages, just standing waiting to get a glimpse of him. There were hundreds of people outside, traffic was at a standstill, and pressmen were fighting for a vantage point. Sunderland hadn't seen such a crowd in the High Street before.

The roar was tremendous when the star stepped out of the car. His huge sunglasses helped everyone identify him. Thankfully, ample police were available to expertly control the mass of people and escort Alan Freeman to the top floor where we'd arranged a table for him to sit and sign autographs for the fans who had patiently queued for hours. To say he gave value for money was an understatement. Except for a lunch break (I took him home to Hetton away from the crowds), he sat non-stop for five hours writing autographs and speaking to the fans. At the end of the day he must have been exhausted, yet didn't show any sign of fatigue. Finally, the store closed, crowds dispersed. Crowds of fans had prevented shoppers getting into the store, shoplifting had been excessive, and breakages extremely high. The only person who seemed to have gained from the day was Alan Freeman who, by now, was flying back to London—at our expense. However, within a week we found an upsurge in business. The tactic had paid off—it had made people aware of Sunderland Co-op. Over the next few months we often used the same tactic and each celebrity helped to push the sales to an even higher level.

Simon Dee attracted even bigger crowds than Alan Freeman, but he spent less time signing autographs and speaking to fans. Nevertheless, his visit produced the same results.

The Bachelors were extremely popular and spent more time talking to people than just sitting and writing autographs.

In addition to giving a huge boost to trade, the effect on staff was marvellous. They were now full of enthusiasm, not only looking for the next activity, but actually recommending ideas to boost the trade. It was hard to believe the change in both managers' and staff's attitude in only six months.

Bachelors' visit, Sunderland Echo

Crowds at Sunderland Co-operative Society listened to the rich Irish voices of the Bachelors on record before the famous trio appeared in person —45 minutes late—to open a new record department at the store on Saturday.

When it was announced that the singing group would be delayed half-an-hour, most of the young members of the crowd moved on, leaving older fans waiting.

As time passed there were some bitter comments from bystanders who had hoped to get a glimpse of the Bachelors, but all was forgiven and forgotten when John, Dec and Con arrived to sign autographs.

Above: First to meet the Bachelors, who are appearing at Newcastle, were twin sisters Janette and Jacqueline Fish, of Ewesley Road, Sunderland.

We had had an eventful six months. All branches had been converted to self-service, the departmental store had been revitalised. Sunderland Co-op was now back in business.

I was feeling quite pleased with the progress of my first assignment as a 'troubleshooter'. It had been hard work and I'd worked an incredible number of hours. Maybe I could now ease off and see a bit more of my family.

4

STOP THE LOSS—OR ELSE!

Out of the blue came a call to attend an urgent meeting at Manchester. Philip Thomas was not an enthusiast for meetings, so I thought it must be something of importance.

The first surprise was to be told the meeting was in the board room and not in Thomas's office. My next surprise was to see other people sitting round the table, and I was more than surprised when Philip Thomas motioned for me to join him at the top of the table. The other five people were total strangers.

'Gentlemen, this is David Hughes. He is our "Special Executive" operating in the North East,' Philip Thomas opened the meeting. He then introduced me to men who represented the Co-op Bank, accounts department, property section and the financial services. All were dressed in dark business suits and none under 50 years old.

'These gentlemen and their departments will be available to give any help you need,' he said. I was puzzled but thought I'd wait to see why I was expected to need such extensive assistance.

Thomas turned to a mountain of a man, who was casually dressed and in his mid-forties.

'This is Arthur Trotman. He will be your liaison here in Manchester. Anything you require, Arthur will provide.' I nodded to Trotman, received a reassuring smile and was now convinced this was no ordinary meeting. Whatever was coming, it seemed I was to be an integral part.

A woman arrived with coffee and I sat on tenterhooks waiting for the meeting to resume, said a few words of small talk, but my mind was preoccupied with the possibilities to emerge after coffee.

The meeting resumed with Philip Thomas handing out papers on which were listed fifteen north-eastern Co-op societies and beside each name was the amount of their indebtedness to the CWS. The total amount was several million pounds. At the top of the list was Ryhope and Silksworth Co-op, followed by Newbottle, West Cornforth, and other Co-ops well known to me. Philip spoke very sombrely.

'None of these societies could pay us their debts if we demanded.' He continued: 'David has already turned things round at Sunderland and stopped the losses, now we're ready to move on to this lot.'

I was dumbfounded. There were societies on the list I thought were absolutely safe, including the society of David Jones, the man who'd called me 'an impetuous youth' during the early days of my career.

'Ryhope Co-op will be first, and I hope the others can hold on to allow David to take over one at a time,' Thomas continued. 'But they could all collapse together, so we've got to be prepared to give David all the help he needs.'

A great deal of time was spent on the legalities of taking over a Co-op, the most important being the requirement that each society must 'request' my services. Without such an 'invitation' to take over I could not get involved, even if it meant standing by and watching a society go bankrupt. Hedley Whitehead would be permanently assigned as the CWS director who would approach each society's committee. The terms of take-over of each society would be identical: the local committee would relinquish control, I would take over as chief executive officer with total control of trade, staff, and finance. I now had a team of experts here in Manchester to call on if required.

The meeting eventually closed with Philip Thomas stressing the need for confidentiality. Even officials of societies listed hadn't a clue. There would be hell on if the news was to break before consultation. The press in particular should not get an inkling or they'd blow the story out of proportion. Thomas motioned for me to stay behind as everyone left the board room at the end of the meeting.

'How do you feel about the job now?' he said with a smile.

'It's now far bigger than I'd expected,' I answered. 'The implications for the North East are unbelievable.'

'One day there will be one Co-op in the whole of the North East,' he replied. 'How soon that happens, depends on how quickly you can sort out the weak societies.' As I left, Philip Thomas again promised me complete freedom to get on with the job. His parting words were:

'Whatever you need to do this job, go ahead and get it, and good luck!'

The drive home was automatic; my mind was a whirl at the prospect of taking over and sorting out so many Co-ops in addition to Sunderland Co-op. I thought of the managers of those listed societies, many of whom I'd clashed with at various meetings. I thought of all the work I'd had in sorting out Sunderland Co-op. Would this be repeated fifteen times over? I never doubted my ability to do the job—I'd

Philip Thomas

learned a lot in only six months at Sunderland. But one thing was for certain—I needed help to do such a huge sorting exercise.

May couldn't believe my news when I arrived home. She was concerned about my workload and the animosity involved in such take-overs, but she understood that the challenge for me was unavoidable. I'd been put in a position where I could help to shape the future of the north-east Co-op movement. Even in my wildest dreams, I hadn't foreseen that possibility during my days at Hetton Co-op.

No one could be told of the CWS plans. When I attended various meetings in the next few weeks I mentally ticked off the Co-op managers present against those on my list. I listened to their arguments and proposals that I knew were meaningless in the light of my knowledge of their future survival.

One man who always seemed to talk with common sense was Bill Fish. He had recently been promoted to manager of a small Co-op society in Durham. He was younger than me, had attended a short course at college while I was a full-time student, and we had got to know each other quite well—so I decided he could be the man to help in the massive programme coming up. Could I persuade him to step down from being a general manager to be my assistant? One good argument was the fact that his society was on my list, but I couldn't give him that information until he joined me.

'Hello Bill,' I said as I entered his small office. I hadn't explained my reason for wanting to see him, so I wasn't surprised when his response was an immediate query as to why I was there. I gave him as much information as I could concerning my job and tried to paint a picture of the future without giving him confidential information.

'This society is small, and I'm sure you know trade and profits aren't good,' Bill said with concern in his voice. 'Will we be taken over?' he asked.

'I'm sorry Bill, I can't give you that information,' I replied. 'One thing I will say, the job I'm offering you will be secure and will pay more than you're earning now!'

'I'll need to think about it and talk to my wife,' he replied. We parted and I was still convinced he was the man for the job. He kept me waiting two days, then a phone call clinched the deal.

In all my career I would never make a better move than to make Bill my assistant. Immediately he joined, I gave him a complete briefing on the situation at Sunderland Co-op. When the time arrived to take over other Co-ops, I wanted him to keep control of our current success.

Within a few days of Bill's arrival as my assistant I was called to yet another meeting at Manchester to be given a briefing to take over Ryhope and Silksworth Co-op Society Ltd. I was to contact Bob Mason the general manager and 'request' that Hedley Whitehead and I be invited to attend their next board meeting.

The meeting had been in progress almost an hour. Hedley and I were patiently waiting on hard chairs in a drab, dark-painted adjoining room. There was no heating and only a single light bulb produced dark shadows in every corner. Our plan, when we eventually met the committee, was that Hedley would do all the talking. I'd only answer any questions on business. A sound of footsteps and a creaking door produced a very small, immaculately dressed man in his early sixties with a balding head and a very courteous manner. He ushered us into a smoke-filled board room that immediately reminded me of my interview years ago for the job at Hetton Co-op.

'Well gentlemen, we are honoured at your visit to our meeting. We've never had a CWS director, and Mr Hughes we know by reputation. But we're at a loss to understand why you're here.' The chairman was a very clear and forceful speaker as he bid us welcome. At the same time he gave a clear impression that he was in charge. Hedley asked permission to address the meeting and, with nods of agreement, he rose to his feet to speak. He did a brilliant job of analysing their financial position and detailed the amount of their debt to the CWS and indicated the concern of the CWS board on Ryhope's ability to pay their debts. Without actually saying the words he clearly indicated they were a bankrupt business. Hedley concluded by saying:

'The CWS are very concerned and, to avoid us pressing you for payment, I'm here to formally ask if you wish Mr Hughes to take control of your society.' For a few moments there was complete silence then I thought the chairman would explode.

'Who the hell gives you the right to come here and tell us we're in difficulties?' he shouted. 'This is our society, so get out of here both of you. We don't need your interference.'

In next to no time we were out in the street. I hadn't uttered a word and Hedley was quivering with rage.

'It's obvious the bloody manager hasn't told them the facts of life and the true position of their business,' he said.

'Well, we won't get back until they know how serious a situation they are in,' I said. 'I suggest you leave me to speak to the manager.'

'OK, David. Let me know if you're successful,' was his parting comment as he drove away.

The next morning I waited until 10 o'clock to give Bob time to get settled in his office.

'I'm sorry the way you were treated last night,' he said in answer to my phone call.

'Don't talk too much on the phone,' I replied. 'Any chance of meeting you for lunch today?'

'Yes, I'll meet you anywhere but here,' he said.

We met at the Roker Hotel, had a salad lunch, and were being served coffee when I said:

'It's time to get down to business, Bob.' He didn't speak, no doubt waiting to hear the reason for his free lunch.

'Bob, if the CWS were to demand immediate payment and the Co-op bank called in your overdraft you'd be bankrupt.'

'Yes,' he interrupted me, 'But so would most Co-ops if you gave them the same pressure.'

'The problem is that your position is getting worse every day, and now that Silksworth pit has been closed, you could be facing disaster,' I replied. He remained silent, so I continued. 'A serious situation can develop very quickly. If you're declared bankrupt everyone is going to lose, including the members. If we can act quickly, something may be saved.'

'Look, David,' he replied with exasperation. 'You've seen the committee. They control things, there is no way they'll allow you into the society on your terms.' I looked at him for a few moments as I drank my coffee, then said:

'How old are you Bob?'

'I'm waiting patiently for my pension,' he answered with a sigh.

'Bob, I must tell you the CWS are going to demand payment, the bank will recall your overdraft.' He was about to say something but I asked him to hear me out. 'When you're declared bankrupt you personally have a lot to lose.' He just gave me a steady look and said nothing, so I continued. 'If you can get your committee to "invite" me to take control on behalf of the CWS, I will guarantee that you can retire immediately.'

For the first time I saw a spark of interest. I had given him a way out.

'You've seen our chairman: how the hell do you expect me to persuade him?' he said with alarm in his voice.

'Simple,' I answered. 'Tell him the true position of your society, show that they have no alternative except to be declared bankrupt.'

'I won't be allowed to retire, I'll get the bloody sack,' he said in a whisper.

'No you won't,' I reassured him. 'You'll be allowed to retire early.' He looked at me long and hard but didn't speak. I felt sure he was wondering if he could trust me, and visualising the reaction of his committee, particularly the chairman, after he presented them with the true state of their business and the alternative options available to them. I didn't envy his position. Eventually he emerged from his thoughts and said:

'Can I have the deal you're offering in writing?' He didn't trust me, but I answered:

'I don't think that would be a wise thing to do Bob, but don't worry. If you get their immediate agreement for me to move in, you'll be retired within a couple of weeks.'

I parted from a troubled man and made my way back to my office where Bill Fish was keen to know the outcome.

We then discussed the Ryhope situation, assumed it would soon be our responsibility and decided we would need a team of people we could trust to help the mammoth reorganisation facing us.

John Love, a short well-built man, always bubbling with enthusiasm and very ambitious, was wasted in the coal depot. He could control the departmental store. This would give Bill Fish more time to work with me.

Arthur Belton was the non-food buyer at Hetton Co-op, I knew he was honest, very good at his job, and could be invaluable in the team if he could be persuaded to leave Hetton.

Eddie Weirs was the regional union organiser. He'd progressed as far as he could in the union and was a local councillor. Ryhope Co-op had been completely dominated by the union for years so I could see problems ahead. Eddie would be ideal to help smooth the waters if he would leave the union and join the team.

Bill Edmondson was now a man with great enthusiasm and could quite easily combine the job of secretary and financial control for both Sunderland and Ryhope Co-op Societies.

Arthur came with a new title, more money, and a new purpose in life. Eddie resigned from the union, and accepted the title of member relations officer with a much bigger salary than he'd expected.

Decisions were made and implemented in record time. I had no committee approval to worry about and no one at the CWS pressed me for reports. I never volunteered any information other than a trade and profit statement every four weeks.

While all this activity was going on, Bob Mason had made progress with his committee at Ryhope Co-op. A couple of weeks after our lunch at the

Roker Hotel, Bob phoned me with an 'invitation' for Hedley Whitehead and me to visit their society to meet the committee. This time we weren't kept waiting, and were quickly given chairs at the head of the table, next to the chairman.

The room was full and laden with smoke, and to my surprise I could see some cans of beer in the centre of the table. Still, it was their business (for the moment).

The chairman was on the defensive, although he made no apology for his disgraceful outburst at our first meeting.

'The manager has finally given us the true position of our society,' he began. 'We're all very shocked. We didn't realise things were so bad.' He had the chair and continued to speak on behalf of the whole committee. 'Mr Mason has requested early retirement, so we'll be happy for Mr Hughes to take his place.'

I quickly looked at Bob, who looked at a fly on the wall. I didn't like the sound of this one little bit, but Hedley Whitehead suddenly interjected:

'Mr Chairman, if you are asking for CWS management to try to save your society, then Mr Hughes is prepared to move in and take complete control. He will be chief executive officer with absolute authority and your role as a committee will only be in an advisory capacity.' One of the committee men sitting on my left said:

'Do you mean to say, Mr Hughes can do anything he wishes with our society and we have no say in anything?'

'You can give him advice, which I have no doubt he will note, but he answers only to Philip Thomas.'

I still hadn't spoken, but for now I was quite happy with Hedley's performance.

'In that case we may as well stay at home and let him get on with it,' someone else at the table commented.

'Hold on, we haven't agreed to hand our society to anyone yet,' the chairman reasserted his authority. Turning to Hedley Whitehead he said, in a more aggressive voice: 'What other alternative can you offer than a complete take-over?' Hedley slowly stood up to his full six feet, no doubt to make his response seem full of authority.

'Gentlemen, if we leave this room without your formal "invitation" for Mr Hughes to take full control of your society, and without your agreement to be advisors only, then your society will be declared bankrupt within a week. This is not negotiable and there are no other options.' Hedley had spoken slowly and precisely, no one was in any doubt about their position as he quietly resumed his seat.

The only sound in the room was some whispered conversation at the far end of the table. The chairman and Bob Mason were silent and motionless. Within an hour, the formal discussion was completed in an atmosphere of total capitulation, a letter had been written and signed 'requesting' my services, the committee ceased to have authority, Bob was granted his retirement, and Ryhope Co-op was now my responsibility.

The organisation was immediately set in motion. The team I'd created moved into Ryhope Co-op and the local press did me no favours by publishing some very disruptive stories. The local union had a ball. They threatened total stoppage and disruptions unless I guaranteed everyone their jobs. Within a few days I had sufficient information to realise that the situation was much worse than I had expected. Losses were high, expenses high, and money so short that unless the bank honoured the wages cheque, the staff couldn't be paid.

I would have to do something quickly and effectively to stop the losses —or else Ryhope Co-op had no future.

Ryhope & Silksworth Co-op

5

CLOSE IT DOWN!

'I'm sorry David, that's his decision.' I was dumbfounded; I couldn't believe the news that Arthur Trotman had just given me.

'Arthur, he can't do that, doesn't he realise the effect it would have on every Co-op society in the north of England?'

I had been in control of Ryhope Co-op only three weeks. Stock sheets were fictitious, members' debts were horrendous, and capital withdrawals by shareholders were escalating. The business was bankrupt. Only the goodwill of the CWS and the bank was keeping it open. Now, after only three weeks, the response of Philip Thomas was an incredible—close it down immediately! I'd talked it over with Arthur who confirmed that Thomas was determined. He absolutely refused to subsidise any more Co-op societies, and particularly Ryhope Co-op, which was an unacceptable drain on cash flow.

I phoned Philip Thomas' secretary and asked for an urgent appointment.

'Eight o'clock tomorrow morning, Mr Hughes,' she said after speaking to him on the intercom. If Ryhope was declared bankrupt there would be panic among shareholders of Sunderland and other north-east Co-ops. People considered the Co-op as a totally safe haven for money, confidence in the Co-op would go, and I had no doubt that share capital would disappear like snow on a hot day. The whole Co-op business could collapse.

I didn't dare let anyone know the position: that Ryhope was in trouble, Thomas wanted to close it, and that I had fears for other Co-ops.

Somehow I had to get him to change his mind, and I had less than 24 hours to build a case.

Bill Fish and I collected all the information and accounts we needed and arrived at the Piccadilly Hotel in Manchester about 3 o'clock in the afternoon. We would be well away from phones, day-to-day queries and curious colleagues. We had only 17 hours to come up with a convincing argument to change the closure decision (assuming we didn't sleep). We knew we couldn't make a profit at Ryhope, our aim was to stop losses. Somehow we had to convince Philip Thomas that it would be better to save part of Ryhope Co-op than declare it bankrupt, with all the knock-on repercussions. Bill and I examined the figures for every single section, with the aim of ruthlessly eliminating loss-making units and saving those sections that were at least breaking even.

All office work and administration could be integrated with Sunderland Co-op, and excessive staff bonus schemes eliminated. Major cuts in senior management could be carried out by combining the two societies. Our proposals to Philip Thomas were finalised at about 6 o'clock in the morning. We were shattered and were due to meet the man in two hours' time.

'You know Bill, we're mad,' I said. 'Even if Thomas accepts this proposal, there'll be hell on when we get back and try to implement it.'

'We've gone this far, let's wait and see what he has to say,' he replied. The proposals we listed were very severe but it was the final item that might be more than even he or the Co-op movement could accept. I had done a few spectacular things in my time but if accepted, this would create the biggest stir of all.

Right on time we walked into his office to be given a cup of coffee by Philip's secretary. I deliberately let him know that Bill and I had been up all night, to indicate how important I considered this meeting. Of course, to Philip Thomas Ryhope Co-op was only one small Co-op of very little significance to his grand, nation-wide scheme of things. The next half hour would change his mind (or so I hoped).

First I dealt with the knock-on effect there would be if I had to go back, close Ryhope Co-op, and put 600 people out of a job. He didn't speak, didn't interrupt, just listened. When I started to list the individual items of cuts, closures and redundancies, he stopped me and spoke for the first time.

'David, individual details are your responsibility, just give me the overall picture.' I answered without having to refer to notes.

'It will mean a 30-per-cent cut in trade, a 50-per-cent cut in staff, and will take six weeks to implement. It won't produce profit but should get to break even.'

'How many staff to go?' he enquired.

'Nearly 300.' I replied. 'There's one more proposal,' I continued before he could ask another question. 'Since the local pit closed there's been a steady withdrawal of share capital from Ryhope Co-op. In fact withdrawals are escalating and spreading to Sunderland Co-op.' Thomas didn't comment, just waited to hear my proposal. 'If you agree to the cuts I've recommended, it could create panic by shareholders so I believe that all cash withdrawals should be frozen—immediately.'

'What if we don't freeze capital?' Thomas queried.

'We'll simply run out of money.' I answered.

Bill had not said a word since I had introduced him to Philip Thomas at 8 o'clock. We now sat in silence waiting for the response. We'd done all we could to avoid the closure of Ryhope Co-op. If the answer was still no—so be it. It seemed an age while Thomas considered my comments. Would he change a decision he'd already made? Suddenly he picked up his phone, asked to speak to the head of the legal department, and said:

'We're thinking of freezing all cash withdrawals at two retail societies. Any legal problem?' I couldn't hear the answer. I looked at Bill, who lifted his eyes to the ceiling. At last the man spoke.

'David, I don't think you can win this one. I've got to make a stand and stop subsidising inefficient Co-op societies. I appreciate all you've both done trying to save Ryhope, but it may be best to cut our losses and get out now.'

I suddenly felt very tired; loss of sleep was catching up, particularly when it now seemed to be in vain. Suddenly, I became alert when Thomas continued:

'However, I'll tell the bank to honour the cheques for eight more weeks. If the losses aren't stopped by then I want you to close Ryhope Co-op down without any more discussion.'

'What about the freezing of cash withdrawals?' Bill spoke for the first time.

'Go ahead with your full package, and good luck. I'll be watching the press,' he said with a smile and a handshake.

'Well he's given us a free hand to do the job,' Bill said with a grin, as we entered the lift on our way out.

'Be under no illusions,' I answered, 'He's given us plenty of freedom to carry the can if we don't succeed.' Poor Bill, my comment worried him for weeks.

Our lack of sleep was forgotten, the long ride home was filled with discussing our programme to save Ryhope Co-op. Eight weeks wasn't very long—still, it was two weeks more than I'd said was needed to reach break-even. I had no illusions: Thomas would pull the plug in eight weeks' time if I hadn't stopped the losses and, in the event of that happening, I felt certain that Sunderland and other Co-ops in the North East would soon collapse.

The enormity of what we were heading north to implement really sank in when we started discussing the 50-per-cent staff cuts.

'We'll certainly have union trouble,' Bill forecast.

'Now is the time for Eddie'—our 'member relations officer'—'to earn his money. Maybe he can tell us the best way to handle his ex-colleagues,' I replied.

The timing of each action of our plan was crucial if we were to avoid total collapse of the business:

Shareholders could panic to withdraw cash!

Suppliers could stop credit and demand cash!

Unions could launch strike action!

Customers could simply go elsewhere!

The impending staff cuts could spark off major problems, so it was necessary to condition everyone to the fact there was 'Crisis at the Co-op'. Once this atmosphere was created, the negotiations with the unions would be more amenable.

The first move would be to freeze all cash withdrawals, because at Ryhope Co-op withdrawals were accelerating daily. Redundant miners were needing their savings and, unfortunately, in the process they were bleeding their Co-op to death by creating a major cash-flow crisis. To avoid breaking the law, no one must be allowed inside information and withdraw capital before the freeze, so immediately on returning to the office, Bill organised a meeting for half an hour before opening time the next morning. The secretary and chief clerk of both Sunderland and

Ryhope Co-op would meet in my office. In addition, I invited the chairmen of both advisory committees and a press statement was prepared.

Everyone was on time and I opened the meeting by giving a summary of the Co-op problems and the deadline of eight weeks to stop losses. Without giving any closure details, I hinted that drastic action was unavoidable.

'Gentlemen', I continued, 'I've called this meeting to implement the first move. From this moment, no one will be allowed to withdraw capital for any reason. It is frozen until further notice.' There was total silence, until slowly it dawned on them what I'd just said.

'But it's members savings—you can't stop them getting it,' the chairman of Ryhope said with disbelief.

'Maybe it is savings, but it's invested in their Co-op—and it's bankrupt.'

'Some people deposited money only yesterday and now it's frozen,' Bill Edmondson said.

'Look, we'll all hear heartbreaking stories, but I intend to see every person with a problem and see what we can do to help, short of withdrawing money. Don't forget,' I continued, 'the alternative is closure now, which would be much worse.' I think I was saying the words not only to convince them, but to reassure myself that I was doing the right thing.

Within half an hour of the news breaking, it was obvious I would be besieged with worried and irate members demanding their money, so I arranged to devote every afternoon to seeing anyone with a problem.

The freezing of capital was only the first move to save Ryhope. I was going to depend on Bill Fish and the team we'd created to implement the rest of the programme. We were already eight weeks minus one day. Before we made any moves on closures or staff reductions, the union had to be consulted. If they created problems or caused delay, it would be curtains. Eddie, our ex-union organiser, came up with an idea that was to prove brilliant.

'The union knows they've been squeezing Ryhope Co-op for years,' he said, after I gave him all the details. 'They can't ignore the facts, but we've got to let them be seen by the staff to have done their best.'

On his suggestion, we covered the board room table with every ledger and account book in the office. A cash-flow report, stock sheets—in fact anything we could get our hands on. After the union representatives had settled down, I proceeded to give them an overall picture of the state of the

THE CHILL WIND ROUND A CO-OP

Freeze will ease — but slowly

Savings frozen for 47,000 as Co-ops prepare merger

From The Northern Echo, September 26, 1967.

A THAW in the seven-month "freeze" of £516,000 share capital belonging to members of Sunderland Co-op seems likely within the next two months. This should be some consolation to the 47,000 members of the old Ryhope and Silksworth and Sunderland Societies, which merged just after the freeze.

But any withdrawals will be restricted by the little-known society rule that only 10 per cent. of the members' share capital can be withdrawn in any year. The freeze announced last September as a temporary measure has brought some hardship, particularly to pensioners.

But the Society's chief executive, Mr. David Hughes, who guided the merger through, said yesterday, "I was faced with freezing the share capital, or the alternative of liquidation, when I took over about the middle of last year, was that there was a desperate shortage of liquid capital, although there were ample funds in the form of stock, bricks and mortar. About three months later, we were over Ryhope and Silksworth where there was an additional shortage of capital and trading results were not profitable."

Asked about members' fears that they have seen the last of their money, Mr. Hughes replied, "Their money is not in jeopardy. It is purely a question of the availability of liquid capital In six months, the position has improved considerably, and is now under consideration by the management committee. The executive committee and four full-time directors of the CWS Manchester, but none was available for comment yesterday.

To effect an improvement and produce more liquid capital, uneconomic units had been closed, surplus staff unnecessary vehicles, surplus properties and surplus stocks had been disposed of.

The balance sheet was now being printed, but at present Mr. Hughes said he was not in a position to reveal any figures. Would the freeze lead to distrust among members? "I'm confident that once we have we have cleared this hurdle and proved to members that we are a progressive and profitable group, confidence in the Society will return. And he did not think there would be panic withdrawals.

Mr. Hughes said it was true that the Society was holding credit notes against members' share capital for funeral expenses. "Our aim has been twisted on this because members with share capital sometimes want to pay." Several old people looked upon their share capital as personal "burial money" and were worried at the thought of it not being available.

But Mr. Hughes said he was assured many old people that if they die their funeral expenses will be paid out of the money they have in the Society."

Sunderland Co-operative Society's store.

Old people hardest hit

COMPLAINTS—and fears—about the frozen assets, which range from £20 to £843, were easy to find. None of the people to whom we spoke seemed aware of the 10 per cent. withdrawal rule.

Equally, they were unaware of the possibility of the Co-ops going into liquidation six months ago. But one of the things we merge from the enquiries was that all of them still shop at the Co-op.

Typical of this attitude was Mrs. Cope, of 57, Cordon Avenue, Castletown, who was widowed last December. "I still buy at the store because it is the only way we have a chance of getting our money back." She has £843 in share capital left by her husband. "And I can't touch a penny of it."

She and her husband saved up through the Co-op to pay for a wedding reception for their only daughter who was married last September. The Co-op froze the money the day after the wedding. "I wanted to draw £200, but couldn't get it," said Mrs. Cope. "I wanted to pay the bill for the hotel and was told to go back and wait and refer them to the Co-op. Pride would no let me do that. I went to see Mr. Hughes and he told me that he would verify for the hotels that I had the money to pay, but they would have to wait until it was sold. Then the only way we have a chance of get-

ting our money back."

Mrs. Cope said when the bill came in from the store for her husband's funeral in December, she refused to pay it. "I went to see Mr. Hughes and he said, "on't worry about it. In the end insurance money paid for the funeral."

Mr. Gladstone Moore, of Riverdale, Castletown, 63-year-old redundant miner, said: "This doesn't affect me very much, although I have £90 in the store. But as Society steward of Castletown Methodist Church, I come into contact with many of the older people in the village. They are living a bare existence and cannot get any essential extra because their little bit of money which would make life easier is frozen.

The Northern Echo, 1967

Co-operative Societies in cash "squeeze"

CWS 'squeeze' crisis societies

DIRECTORS of the Co-operative Wholesale Society have ordered a clampdown on withdrawls from two struggling East Durham societies.

business. I explained the time-scale I'd been given and the drastic measures to be taken. I asked for their help and co-operation to save as much of the society as I could.

'I think we should call an immediate all-out strike to demand every job is guaranteed,' a tall ginger-haired shop steward shouted from the back of the room.

'It's entirely up to you,' I said, 'but be in no doubt about my intentions. Things are bad enough, but if you call a strike then I have no alternative but to declare Ryhope bankrupt. Members will lose their money, staff will lose their jobs, and I'll make damned sure the press gets the full story of the union's contribution to this sorry mess.' There was no response, only a lot of muttering and whispered conversation.

Eddie stepped forward. He had known and worked with these men on union business for years. I doubted whether they trusted him now that he'd 'gone to the other side'.

'Mr Hughes has given you the full facts but in addition has agreed to my suggestion that you be given total access to all the accounts. They are in the board room for your inspection and if you can provide a better solution to save some jobs, he'll be delighted to listen.'

It was obvious by the look on their faces that this unexpected facility was acceptable, so they trooped off with Eddie into the board room. After a couple of hours they were supplied with tea and sandwiches and finally, after almost four hours, emerged with sober faces, claiming that 'things couldn't be worse' and they would support 'whatever action was necessary'.

God knows what they'd done. There wasn't an accountant among them. All I got from Eddie was a smile, a wink, and assurance there would be no union trouble. Amazingly, there never was.

The union called a meeting of all the staff and reported that they had had long negotiations with me, that I'd given them full co-operation and access to any document they had 'demanded' and, sadly, conceded that drastic measures were needed to save as much of the business as possible.

Well done Eddie! If he never did another thing he'd earned his pay.

The area of major loss was a fleet of 29 mobile shops.

Due to union pressure on the Ryhope manager, two men were on each mobile shop and were paid a generous bonus on sales, even though they were losing money every day they were on the road. To eliminate these would involve 80 staff (including warehouse and admin staff). We would convert nearly £20,000 worth of stock into badly-needed cash, vehicles would be sold, and an area of loss eliminated. This would go a long way to my target. Six small branches were closed, a café and a ladies' hairdressing shop were put up for sale and an item listed as a 'farm' was sold (it was only a one-acre small holding).

An army of eighteen credit club collectors had an incredible contract. Even if a customer paid at a branch, the nearest collector received credit and, of course, a generous bonus, even though he did nothing. The union had negotiated a deal for them that was so good, it would now put them out of work. All payments would now be paid at branches and, unfortunately, eighteen more staff were unemployed. We were well on target and well within the time schedule. I had no doubt that loss units would be eliminated and break-even achieved. A much-reduced Ryhope Co-op now had every chance of survival.

Sadly, the misery and heartache created by the survival programme was immense. Closing shops and sacking people produced a terrible time for everyone involved.

The argument by Philip Thomas to refuse help to societies that were inefficient and badly managed was understandable, but I questioned whether it justified such hardship and suffering by so many people. I am certain I could have done a better job if the CWS had injected adequate cash into the retail sector.

The employees' union had a lot to answer for. They had had sympathetic men on the committee and exploited weak management by securing wages, bonus, and deals far in excess of the going rates.

While all this was going on, my biggest problems were handling press headlines, letters, phone calls, and threats against me. I had planned to devote every afternoon to any members with problems arising from my freezing of capital withdrawals, expecting the furore to abate within the first four weeks. In fact, long after the eight-week deadline given by Philip Thomas, I was still spending time dealing with financial problems of members of both Ryhope and Sunderland Co-ops. The afternoon pattern was always the same. I could have delegated the task to someone else, but the general request was to see 'the man who froze our savings'. Every afternoon at 2 o'clock a queue of people was outside my office, all of them with different problems. My secretary had a full-time job supervising the crowd of members.

A couple had all their savings in the Co-op to pay for their daughter's wedding reception at the Roker Hotel. I phoned the manager and guaranteed to pay the bill when the capital was released. He refused.

Two old ladies wanted a guarantee I would pay for their funeral if they died before capital was released. I was able to give them peace of mind and my assurance.

The vast majority were people with outstanding accounts: we would clear the debts when capital was free. Unfortunately, in spite of my personal assurances to pay outstanding debts when capital was unfrozen, I couldn't persuade local authorities to wait for rent and rates. Electricity, gas, and water authorities were equally unco-operative. So it went on, day after day. Some cases of hardship I couldn't help, but in by far the majority of cases I was able to reassure and find a solution, stressing that their cash was only temporarily frozen and would be available as soon as we could manage. A problem arose every day after 3 o'clock when the pubs closed. Fathers, sons and husbands headed for my office much the worse for drink. After some ugly incidents, I arranged for two of the heaviest staff I could find to stand outside my office.

At the end of eight weeks the threat of closure was lifted, Sunderland was making a modest profit and Ryhope, although much smaller, was no longer producing losses. Within six months I was preparing the way for an official amalgamation of the two Co-ops, although in reality many of the activities were already integrated. Nevertheless, a legal merger could make way for even more economies. In July 1967 after separate meetings of members of each society, Ryhope and Silksworth Co-op ceased to exist and became part of Sunderland Co-op. It was a good move for taxation and trade location purposes. The new enlarged Co-op had a turnover of £3 million per year.

Now maybe the scene was set to develop the business and hopefully we would be able to release the share capital to members in the not too distant future.

SOCIETY SET FOR RECOVERY

Co-op boss says 'I knew I'd be unpopular'

OUR SUNDERLAND STAFF

SUNDERLAND Co-op is now saved and on the road to future success, said Mr. David Hughes, the store's chief executive officer, last night.

Mr. Hughes was speaking to members of Silksworth Women's Guild about controversial issues affecting the Co-op, which took over the Ryhope and Silksworth Society last year.

He told them: "I was under clear instructions to save the Society and as many jobs as possible." He said the pit had closed and money was being withdrawn from the Society at a fast rate.

"The Society was still trying to give the same services—credit, delivery and the like, even though costs had gone up considerably in recent years.

"The grocery section was losing hundreds of pounds every week, sales were going down and there was such a shortage of liquid capital that the Society literally had to borrow to pay wages—and remember the Society already owed the CWS over £100,000."

Unpopular man

Mr. Hughes added: "Unless I could stop the slide very quickly the Society would have had to close down. Then every employee would have been unemployed and the value of the shares could have been much less than £1.

"I realised that no matter

Sunderland Echo, *1962*

Price Cuts Will Follow Big Wearside Co-op. Merger

WEARSIDE'S two biggest co-operative societies are to merge. Joining Sunderland! will be the Ryhope and Silksworth Co-op, and together the combine will have 47,000 members and an annual turnover of £3 million.

Heading the new group will be 41-year-old Mr David Hughes, of Hetton, the C.W.S. advisory officer at present with the Sunderland Society. He told the Echo today: "We aim to make the Co-op a force to be reckoned with on Wearside. There will be more price cutting."

For some time now the Ryhope and Silksworth Co-op, with 23,000 members, has been negotiating with the C.W.S. on the possibility of a merger. Said Mr Hughes: "Integration was thought desirable, because the two societies were, in fact, competing with each other and covering the same ground."

PRICE CUTS

The merger will take place at a date to be determined by the members. Meanwhile, Mr Hughes will be the chief executive officer. Ryhope and Silksworth managing secretary Mr J. Mason, who has not been in good health for some time, will vacate his position at a later date, but will act in an advisory capacity until then.

What will the merger mean? Said Mr Hughes: "With buying power of this dimension we will be able to make more price cuts and stand on equal ground with any store in the area. The Ryhope and Silksworth members will immediately benefit by the cuts already made at Sunderland."

The new group will have 700 staff and a share capital of £300,000.

MR DAVID HUGHES

Sunderland Echo

6

THE EGG WAR

For a number of months the whole media attention had been critical of the Co-op in general and me in particular. Of course with cutbacks, closures, redundancies and financial problems, they didn't need to look very far for a critical story.

I needed something to get more emphasis on the positive aspect of our trading activities. By pure chance, an opportunity emerged that was ideal for my purpose. In 1967, all eggs were sold under the control of the Egg Marketing Board, who had their lion stamped on every egg. Any eggs sold without the lion stamp made the egg producer liable to prosecution. (The retailer had no liability.) Most poultry farmers were discontent, claiming the board was pushing prices too low. A farmer from Cleadon approached me to se if I'd buy his eggs—without a stamp—and sell them at a premium price as 'Farm Fresh Eggs'. His only concern was that at no time would we disclose our source of supply. I could see an ideal public relations opportunity to serve our purpose and obtain some positive media attention.

At Hetton Co-op I'd created a stir by breaking the Retail Price Maintenance control. Here was another bureaucratic system to tackle—the Egg Marketing Board. In fairness to the poultry farmer I explained my plans. His only comment was: 'For God's sake, don't tell them who your supplier is or I'll be out of business.'

The first supplies arrived. A large area of the supermarket was devoted to 'eggs direct from the farm—no lion stamp'. No retailer had done this previously, assuming (wrongly) they'd be prosecuted. There was no need

Co-op wages war on the 'lion'

REBEL MARKET FOR UNSTAMPED EGGS

A CO-OP and 20 North-East poultry farmers are going to work — on the Egg Marketing Board. For the Sunderland Equitable and Industrial Society's chief executive, Mr. David Hughes, plans to buy unstamped eggs from "rebel" farmers.

He said yesterday : "Twenty poultry farmers have agreed to defy the Egg Marketing Board and supply 40,000 eggs without the "lion" stamp each week to Wearside families."

The suppliers face "disciplinary action" and a possible fine from the Board. But Mr. Hughes added: "I will not reveal the source of my supply. As a retailer I am not required to say where they are coming from."

A Board spokesman said : "We can't do anything about a retailer handling unstamped eggs. This is a loophole in the

OUR SUNDERLAND STAFF

regulations." However, the sale of unstamped eggs would be brought to the notice of the appropriate authorities.

The spokesman warned that any farmer selling unstamped eggs to a retailer could be brought before a disciplinary committee and fined. "Although the retailer cannot be forced to reveal his source of supply, we have power to send investigators to the North-East," said the spokesman at the Board's Leeds headquarters.

Mr. Hughes, head of the cut-price Co-op, countered : "I think there is something wrong somewhere when egg producers want to sell unstamped eggs and housewives want to buy them, but an authority says they must be stamped."

The eggs — at 3s 4d to 3s 6d a dozen to the housewife — will be sold from a special "24-hour fresh" centre at the store.

Mr. Hughes recognises that his

suppliers face fines from the Board if they are caught by-passing the authority. "All I want to do is give the housewife what she wants — and there is a terrific demand for unstamped eggs.

"I was first approached by a 'rebel' producer who offered a small amount of eggs. I thought it would be unfair if only a few of our customers could have them. So I investigated the situation and was surprised at the number of farmers willing to supply unstamped eggs in defiance of the Board."

Mr. Hughes added: "We aim to collect the eggs and get them to the housewife within 24 hours. Initially 20 farmers will supply us, but I have others willing to send more."

Last week Sunderland Co-op announced they were going to cut out the "middle men" and deal direct with manufacturers and producers.

But for any of the 40,000 members who want them "little the lion" eggs will be available.

Mr. Hughes

A CUSTOMER looks at the latest batch of non-lion eggs.

The Journal, *1967*

Egg rebels risk £500 fine

By Journal Reporter

A GROUP of poultry farmers in the North-East are preparing to play "cat and mouse" with the Egg Marketing Board, and sell eggs unstamped and without official authorisation.

Twenty farmers have agreed to supply the Sunderland Co-operative Society with 40,000 unstamped eggs every week for sale over the shop counter.

If the rebel farmers are caught in the act they face fines of up to £500 each.

Because of this the "rebels" are keeping their identities secret. The society's chief executive officer, Mr. David Hughes, confirmed that the "cloak and dagger" egg sales operations would remain, as far as the Co-operative was concerned, strictly secret.

DEMAND

Last night he said: "I can only say that the eggs will be collected by an arrangement we have worked out. As I understand the situation, they face a fine from the Board if they are caught by-passing the authority."

He continued: "I think that if people want to buy unstamped eggs, and there is a great demand for them, then the farmers, who are quite willing, should be able to supply them.

"I have been surprised at the number of farmers willing to take the risk of supplying unstamped eggs in defiance of the Board."

The Journal, *1967*

to spend money advertising eggs: within 24 hours local and national press were broadcasting the news that Sunderland Co-op was challenging the authority of the Egg Marketing Board. People flocked to Sunderland

Co-op to buy 'fresh' eggs—as if the lack of a lion stamp made them superior. Within a short time an official from the Egg Marketing Board was at my door demanding the name of our supplier. He was politely told to go away. Of course his visit made our supplier very nervous and said we'd have to collect the eggs, he wouldn't risk delivering. At that time we had four CWS trainee managers operating at Sunderland. I arranged for two trainees to take an unmarked van—in darkness—to collect the eggs every day. The amount of subterfuge seems incredible, but in the 1960s we were breaking a government control which was quite critical.

It certainly changed the type of publicity we'd been receiving, which was the object of the exercise. It became such a major issue that I received an invitation from BBC Television to appear on a discussion programme for a confrontation with the chairman of the Egg Marketing Board, with Ludovic Kennedy as the presenter. I had appeared on television a number of times, so I wasn't feeling nervous, but I was utterly amazed to see Ludovic in tatty old slippers and crumpled baggy trousers only fifteen minutes before transmission.

'We're only seen from the waist upwards,' he explained with a smile as we briefly discussed the format of the programme. The chairman was in London so the discussion was me arguing with a television screen and Ludovic Kennedy prompting questions. Afterwards I was assured it had been a lively discussion, but for me it was just another public relations exercise to improve the Co-op image.

After a few weeks, unstamped eggs were no longer news. Other retailers jumped on the bandwagon. Eventually the Egg Marketing Board with its little lion disappeared.

It all began because I was looking for a good publicity gimmick.

7

HI-JACKED!

To avoid the risk of members of staff carrying cash to a bank near their shop, I organised our own security van to call at every shop. By the time it had completed the journey, the van could be carrying up to £50,000, depending on the day's takings.

At 3p.m. one Friday afternoon, a frantic phone call informed me that the driver and his mate had been overpowered, the van hijacked and the money was gone. It had been carried out at our Castletown branch, a fairly remote part of Sunderland. It was the last call of the day and the van was estimated to be carrying over £35,000. Thankfully, no one was hurt. We were fully insured, so I wasn't unduly concerned. No doubt the police would deal with the robbery. Over the next few days of inquiry, the police were convinced it was an inside job and interviewed many of our staff.

'You're not going to believe this!' Bill Fish said on the phone a few days after the robbery.

'What now, Bill?' I replied.

'The mastermind behind the cash-van robbery was an employee.'

'You must be joking,' I answered.

'No, he's been arrested, he's in jail and will be charged tomorrow.' I could not believe Bill's news: the employee was a trainee manager, only nineteen years old, and a smart, well-dressed and courteous young man. I'd never had a complaint about him and his future as a manager seemed assured. Surely to God it must be a mistake? I understood his father was dead, I had never met his mother, but had no doubt she would be devastated. Nevertheless, he was charged, along with two others who weren't staff and, when they eventually appeared at Durham, they all pleaded guilty. All the money had been recovered and everyone who knew him was shocked: it was so out of character for a man who appeared to be steady and law-abiding.

He was sentenced to eighteen months in prison. Although I was sorry at his downfall and the loss of a career, it was of his own making. In any case, I had much more important things to see to.

May and I had been out to a function and returned home one evening at about 11 o'clock.

'The governor of Wakefield prison has been on the phone trying to speak to you.' My son David liked his occasional joke, so I didn't know whether or not to take him seriously as I took my coat off. 'He's phoning back later tonight,' David said, 'then you'll know I'm not kidding.' We were having a cup of tea when the phone rang and a quiet, well-educated voice said:

'This is the governor of Wakefield prison speaking.' If my life depended on it, I couldn't guess what on earth he required of me. 'I have a young man here, who has been with us six months. I don't normally do this sort of thing, but you can help him—are you still there Mr Hughes?' I hadn't spoken, I couldn't believe what I was hearing.

'Yes, carry on,' I replied.

'In all my career I've never known prison affect anyone as it has this young man,' he continued. 'I'm prepared to recommend his immediate parole, but he must have a job and he claims that you're the only man he can turn to.'

'Are you asking me to take him back?' I almost shouted down the phone.

'I realise what I'm asking, but I'm utterly convinced he'll not let you down,' said the governor.

'No way,' I said. 'I've enough problems! You can't expect me to give him a job again—Good God, man, he planned a bloody hijacking of our money, and you want me to take him back!' I was boiling with anger at the audacity of the man.

'All I'm asking is for you to think about it. You could get him out in a few days, otherwise he'll serve his time here.' I had calmed down as he was speaking.

'I can't give you a promise,' I said, 'you're really asking too much.'

'Well, I'll wait to hear from you, one way or another. I'm sorry to have given you such a problem,' he said as our conversation came to a close.

I was surprised when neither May or David offered an opinion after I'd related the conversation. May's only comment was:

'Fancy, he is almost the same age as our David.' David kept quiet.

I had no sleep that night, thinking of the risk I'd be taking if I got him out of jail. It was all right saying he wouldn't let me down; what would Co-op members have to say?—They couldn't withdraw their cash, he'd tried to steal it, and here I was, even considering taking him back. No way!

'He's very near David's age,' May's words kept coming back to me. I couldn't stand the thought of David in a position where he depended on someone else. Damn it, no—I couldn't trust him. In any case, another twelve months wasn't that long to be in prison. I'd made my mind up, I refused to take the risk.

At breakfast next morning, it wasn't discussed. When I got to the office, I asked Bill for his opinion, but he replied by giving me two sides to the problem—some help! I phoned CWS director Hedley Whitehead for advice. He flatly refused, saying:

'David, it's your problem, but I'll support your decision to take him back if he remains honest from now on.' Some advisor was Hedley! I made my mind up, the answer was no. I'd have a cup of tea, then speak to the governor of Wakefield prison on the phone. My secretary brought me a cup of tea and said:

'There's a lady been waiting for some time to see you, but she won't tell me what it's about except that it's very private. She looks quite ill.'

A woman of about 45 years old slowly walked into my office and sat down in the chair I offered. Although not well dressed, she was tidy in a dark blue coat, her sallow complexion stood out from her jet black short hair. She had the most sorrowful expression I'd ever seen.

'What can I do for you?' I asked. She lifted her sad eyes and in a whisper said:

'I'm his mother.' Then she burst into an uncontrollable flood of tears. It took a long time for her to calm down, have a drink of tea and explain the reason for her visit (although I was almost certain I already knew the reason). She had visited her son the day before, he had explained to her about an interview he'd had with the governor and that I was the key to his cell. She was ashamed of what he'd done, but he was her son and she felt some responsibility for his mistake. With tears rolling down her cheeks she sobbed:

'Mr Hughes, he's learned his lesson, he wouldn't let you down again. Please get him out of that awful place.'

In spite of my decision already made, against my better judgement, I picked up the phone and said:

'Please get me the governor of Wakefield prison.' The girl on the switchboard sounded surprised and repeated it before getting the call. I smiled and said:

'You can stop crying, I'll get him out.' My comment only provoked more silent sobs. He would be released in one week: the governor thanked me and said he was available if there was a problem. A smile came when I told his mother the news. I arranged to see them when he was free.

She left my office a different person from when she entered. I was sitting at my desk after she'd gone thinking: 'David, you've been stupid. You'll live to regret this day.'

The following week the young man was released. As arranged, he came to my office with his mother. I didn't mention the robbery, but made it clear that I'd put my reputation on the line, the governor of Wakefield prison had stuck his neck out, and his mother looked as if she could take no more. He promised that he wouldn't let us down, so I gave him a job as an assistant at a small branch at Lumley in Durham, well away from his previous work place.

I asked the area manager for regular reports, all of which were faultless. He'd been good before the robbery, but now he was clearly out to prove something. His dress, manner, time-keeping and work-rate were of the best, and within six months the area manager promoted him to section head. I didn't comment. Everyone was aware of his record and as a section head he would still be well supervised.

When a vacancy occurred a few weeks later and he was recommended to be a holiday relief shop manager, I had to intervene.

'Mr Hughes, without any doubt, he is the best candidate for the job and deserves the chance.' Peter Clennell and I had worked together since the collapse of Moorsley Co-op. I had total confidence in his judgement as an area manager, but I wasn't happy about this recommendation. Eventually I agreed, but said:

'Peter, for God's sake keep an eye on him.' Reports still continued to be excellent, and at last the niggle of worry was leaving me. Maybe I'd been right after all in getting him out of prison.

With so many branches it was almost an everyday occurrence to have a robbery somewhere. We had a set procedure: our insurance cover was adequate, so I didn't personally get involved except to read the reports. Suddenly, robbery at shops took on major priority in my daily routine. The last three robberies had all occurred at branches where the young man had been holiday relief manager. On each occasion the police had whipped him into the station for interview and on every robbery he was cleared of all blame. Still, he was always producing excellent results and deserved his promotion to store manager at Hylton Castle, a very busy shop just outside Sunderland. His promotion coincided with his wedding and acquisition of a flat above the shop.

He was now one branch manager among 54 others. Suddenly, he was again in the spotlight. A second hijack of our security van occurred with a similar method to the first. It was a Friday afternoon, over £20,000 was in the van, but it occurred at a different branch—Hylton Castle—the branch where he was the manager. I couldn't believe it. No one could be so stupid twice in a lifetime, but the coincidence was incredible. He was in and out of the police station for weeks. Although the police suspected an inside job, they had little to go on.

I was a bundle of nerves. If he was guilty a second time after I'd got him out of prison, not only was my reputation on the line, but even my job could be in jeopardy. Eventually, I could take the worry no longer, he hadn't been charged, nor had he been cleared. I asked him to come to my office.

'In our business there is always shoplifting and burglaries,' I said as he sat opposite me. 'With your record the police are always going to take you in for questioning.' He didn't speak so I continued:

'I think it would be better for you to work for a company that didn't have our problems, then maybe it will get the police off your back.'

'The police don't bother me,' he answered with an uncharacteristic bluntness.

'Maybe,' I said, 'but they certainly bother me. Anyway, I've got you a job at the Co-op laundry in a junior management capacity. If you'd like to change your job, it's the same money and—'

I got no further. He leapt to his feet, gave me a glare and, pointing a finger, he shouted:

'You're all the same, you're condemning me without any evidence. I'm innocent this time but neither you nor the police will give me a chance.' He stormed out of my office and banged the door shut before I could say another word.

He didn't go back to work. He left our company and took up the laundry job. He eventually moved out of the flat above Hylton Castle shop. I never saw or heard of him again.

Some six months later the local police inspector phoned me to say they had caught two robbers who admitted to our hijacking, although only a small amount of the money was recovered. 'What about our man?' I asked with some apprehension.

'He's been as clean as a whistle since he came out of prison,' he answered. 'No, I don't think we'll have trouble from that young man again.'

I very slowly replaced the phone.

8

CONSULTATION

With almost 1,000 staff it was routine to have regular consultations with the union representative. During the first few months our contact was like two boxers trying to weigh each other up. We were quite polite with each other, and the exercise at Ryhope was very constructive in establishing an understanding. As time passed I realised that consultation was a ritual exercise with procedures that had to be observed in order to preserve harmony.

The union organiser and I became very good friends, but few people would believe it at our consultation meetings. A stocky man, tidy dresser, and always quick to smile, he attended a monthly consultative meeting supported by six shop stewards. Being the full-time union man, he did all the talking; the others were usually satisfied with nodding or shaking of heads, like puppets, in support of his particular argument. In front of his shop stewards he was aggressive, demanding, and sometimes abusive. Each month they presented a list of problems or requests, most of which were petty and could have been dealt with by area managers. In return I had a list of my future proposals. At the end of the performance, the meeting broke up, honour was satisfied, grievances had been aired. It was always proposed that he and I would meet before the next meeting in order to review progress.

'You went on a bit strong last week,' I said as I handed him his usual cup of tea at our 'progress' meeting.

'Well, you'd just closed a couple of shops and the lads were expecting a bit of a show,' he replied.

'I've a surprise for you,' I said. 'You can have everything on last month's list. I want no objection to my plans, but our next meeting can produce some disagreements if you wish.'

'That's OK by me,' he replied. 'Can you do a favour for me?' So long as I could help him to be seen as an antagonist and occasionally win some concessions I'd have no problems. Throughout my time as a 'troubleshooter' I never had one day's union trouble because I always observed the ritual.

'So what's the favour?' I asked.

'You know our shop steward?'

'Of course I do,' I replied. 'He's a nuisance, a real stirrer. How on earth did you let him be shop steward?'

'David, it's called democracy,' he replied. 'He's undermining official union procedures. Any chance of moving him away from Ryhope?'

'No problem, leave it to me,' I replied. The tone of our meetings was always of a friendly and amicable nature so long as no one else was in attendance—then it was a different matter.

Bill Fish came up with an idea when I mentioned the request.

'Why don't you use the army trick and promote a troublemaker?' he said. We have a management vacancy here in the store. He'd have to leave the union but the wage is good.'

'OK, offer him the job and see how he does,' I replied. The man accepted the job and resigned from the union, but after a few weeks found the job far beyond his ability. The union wouldn't have him back after deserting them to be manager, so he left the Co-op to work for another company.

At the next consultative meeting, the union organiser said, with some feeling:

'The union is very sorry that the Co-op has lost such a fine employee and we've lost a good shop steward.' Our eyes briefly met, but further comment was unnecessary.

A short nattily-dressed man, full of his own importance and about thirty years old, was manager of a small branch. He did an adequate job, he kept the shop well organised, staff under control, and followed company policy to the letter. On first acquaintance I expressed surprise that he didn't have greater responsibility. This provoked an immediate tirade against the previous general manager. I made no comment, thinking maybe one day he might get promotion.

'I'm surprised this man isn't one of your shop stewards,' I said at one of our private consultative meetings.

'He'd have to toe the union line if he was elected, and that's not his style. He's one of the real troublemakers. He'd do anything to undermine you or me,' the union organiser continued, with bitterness in his voice. 'He won't be part of the union, but does his best to stir things at every opportunity. Just wait until you have a staff or members' meeting—then you'll see what I mean.'

'So what the hell does he want?' I asked.

'Promotion and power,' he replied, 'He believes everyone's against him, and he could be right. He has an incredible ego.'

I kept an open mind. After all, if his aggression could be controlled he might be an asset to the Co-op—he certainly did his job well. I'd heard that he was organiser of an unofficial branch managers' meeting at a pub in Ryhope, but I took little notice. If they did their job properly, it was no concern of mine how they occupied their personal time. My first eye-opener was at the members' meeting called to amalgamate Ryhope and Sunderland Co-ops. During the members' question time he rose to his feet and hurled abuse at the Ryhope management and committee, followed by sarcastic comments about the CWS. It was hard to believe he was an employee—some of his words were beyond decency for a public meeting. If I'd had grounds, I'd have sacked him on the spot.

The final straw came a few weeks later at a full staff meeting organised by the union, at which I'd been invited to speak. I was waiting outside the hall and couldn't avoid hearing the comments of the more forceful speakers. Bill, my assistant, nudged me to listen. This manager was on his feet, mouthing vitriolic abuse against me. My anger (at such unwarranted abuse to feed his ego) was too deep even to show emotion. I fulfilled my speaking commitment and said to Bill as we left the building:

'If he hates me now, he'll really have something to shout about when I'm finished with him.'

With such outspoken opinions by a branch manager, I didn't think it was in the interest of the business that he should remain in a position of responsibility one day more than necessary. I had no grounds to demote him; in any case, after his comments to staff, any action on my part would appear to be victimisation. He had to go, but it would have to be his decision—but how?

I decided to concentrate on his ego. When visiting his shop I made him feel ten feet tall, by my praise for his ability. I indicated that he was wasted in such a small shop and that his promotion was inevitable. Sure enough, the first vacancy for a much bigger job produced his application. I gave him an excellent interview, included him in the final interview with another applicant, then gave the job to the other man. I later phoned to commiserate, but said there would soon be another opportunity for a man with his ability. Five vacancies occurred during the next few months. He applied for them all, always progressed to the final two, and then failed. His ego couldn't take such set-backs and slowly he realised he would never get promotion. People he considered his inferior were now senior to him. The day he gave his notice to leave and work for another company, he said to Bill Fish:

'I always thought I'd get promotion from Hughes.'

'Maybe it's something you said,' Bill replied.

9

TURNING A BLIND EYE

The most profitable section of the business was the funeral department: every year it showed improved trade and profits. Consequently, with all the other problems in the Co-op, I left it free of interference.

Eventually, its turn came, so I asked Bill Fish to spend some time to 'just give the department the once-over.' After a few days he came back to me and said:

'There's a procedure operating that you should be aware of. The funeral director draws over £200 per week as petty cash, but he's got no receipts.'

'You mean to tell me he can't prove where £200 a week goes?' I asked.

'That's right, he can give you a list of where the money goes, but that's all.'

'Are we losing £200 a week?'

'No, no, it's built into the funeral bills—the customer pays,' Bill replied. 'In fact, he claims the business will grind to a halt if he didn't hand the money out every day.'

'Bill, do you mind telling me what the hell we're talking about?'

'You're not going to believe it, but I've checked and double checked.' I didn't answer; Bill was making a meal of this.

Although the image of a funeral department is of a sedate, tranquil and caring service, there are two elements of the funeral business rarely noticed by the general public:

1. It is a very competitive business;
2. It is subject to precise timing.

There is such a profit that a variety of practices are used to capture business. No matter what happened to the rest of the business, the Co-op funeral business was unaffected. Timing was all-important!

If a funeral time is given to a family, they expect it to be implemented to the minute, not half an hour early or late. Little does anyone realise how many elements are involved to achieve this precise timing: hospital porters, police, doctors, drivers, and even clergymen. Without their co-operation, the timetable couldn't be maintained.

'Do you mean that some of these people get a fee from funerals?' I said with incredulity.

'Correct, no receipts,' Bill replied.

'Well it stops from now,' I said. 'Give him a small book and I want to see a signature for every penny paid out.'

Four days later Bill and the funeral director were waiting for me when I arrived at the office. Bill was agitated.

'Trying to get signatures is creating chaos,' Bill said, before I had time to sit down. 'No one refuses to give a signature, they just refuse to accept the money.'

'Fair enough,' I answered. 'It'll save us some money.' The funeral director spoke for the first time, in a tone of exasperation.

'Mr Hughes, without payment, porters find other important duties, doctors ask you to call back later for a death certificate, and the clergy find difficulty keeping the schedule.' With a condescending voice he continued: 'Everyone does it, it's gone on for generations and you'll finish our business if you continue to demand a signature.'

'Do you agree with this?' I asked turning to Bill.

'Reluctantly, I've got to say yes,' he said.

Principles or not, I couldn't afford to lose such a profitable part of the business. My instructions were cancelled, problems disappeared.

10

MARY POPPINS

A friend of mine had supplied me with American newspapers for some months. More and more I was reading about the new retail phenomenon of 'out of town' shops that sold everything under one roof. Nothing like it had been tried in Britain. It was thought that people wouldn't travel out of town to shop and the idea of selling fashions, electrical and other non-food in the same shop as food was considered typically American and not for the British, who preferred specialist shops and departmental stores.

We had a branch at Castletown (the site of our first hijack). The building was large and was divided into separate shops, some workshops at the rear, and had ample car parking. It was situated about four miles outside Sunderland, in a housing estate and on a bus route. The ideal site to try an 'American Experiment'.

Dividing walls were demolished, the floor renewed, strip lighting installed, and the store redecorated. The whole store was made self-service. Staff were available to help customers with non-food purchases, but only if requested. Many people expressed doubts about people buying carpets, furniture, and other non-food items on self-service. ('It isn't the British way.') At the rear, a quick-car-repair workshop was set up, and a car-accessory shop created. The idea was that while the woman shopped, the man could see to his car. A small coffee shop was created for long-distance shoppers (we hoped).

The only members of a family not catered for were the young children. A nursery was the answer: somewhere for young children to be looked after—free of charge—while their parents did the shopping.

I was blatantly copying American ideas; it was 1969 and it had never been tried in Britain. Once again an element of luck entered the planning. The film Mary Poppins, starring Julie Andrews, was being shown throughout the country. We needed a qualified nurse for the children's nursery, so we advertised for a 'Co-op Mary Poppins'. The response, publicity and reaction were incredible. Although the whole shopping concept was new, it was the nursery that created the publicity—from press, TV and women's magazines. Everyone wanted to see the toys, facilities and, of course, interview our own 'Mary Poppins'.

We hardly needed to pay for advertising, we'd had so much free coverage—so Britain's first 'American Style' one-stop shop was opened. From day one it was a huge success. Car owners filled every vacant space, buses emptied outside the store, and private hire coaches came from as far afield as Newcastle, South Shields and Hartlepool. Other organisations quickly developed this new selling concept, Woolco was first, followed by Presto and others. Within two years our store was already old-fashioned and we hadn't the money or sites to keep up with competitors. They were getting a good start over the Co-op in modern retailing and there was absolutely nothing I could do about it.

Sunderland Co-op paves the way

THE first in a ring of six experimental out-of-town shopping centres was opened in a blaze of publicity at Castletown, Co Durham, last week by Sunderland Co-operative Society. Based on American supermarket ideas, the centre incorporates many new features and is being watched with interest by other supermarket operators outside the Co-op movement.

Aimed at attracting shoppers from within a six mile radius, the 7,000 sq ft Castletown centre—sited in a small colliery village just outside Sunderland—represents a departure from the conventional British supermarket operation and is very American in style.

Mr David Hughes, Sunderland Co-op's chief executive officer who master-minded the "shopping-ring" idea, told SELF SERVICE & SUPERMARKET that he had been studying reports and literature on American operations for years. He was convinced that the American system would be adopted over here sooner or later and he wanted Sunderland to promote the co-op movement's new go-ahead image by being the pioneer.

NEW FEATURES

Among the new features is a nursery where shoppers can leave young children in the care of a qualified nurse.

In the 5,000 sq ft supermarket Mr Hughes has introduced a new system whereby foods and non-foods are mixed indiscriminately. For example, the paint gondola is next door to the cake section.

Self Service
magazine, 1969

Are you a
QUALIFIED CHILDREN'S NURSE?
Are you a modern
MARY POPPINS?
If you are
WE WANT YOU!
TO TAKE CHARGE OF OUR SHOPPERS' NURSERY AT OUR

NEW DISCOUNT STORE

— CASTLETOWN —

The Store is to open September 12th and will provide *FREE NURSERY FACILITIES* up to the age of five years, while Mother does the shopping. If you are interested apply in writing to Mr D. Hughes, Chief Executive Officer, Sunderland Co-op, High Street West, Sunderland.

PARK THE CAR WHILE YOU SHOP. NO SEARCHING FOR PARKING SPACES.

PARK THE BABY WHILE YOU SHOP. A FULLY QUALIFIED CHILDRENS NURSE IN ATTENDANCE.

CO-OP

Sunderland
CO-OPERATIVE

NEW DISCOUNT STORE

The nursery? Mothers forgot to collect their children until the end of the day, and frequently some were awaiting collection an hour after the store closed. The facility was grossly abused. 'Mary Poppins' got fed up and it closed after six months. However, once again, we'd been first—it would be for others to perfect out-of-town shopping.

'Mary Poppins'—Nurse Marion Hudson—greets a new arrival to the store's nursery, allowing mother to do her weekly shopping unhindered.

MR David Hughes, chief executive officer for Sunderland Co-operative Society, is a man of vision and ideas. And also a man with enough courage to put his ideas into practice. Well versed in the American supermarket scene, Mr Hughes is confident that the trend in America today will be the trend in Britain tomorrow.

With this in mind Sunderland Co-op has embarked on an imaginative programme that is already creating a stir of interest among major supermarket operators.

The plan is to provide a ring of six shopping centres, well served with car parks and designed to meet every shopping need, around Sunderland's perimeter.

Sunderland goes American

The first centre was opened recently at Castletown, just outside Sunderland, a small colliery village with a population of about 5,000. In a rather isolated position, the centre will rely on about 75% of its trade coming from shoppers visiting the centre either by car or public transport.

But the Castletown branch has a potential 30,000 shoppers on five estates (not including Castletown village) within a six mile radius. The estates are Town End Farm, Hylton Castle, Witherwack, Downhill and Redhouse.

The centre lies between these estates and Sunderland town and its attraction to estate residents is a saving in travel, convenience, easy car parking, cheap and comprehensive shopping services — and one of the most attractive features — a nursery where children under five years of age can be left in the care of a trained nurse.

Built on one level, and converted from a former Co-op store, the centre comprises a 5,000 sq ft supermarket plus an area of 2,000 sq ft (under the one roof) divided into a wine and spirits section, car accessory shop, a coffee bar and the nursery. Behind the centre is a garage for customers where a resident mechanic is available to carry out minor car repairs.

very unusual ideas some of which, said Mr Hughes, are very much of an experimental nature.

Chief among them is the policy of mixing nonfood and food items as opposed to stocking them in separate sections. In this way you find in the store items such as paint and cakes standing side by side.

And Mr Hughes is coupling the idea with a complete weekly change of layout.

His theory is that by mixing foods and nonfoods the housewife is forced to see items she might not have the opportunity of seeing in a conventional layout and is prompted to purchase. Following on this, by frequently changing the store's layout pattern the shopper is unable to follow a blind buying habit that is going straight to certain sections of the supermarket, for her goods, week in and week out. Frequent layout alterations means that she has to "search" for the items she requires and in doing so sees other goods outside her normal shopping list which might tempt her to buy.

Paint and cakes stand side by side— one of Mr Hughes' experimental ideas.

THE SUPERMARKET

The supermarket incorporates son

AND 40 CUSTOMERS CAME BY HIRED COACH!

A PRIVATE bus stopped outside the store—and out stepped 40 housewives at 7.30 p.m. for a shopping spree!

Such was the impact of Sunderland Co-op Society's new out-of-town one-stop-shop developed in former branch premises that trading figures in three days passed the previous total for a month of trading in the traditional manner.

The opening of the American-type store on one level turned the sleeping mining village of Castletown, on the banks of the River Wear four miles from Sunderland town centre, into a boom town.

Cars parked around the premises and in side streets. At one point 43 people were counted waiting for one of the 200 wire baskets at the shop to become vacant.

Ad campaign

Leading up to the store's opening was a carefully planned advertising campaign in the local press and handbills, coupled with stories creating sufficient interest to attract national press coverage.

At the helm was David Hughes, chief executive of the society, who told "Self Service Times": "Everything has gone according to plan. The out-of-town shop literally has attracted people out of towns from a wide area."

A quick check to the nearest branch to Castletown—only two-and-a-half miles away—showed no change in trade. Further checks revealed sales increases at the society's other 21 branches.

Added Mr. Hughes: "No one I spoke to was disappointed at making the trip to the shop.

Nursery

"I met one couple who had travelled 12 miles to the store. The husband went off to buy car tyres and a battery while his wife got in groceries. Then they met for a coffee in our cafe—a perfect illustration of what we had aimed for."

The cafe is just one of the features for customers at the Castletown shop.

A popular venture has been the provision of a nursery, which catered for 242 children left by young mothers in the first three days of trading. (See "Men and Matters," page 6).

Some children cried when they had to leave the store's "Mary Poppins"—21-year-old children's nurse Marion Hudson—and could only be placated by a promise that they could come again tomorrow.

The "resident" car mechanic was also kept busy with quick on-the-spot minor repairs, tyre and accessory fittings. The car park was always full.

Undoubtedly keen prices attracted customers. Said Mr. Hughes: "Many people had got a handbill of our prices and then compared them with the grocery bill they were paying each week. Savings of up to four shillings in the pound were being made, they claimed."

The shop covers 7,000 square feet and includes sections for wines and spirits, car parts, tyres, butchering and fresh meat, provisions, specialised fruit and vegetables, and there is a 300-foot run of non-foods.

In the first two days refrigerators and 12 beds were sold, many being collected by customers with their own transport. There is no credit. Deliveries are made, but there is a charge.

Average purchases have been £2 15s. a head at the self service and counter sections.

How has the new-style shopping for the area been received by old-style Co-op members?

Two shoppers, Mrs. A. Trotter and Mrs. J. Crossley, of Castletown, both branch members for over 50 years, were delighted.

Said Mrs. Trotter, aged 79, pushing her trolley: "The prices are helping pensioners. I think this should have happened years ago."

Added Mrs. Crossley, (72): "I like this idea much better than the old shop."

UNOFFICIAL BUILD-UP OF CO-OPERATIVE SUPERS

A STRONG unofficial campaign is building up throughout the Co-op movement to increase the number of supermarkets operated by retail societies, reports Clive Beddall.

This important step to assist in restoring the co-op's image in the High Street has come about following several significant moves by retail societies in various parts of England and Wales and there are hopes of an even more dramatic build up in the months ahead.

One development which could be of great influence on the build-up came about this week when Sunderland Society opened the first of its planned string of American style shopping units.

Situated at Castletown, the 7,000 sq. ft. unit opened on Thursday.

Sunderland chief executive Mr. David Hughes told me: "Throughout the country there are lots of traditional co-op premises trading in a traditional co-op fashion. With these new units we are trying to introduce a more modern image."

A string of retail societies are believed to be watching the Sunderland operation with interest. In fact one prominent co-operator said this week that the North East unit could well be the shape of things to come for many other societies.

The Grocer, *1969*

SUNDERLAND CO-OP FINDS ITS 'MARY POPPINS'

SUNDERLAND Co-operative Society has appointed a real life "Mary Poppins"—complete with her own nursery — for the society's first American-style one-stop shopping centre which opens at Castletown on September 12.

She is 21-year-old Miss Marion Hudson, an attractive brunette chosen from a list of 14 applicants—all qualified nursery nurses. For the past nine months Marion has been working as a nanny looking after two children in Rome, where she had to learn to speak Italian. Before that she served at two nurseries in Sunderland.

At the new store, mothers will be able to leave their children in the nursery while they do their shopping in peace.

Says Mr. David Hughes, the Society's chief executive officer: "We advertised for a modern Mary Poppins who the children would like. We got applicants from as far away as Cheshire. Marion really fits the bill and the nursery should be a boon to mothers with young children who find it difficult to get out shopping."

Five stores like the one opening at Castletown are being planned.

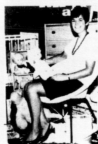

Sunderland Co-op management conference, 1969

11

COLLAPSE

The marketing exercises of eggs, an out-of-town store, and many other gimmicks all helped to divert media attention from my main activity of rationalising the business and getting it on to a very firm base ready for future development.

The concern of Philip Thomas that a number of Co-ops would collapse was well justified. In quick succession a number of Co-ops 'requested' my services to take control. There was no need for a CWS Director to persuade them: the situation was too desperate for that.

The lessons learned at Ryhope and Sunderland were invaluable, a team of managers was now well experienced in sorting out our problems. The take-over procedure didn't alter: the board members of each Co-op became advisors without authority; I took over as chief executive officer, and with only one exception (West Cornforth) the senior officials were made redundant.

At the peak of take-overs I was in control of five Co-ops at the same time.

The workload was mammoth, the pressure intense, and always the media kept our activities in front of the public. I tried to maintain an image to staff, customers and media of calm and control, but the true state was slightly less. For months my daily routine was to face decisions on staff redundancies, shop closures, reorganisation of take-overs, and the never-ending problems of capital (or lack of it).

The amalgamated society of Sunderland and Ryhope improved considerably and I was able to release members' capital. This served two purposes: we received favourable reports in the press—at long last the Co-op image was improving; it also gave us credibility. People now realised that if Sunderland could be saved maybe their society could be saved. Consequently, even more Co-ops were lining up for take- over.

The rare outward indication of praise from Philip Thomas was a telegram of congratulations on our progress, which I used as an excuse for a huge staff party. However, he maintained his rule of no financial assistance to any Co-op taken over and no interference in my management control.

Inevitably, with such a considerable amount of activity, a number of incidents occurred that will never be forgotten.

When faced with strict stock controls, all nine butcher van-salesmen walked out, each man hired a van, became self-employed, did their usual customer calls—and the total butcher trade was lost to the Co-op.

In the main street of a town in West Durham, the Co-op business was duplicated by having two shops selling identical products. One was patronised by Catholics, the other by Protestants. After discussions with both groups I spun a coin and the Catholic shop closed. The other shop supplied all residents, but for a long time each group shopped on different days.

When checking stocks at bankrupt Co-ops we found—shoe boxes in stock rooms without any shoes inside; cycles with only one wheel; dresses that had obviously been worn; masses of broken toys; canned goods covered in rust; biscuits two years old; televisions that didn't work; etc. etc. All were listed on stock sheets as saleable goods at full price. We were sorting out inefficiency that had accumulated over many, many years, I was now stopping bad practices and inefficiency, but the cost in financial terms was very high and, in human terms, unacceptable.

The collapse was escalating and we were nearly overwhelmed with problems. Every corner seemed to produce even more and bigger difficulties. Philip Thomas had a grand plan for only one Co-op to cover the whole of Britain. If many other Co-ops were in the same state as those I was sorting, then his dream was many years ahead.

By now I'd had my fill of media attention, pressure of business was at a peak—suddenly everything changed.

Flying home, after visiting his daughter in South Africa, the plane crashed. Philip Thomas was dead!

The man was gone. His replacement didn't have the same drive, determination, or vision for the Co-op movement. It was obvious that the situation in many north-east Co-ops was serious. Consequently the few large Co-ops (Darlington, Newcastle and Blyth) floated the idea of one huge Co-op to be called 'The North Eastern Co-op Society'.

The CWS pledged that the five Co-ops that I controlled would transfer to this new Co-op society. My days as a CWS advisory officer in the north-east were numbered. I could stay with the CWS and do the same job elsewhere in the country, or I could join the new Co-op being created.

I was now 45 years old. I'd really had enough of the job but, more important, there was no way May and I wanted to move to another part of the country. I resigned from the CWS, joined the North Eastern Co-op as an 'executive with special powers'. Financially I was no worse off, responsibility would be considerably less and, I hoped, I'd be helping to build something for the future in the north-east of England.

I'd been in retailing 30 years from shop boy to chief executive officer, but the next phase of my career would expose me to big business—ruthlessness, intrigue and power that was greater than anything I could have imagined.

'Last hope' talks today for small stores

Now for a £70m. Co-op?

By HOWARD COATS, Our Industrial Correspondent

PLANS for the creation of a North-East Co-operative Society will be finalised in Newcastle today when top CWS officials meet managers from 30 societies and union leaders, representing 10,000 employees.

The new Co-op giant will take over the purse strings of 1,300 shops with a total £70m. turnover to become one of the biggest retail businesses in the country.

At one of today's meetings, Mr. Alfred W. Allen, general secretary of the Union of Shop, Distributive and Allied Workers, will meet representatives of union branches in Northumberland, Durham and Teesside.

Though the chance of redundancies following such a massive shake-up have not been ruled out, USDAW favours the plan in general. It is seen as being long overdue and for some small struggling societies the final hope.

USDAW gave its blessing to the idea as far back as January, 1968, when the Co-operative Union — the central advisory body of the Co-op movement — recommended that 50 regional societies should replace the present 467 in England, Wales and Ireland.

The North-East plan was put to regional Co-op chiefs in October by Mr. Denis Greensmith, deputy executive officer of the CWS, who will make final details public today.

Mr. Greensmith said then: "Once policies are settled, the CWS will put its resources squarely behind the project to achieve positive expansion of trade in the North-East."

Many societies in County Durham have been hit by pit closures and the need to work as larger units has grown with modern methods in commerce. The movement has failed to keep its share of the growing retail trade.

The large, modern Co-ops of Darlington, Teesside and Newcastle have led the way. Under the new plan, less than a dozen regional units would take over the process of streamlining in the face of continued decline.

Mr. David Hughes, chief executive of the 59,000-member Sunderland Co-op said: "It's the greatest thing since I joined the movement 30 years ago.

"The potential is tremendous. It could be the beginning of a great future for the Co-op. This has to be agreed by the members, but we have no reason to believe they will not be delighted with the formation of the new society."

12

NECS

The North Eastern Co-op was created from sheer necessity and a fear for the future of the Co-op movement in the north. Already I'd taken over five Co-ops just to save them from bankruptcy, but it was estimated that anything up to 70 per cent of the Co-ops in the north east were in the same position, and might not survive for much longer.

Now that Philip Thomas was dead, the CWS lifeline was in danger of being withdrawn and unless something was done the Co-op was in danger of collapse. Newcastle, Darlington and Blyth Co-ops were the most successful in the north. At the instigation of the CWS, these three became the focal point of a new society. The theory was that their strength, plus the five Co-ops I controlled, would attract others in the north east to join.

The top jobs were given to the officials of the three large Co-ops as an incentive to create the new Co-op. Harry Jennings from Darlington became chief executive officer with Harold Whitehead from Blyth as his deputy. Martin Reed from Newcastle became society secretary. So the three top jobs were closed to anyone else, but it ensured there was no objection to the amalgamation. At the same time other top jobs like personnel, services, funerals and finance were filled before the NECS had even been formed.

What was left for me? Initially I was promised the food controller's job but, after I'd resigned from the CWS, Harry Jennings reneged on his promise and gave the job to an ex-Marks and Spencer's manager. I was offered a job as 'executive with special powers'. It was a grand title to cover a multitude of activities, it guaranteed the same wage as I had had at the CWS plus a car and, although disappointed that Harry didn't keep his promise, I accepted the job and hoped.

Everyone of the team I'd created at Sunderland was placed in acceptable jobs, including Bill Fish, my assistant, who became an administrative executive. So the hand-over of the societies I controlled to the new Co-op went quite smoothly and I was now one of the executives of this potentially mammoth Co-op society. No longer was I the top man with full authority, nor did I have the responsibility and worry. I had had enough and was quite happy to let others take over. I would take a lesser role—for a time.

These moves had taken place and decisions had been made long before the 'official' formation of the 'new' Co-op. The first public action taken was in 1970 when a meeting was organised by the CWS of every north-eastern Co-op society. The theme of the meeting was that it was 'the last hope for small Co-ops'. The CWS promised massive financial assistance (directly opposite to the Philip Thomas policy), promised jobs for all officials, and generally painted a rosy picture if everyone agreed to join the North Eastern Co-op.

The hall was packed with officials of the 30 north-eastern Co-ops, and there was an air of optimism and euphoria. Everyone could see a way out of their gloom. Most of the officials were over 55 years old and already counting the days to retirement, so golden handshakes would be very acceptable. The principle of one huge Co-op was accepted, but the formality of members' meetings needed to be organised.

The day after the meeting I was called to see the chief executive officer. I had known Harry Jennings in my days at Hetton Co-op, when he was at Darlington. He hadn't been as antagonistic as other Co-op managers, nor was he an enthusiast of my methods, but now he was my boss.

'Good morning, David,' he greeted me with a very friendly smile and a warm handshake. 'Now we're going to work together to create something big.' I only smiled but didn't comment. I didn't trust Harry—he'd already broken one promise. He then made a strange comment.

'As you know the CWS is putting a few million into the kitty but is demanding two places on the board and of course you are an executive.' I made no reply. I got the impression that he assumed I was aware of the CWS deal and that somehow I was still involved. In fact, since resigning, I'd had no connection or contact with anyone at the CWS, but if Harry was under the impression I was involved in some way with the financial package, it would be to my advantage to ensure he wasn't disillusioned. I didn't contradict him, I just waited for him to continue. He then handed me a letter and said:

'This gives you full authority.' It was a brief directive, addressed to all managers and staff in the North Eastern Co-op, giving me authority to check, investigate, or audit any shop, section, or department, anywhere in the society, at any time. It was signed by Harry.

The word 'troubleshooter' wasn't to be seen, but there was no doubt what 'executive with special powers' meant. I was to be a roving 'troubleshooter'.

'Over the next few months there'll be a hell of a lot of reorganisation going on, and the CWS insist we have someone in the field keeping an eye on things." he said.

Now I knew why he'd broken his promise. Now I knew the CWS was really pulling the strings, and now I knew why he assumed I was involved. Harry wasn't in total control and I wasn't going to make it any easier for him by denying involvement with the CWS. I just kept quiet.

I was to be responsible directly to him to check on anything, anywhere, and make recommendations on closures, organisation, and efficiency on any item I selected. I was given a roving commission without any responsibility or accountability. After the graft of the past few years it sounded like a holiday, but at the back of my mind I wondered how long such a job would continue. It seemed too good to be true.

The first action was to oversee the organising of members' meetings at each individual Co-op, for them to formally vote the transfer of their society to the new North Eastern Co-op. Although some societies had lively meetings, the vast majority showed only apathy; in fact in some instances there were too few members for a legal quorum, so nearby pubs were visited to 'encourage' members to leave their drink for a few minutes to vote. After some weeks only Chester-le-Street, Seghill, Townley and Stanhope Co-ops refused to join, preferring to remain independent. The North Eastern Co-op was now a single Co-op, comprising 1,300 shops, 10,000 staff, and a combined turnover of £70 million a year.

Before the formation of the North Eastern Co-op, I was aware I had developed an image of being a hard manager because of my actions at Ryhope and the freezing of capital. Now I was to learn how ruthless and uncaring a multi-million pound business can be. It was absolutely essential I learnt how to survive within such a huge and complex business.

Before this job, I had always been the top man, making the decisions and determining other people's futures. In the army as a sergeant I had had a lot of freedom. In my own shop I answered to no one. Although I had a chairman and committee at Hetton Co-op, I had a free hand. Under Philip Thomas at the CWS I had more freedom than ever before. Now I had a boss who wanted a weekly report, and I was part of a new developing business where each executive would inevitably build his own empire around him. Although I was an executive in name, I could do little to create a base because I had a roving commission and no staff.

Another complication had to be allowed for. In the past I'd antagonised most of the Co-op managers in the north east due to my business methods. Now these same men would be my colleagues, and a few even blamed me for their downfall. I had a feeling that the next few years would not be smooth (even if I managed to survive).

The first management meeting was a shambles. It was before any reorganisation and each society still had its own team of managers, so there were 30 of every position. (manager, secretary, accountants and buyers). The meeting was held in the board room and, even with everyone standing and crushed like sardines, some were left in the passage outside. Harry Jennings went on and on, painting a picture of success and a good future for all. A CWS director followed him and spoke of his delight at the formation of a regional society and he went on until the room was like a Turkish bath, everyone trying to look interested but wishing they hadn't been so keen and had been left outside in the passage.

Any fool knew that the promise of 'Jobs for All' was not possible. The whole idea of amalgamation was to cut costs and in fact every management meeting that followed saw a significant reduction in numbers. After each meeting parting managers could be heard hoping they would still have a job by the next meeting. In six months the management team was reduced from about 250 to 45. (So much for the Jobs for All promise!)'.

After that next management meeting all executives were invited to stay behind for a further meeting. As managers filed out of the room I was very surprised to see four CWS people and a director (all from Manchester) enter the board room. I knew them all on first name terms and naturally we stood in a group renewing acquaintances. When asked to be seated (without thinking) I sat alongside Tom Welch, the CWS director, and Bert Rolands, a CWS accountant.

Everyone was introduced, then Harry Jennings detailed the proposed structure of the board, management etc. Not only would the CWS have two on the board, but four people had been seconded to 'assist'. In fact, the CWS was safeguarding its investment—the society was in their hands, for now.

Here I was, sitting in their midst. If Harry thought I still had an allegiance to the CWS, the other executives would have no doubt. It would be pointless denying it, no one would believe me, so I decided to let the myth continue.

'What are Mr Hughes' duties in the society?' the services controller asked, just as the meeting was ending. Harry Jennings gave a full account of my roving commission, which was received in total silence and without comment (which I considered very ominous).

After the meeting I made it my business to speak to each departmental controller. I wanted to assure them that although I reported directly to the chief officer, I didn't intend to encroach on their responsibility; in fact the aim was to assist by being an independent observer. My effort to start off with a mutual understanding was a failure: each controller was courteous, but suspicious. To them I was a spy, to check and report back. (To whom?) Well I'd made my bed, now I'd have to make the best of it. In view of the attitude of all the executives I decided that although I was now part of a multi-million-pound business I'd be a loner. No one would know how much or little I knew about anything, because I'd confide in no one. I'd keep my own counsel about everything.

Within days of the North Eastern Co-op being formed Harry Jennings gave me my first assignment.

'I thought we were going to build a business,' I said with disbelief when he gave me the details of my task.

'We can't build without finance,' Harry retorted. 'In any case, if anyone knows about cutting away dead wood it's you.' I was to identify shops, offices, garages, etc. for closure. He was right of course—if anyone had experience of closing shops it was me, but I had left the CWS believing I was getting away from such misery. Now I was to mastermind a closure programme of mammoth proportions.

'I believe, when we get down to half the number of shops we now have, it will be more manageable,' Harry continued. Good God, I thought to myself, the man's talking of closing over 600 shops!

'What are the criteria for closure?' I asked. 'Lack of profit now, lack of potential profit? What about inefficient management?' Harry stopped me. He didn't want to discuss such details.

'Just give me your recommendations, David, then I'll pass them to the relevant controller to implement.' I didn't bother to discuss it further. All Harry wanted was a list of closures and he didn't seem to care how they were selected.

I left his office, got hold of the latest accounts of all 1,300 shops and sat down to think. I soon realised why there was urgency to close shops: it was the same reason I'd closed shops at Sunderland, Ryhope and elsewhere—to raise finance, liquidate stock, sell property, vehicles, etc.

God knows what my future would be when the CWS lost control. Still, it was too early to worry about that. In any case, a hell of a lot of people would be out of work in the next few months, after I'd selected shops. It suddenly dawned on me that we had newly-installed controllers doing their utmost to create their own empires and I was now going to demolish part of it. Should I tell them? Would it improve relations if I discussed my instructions? (No, they will soon find out, let them come to me. That way I've got the initiative!)

Within a week I'd selected the first ten shops. I had taken great care to spread the list over a wide area from Darlington to Berwick. No area would be hit harder than another. In any case they were all very small shops with no more than three staff. With the list of shops, Harry wanted the value of stock to be liquidated, the book value and market value of the properties, and the amount of expenses savings.

On looking down the list, without comment, Harry put his pen through the two Darlington shops. They were in his previous society and were obviously not for consideration.

'That's fine David,' he said with a smile, 'I'll pass this to the controllers to implement. Keep an eye on how the closures are handled.'

'Do they know how many closures you have in mind?' I asked.

'Would you tell them if you were in my place?' he replied, but didn't wait for an answer because he picked up the phone and told his secretary to convene an executive meeting at four o'clock.

The reaction to my first list was very mixed at the meeting. It wasn't up for discussion. Harry simply gave the instruction that closures were to be implemented—immediately. After the meeting, the non-food controller suggested we work together. I responded by saying I'd consider his closure suggestions but couldn't guarantee to list them all. The personnel controller said I must give her advance notice when it involved staff. I told her to take it up with the chief officer. The food controller produced his ace card. He offered me the job as his assistant.

'What about deputy food controller?' I said, but he wouldn't have that. His assistant was a plum job (or so he thought). I'd already arranged a holiday so, much to his annoyance, I said I'd give him a reply when I returned.

During the holiday May and I discussed the offer at great length and finally decided to reject his offer and stick with what I had, because

a) I didn't like the man and he didn't like me;

b) an assistant can be the can-carrier and never get the praise;

c) if he failed, his assistant would fail.

The minute I returned to work and rejected his job, I knew I'd made an enemy.

For the next few months the major part of my job was to present a list of recommended closures every week. (No matter where I travel in the north-east today I see buildings that are ex-Co-op stores.) The closure programme was down to a fine art. Once the list was presented, each department slipped into gear. Staff were interviewed, unions notified, stock removed, and property sold or rented. The atmosphere created was incredible. I was the last face anyone wanted to see yet, incredibly, the unions did absolutely nothing. The staff were very depressed and apathy was rife. All the stories that the money saved would build new, modern stores was of no consolation to staff being sacked. I was delegated to meet committees of societies and explain the closure plans, which was not the easiest of tasks, and was to have an adverse effect on my career in later years.

After almost a year, even Harry Jennings had to admit that something positive had to be done. Critics were beginning to say the North Eastern Co-op was finished before it had started. His obsession of selling property was doing great harm to our image but, without doubt, finance was being raised in huge amounts. In fact, potential property buyers were actually asking when certain branches would be closed. One 'low-cost discount' chain developed 80 per cent of its 30 stores in branches we closed. Our policy was too crazy for words.

Instructions went out: find a good site for an out-of-town discount store to sell food and non-food. At last we would build something, and I was reminded of my out-of-town store at Castletown and argued successfully for no thought to be given to a nursery. (One Co-op Mary Poppins was enough.) After numerous proposals it was decided at an executive meeting that the best site would be at Annfield Plain. We had a huge old-fashioned Co-op that was the length of a street; so plans were prepared to close down and clear the site to build a brand new store.

The store was closed and a week before demolition, the local authority offered a site at the opposite side of the road at low cost with roads laid etc., provided we gave them the old Co-op building. The deal was accepted, the old building was demolished, brick by brick, and rebuilt as the focal point of a new outdoor museum being built at Beamish. The new store opened and was a huge success from the first day.

Throughout the closure period, I had little trouble with any of the controllers except the food controller. He resented any contact I had with his shops. I understood his feeling but, whether he liked it or not, I had a job to do. One of my responsibilities was to monitor the handling and selling of stock from closed shops. For weeks I had been telling him that his area manager wasn't doing his job right in the Durham area. The area manager was a huge lumbering man who considered himself superior to any Co-op man because he'd been recruited from Moores Stores. The stock was being dumped in warehouses with little effort to sort or dispose of it. Losses would be enormous.

I was fed up trying to get something done through the controller, so in my weekly report I included details of the problem. One of my big mistakes!

Friday 17 March 1972, 11 a.m. A morning etched in my mind like stone. It was the day after I'd submitted my weekly report, and fifteen months after the North Eastern Co-op had been created. An incredible 400 shops had been closed, management streamlined and, I had to admit, the business was more manageable. More important, millions of pounds had been raised, and although the two CWS directors were still on the board, the four 'assistants' had returned to Manchester. I knew my 'troubleshooting' tasks were getting less, so I was watching every move to see if an executive vacancy occurred that would get me a more permanent base in the society.

As the clock chimed eleven I walked into the chief officer's palatial suite of offices to find the food controller already seated opposite Harry.

'Good morning, gentlemen,' I said with as light-hearted a voice as I could muster. Although I got a response, it was hardly very encouraging. I got the feeling the two of them had had an argument. Harry didn't waste time on trivialities.

'David, we've discussed your report on the area food manager in Durham, and after this meeting he will be dismissed.'

'But all I wanted was something done about the problem,' I protested.

'We're going to do something,' he replied. 'I'd like you to join the food group.'

I turned quickly to face the food controller, but he didn't respond. He'd already filled his assistant's job, so what was I expected to do? I didn't have to wait very long to find out.

'We're doing a reorganisation and want you to take over Newcastle area in the food group.'

'You mean to say you want me to step down to area manager?' I said with incredulity.

'It is the biggest area with a turnover of over £20 million,' Harry answered. I was stunned. From executive down to one of four area managers and to have a boss I disliked intensely was too much to accept.

'What's the alternative?' I turned to Harry, looking directly at him.

'Well, the need for your services is getting less every day and there isn't likely to be an executive vacancy for a long time,' he replied. I sat silent for what seemed an age. I felt a mixture of shock, anger and humiliation. I was so near to walking out, but I was 46 years old, the Co-op was my life, and I had to make a living.

'I'd like to think about it,' I said. The food controller spoke quickly:

'There's plenty wouldn't need time to think about such a good job.' I didn't answer, only gave him a long look.

'David, we need an answer today. Go, think about it, you know your contract safeguards your salary, so you'll be no worse off financially,' Harry concluded the discussion.

I walked out and just stood in the passageway for a long time, my mind was in a whirl. My son was working at the non-food head office, which was situated at the far end of the passage. Without more thought I walked in, saw David, and asked if he could get out for a short time. We walked down the street while I told him the story and how I felt. I needed someone to talk to, someone I could trust. Who better than my own son? He hasn't known (until now) how much he helped me over the most difficult moment in my working life.

'If you walk out, they've won. In any case it's still a good job,' he said. Just our talking together was such a help in getting things into perspective, for which I shall be forever grateful. I'm sure that, but for our talk, I would have walked out and would have missed so many pleasures that were to follow.

I went home and told May the news. She was her usual down-to-earth-self. We didn't want to move, the salary was still good and—damn them—I'd stay at the Co-op.

The following Monday morning I set up my office in Newgate Street in Newcastle as 'Area Food Manager'.

13

A TEAM EFFORT

Calling on my previous experience I knew I could do the job. However, within the food group the Newcastle area manager was the 'plum' field manager's job. The area consisted of 128 shops, a mixture of grocery, butcher and freezer centres with a turnover of almost half-a-million pounds a week. It was major business in its own right. I had eight supervisors and an area administrative office to control the area. Most of the supplies to shops were delivered from the most modern and automated warehouse in Europe, sited at Birtley.

A meeting of the four area managers took place fortnightly under the chairmanship of the food controller and his assistant. I entered the board room for the first meeting with a feeling of trepidation, wondering what reception I would face, because I'd been instrumental in getting a colleague sacked and a re-organisation imposed on them by the chief officer, resulting in me controlling the biggest area. My salary was still higher than the controller's assistant, but I hoped this wasn't general knowledge.

I had never worked with anyone in the room so, inevitably, the atmosphere was rather strained until the controller opened the meeting.

'I'd like to introduce a new colleague and wish him every success.' His opening sentence was followed by a most complimentary introduction, outlining my career and experience. To say I was surprised, is an understatement. I was actually being made welcome and invited to be an integral member of the team. I responded by assuring them of my intention of being a team member and concluded:

'I'd like to eliminate a myth that has been created. I have no allegiance to, or contact with, the CWS. I am totally committed to the North Eastern Co-op.' This was well received and created a good atmosphere in which to conduct the business of the meeting.

The food group was divided into four areas, each controlled by an area manager.

Alf Burbeck controlled the southern area, which included the ex-Darlington Co-op. An ex-manager of Harry Jennings', Alf did his own thing. No shops were closed, he bought his own products, and was almost a separate society. The controller seemed to have no authority or desire to intervene.

Joe Brown was the northern area manager, an ex-army sergeant major who still looked the part. Previously a Blyth Co-op manager, he was still in regular communication with the deputy chief executive. Consequently the controller did not have absolute control in this area.

Pat O' Shea, an ex-North Shields man who controlled the Durham area, was inoffensive and methodical.

John Beer, an ex-manager from Stockton, was the assistant to the controller. He was constantly conveying instructions and messages, and the butt of many of the controller's jokes. (Thank God I'd turned the job down, I wouldn't have lasted a week.)

This was the 'team' I'd joined. The most amazing feature was that in practice it was not a team in any way whatsoever. The controller and his assistant were figureheads at head office. Each area manager did his own thing with the minimum of contact with colleagues. It was virtually four separate businesses within one Co-op society.

I settled into the job, determined to create the best area of the four. I wanted to have the same business atmosphere with managers and staff that I had had years ago at Hetton. It was more difficult because of the size and number of staff. Everything was created around each supervisor who I looked upon as a general manager of his own group of shops. The aim was to create high standards of retailing and improve staff morale.

Area was competing with area in Newcastle on shop standards, sales and efficiency. The winners were always given a party night out at the Rainbow Room with their wives. May and I were at every party, together with all the supervisors and their wives. It didn't take long to improve the area into an extremely efficient operation. The high point was a promise that if the area achieved sales of £1 million in one week I'd arrange a dinner and party for all managers and their wives in the whole area. No area had ever achieved such a turnover in only one week.

In the Christmas trade, we exceeded our target. The whole area was jubilant and I got suppliers to contribute amply to the cost of the celebration. Wives received a present, managers were given a medal to commemorate their achievement, and it was the best night of celebration the society had ever seen, particularly when I'd invited executives and other area managers to see what 'we' could do.

The success of my area led to the chief officer thinking of the possibility of creating something similar throughout the society. The idea was created of a 'Millionaire's Weekend'. But, out of the blue, Harry Jennings decided to retire and his deputy, Harold Whitehead, took over. To my delight, Bill Fish, who'd been my assistant at Sunderland, was moved up to be assistant secretary of the society. He deserved his promotion.

Harold Whitehead was an ex-accountant who rarely got involved in field operations, but was an enthusiast for any social occasion, so soon revived the Millionaire's Weekend idea. The food controller's assistant, the northern area food manager and I were delegated to firm up on the idea. We planned a competition throughout the society of every single shop, based on sales and shop standards and covering a number of weeks. Only the best would get the prize.

The prize was a weekend at the Columbridge Hotel at Aviemore, Scotland. We would take over the whole hotel for the weekend, hire a complete train to take us there, plan a gala dinner for the Saturday evening, and organise excursions and activity for anyone wishing to be active—or they could simply laze around doing nothing. It would be completely free for the winning manager(ess) and a partner.

The idea was an absolute success. Staff morale was sky high, standards improved, and the weekend for winners was fabulous. Area managers, supervisors, executives and their partners were automatically invited and May and I had a wonderful weekend, particularly when we won the fancy dress before the dinner (we were dressed as dirty tramps). It all ceased after three annual repeats when the costs became prohibitive and suppliers were getting reluctant to cover the cost.

May and I look back on those Millionaire Weekends as some of our best trips away. For me it helped to create a new image, and I no longer felt an outsider within the society. How pleased I was I hadn't walked out when asked to join the food group!

To my surprise I was allowed to get on without interference from the controller. Except for the regular meetings I saw little of him, but his reputation didn't improve. His approach to reps was at times appalling. He would think nothing of walking out of his office and tell a waiting rep to make another appointment because he hadn't time to see him, the rep having travelled from London for a pre-booked meeting. He made life hell for John Beer, his assistant, but not once did he try to impose his authority on me.

Most of our supplies were delivered from the CWS warehouse at Birtley and for weeks the controller had niggled on about the inefficiency of the CWS warehouse.

'I want full details of every short or wrong delivery from the CWS,' he said at our usual meeting. No one argued—we were aware that there was major inefficiency. We were constantly out of stock of products, so maybe he'd get some improvement. Little did we realise his real motive—or the dramatic consequences.

For the next few weeks we were constantly called to meetings at Birtley, armed with our lists, to listen to reasons and excuses for our complaints. Nothing improved. It was a nuisance, but not a disaster. Our trade continued to improve but, listening to the controller, he made the problem seem out of all proportion to reality.

A phone call from the chief executive officer had me travelling to the board room to attend an 'urgent' meeting. I hadn't a clue why he had called such a meeting; I felt quite apprehensive. When the four area managers and the controller's assistant were all seated, wondering what the hell was going on, in walked the controller, chief officer and the chairman of the board.

'We must be going to declare war on somebody,' Joe Brown whispered from my right.

'Gentlemen, the controller has reported on the very serious situation at Birtley and the dramatic effect on our business.' A slight exaggeration, I thought. 'I'd like your opinion on the controller's proposal to solve the problem,' he continued. I looked over to John, who very slightly shrugged his shoulders to indicate he hadn't a clue what was coming.

We were withdrawing from Birtley Warehouse completely. Each area manager would buy for his own area, and set up his own warehouse and distribution system. I couldn't believe what I was hearing: the idea was crazy and no doubt everyone would say so. Alf had been buying his own products in Darlington so wasn't too concerned. Pat would never rock the boat, so went along with the idea. Joe said he wasn't sure, but I've no doubt he could visualise the perks of being a buyer. Once again I saw myself in a minority of one, but I couldn't keep my mouth shut.

'I'm against the idea. We've no experience of buying, we've no warehouse equipment, so everything will have to be manhandled, everything will be quadrupled, increasing our costs out of all proportion, and there is no guarantee we can do a better job than the CWS.' No one spoke for a few minutes. The chairman looked in my direction, but I had said my piece. If they were determined to commit commercial suicide, so be it.

Each area manager was given a direct instruction: find empty premises for an area warehouse, hire lorries and a forklift truck, and plunder branches for staff. In two weeks we would pull out of Birtley, putting a multi-million-pound automated warehouse out of commission, leaving millions of pounds of food standing idle and about 200 staff out of work.

Every day I expected a call to cancel the plans, but there was only silence as I was interviewing reps, buying stock, overseeing the warehouse, and organising branch delivery-schedules. After Ryhope and Sunderland, I had a good idea what was required and knew there was no chance of buying, warehousing, and delivering over 6,000 products to every shop at least once a week. The other area managers were in panic as day one arrived. They'd never been under such pressure in their lives.

Within three weeks the whole of the food groups was in utter chaos. We were now short of far more products than ever before. Managers, customers and unions were all complaining; at each area we were working flat out but couldn't possibly cope.

Half way into the fourth week, an instruction (via the controller's assistant) informed each area manager to cease buying, close down the warehouse, and revert back to the CWS at Birtley. No explanations were given, but maybe we would hear more at a special meeting called for Monday.

Joe and I were first into the board room and were discussing the chaos of the past few weeks when the chief officer walked in, accompanied by

John Beer, the controller's assistant. Without waiting for the others to arrive Harold began the meeting with a statement that took our breath away for the rapid, ruthless decisions that had already been implemented.

'We will return to the CWS for our supplies and the resignation of the controller has been accepted.' Joe and I didn't speak, waiting for more revelations. 'So Mr Beer will take over as controller immediately and a reorganisation of the food group management will also take place.'

John then took over the meeting to establish he was the boss.

'We're eliminating the four area managers' positions and I won't have an assistant,' he said. (My God, what's happening now? I thought, without making a comment.) John continued:

'We're dividing the society into two. David,' he said, looking at me, 'you'll be regional manager (south) controlling every food shop from the River Wear down to Scarborough and across to the Dales. Joe, you'll be regional manager (north) controlling from north of the Wear to Berwick. We three will now control the food groups,' he concluded.

'What happened to the other two area managers?' Joe enquired. Harold replied:

'Alf at Darlington is redundant and Pat at Durham has been given an office job.'

The speed of their action had Joe and me speechless. I thought to myself: I've survived another purge and, in fact, gained a major promotion in the process. It's a strange world. Eventually, I said:

'John, what do you mean that we three will control the food group?'

'Together we'll plan policy, development, and everything else,' he replied. 'If ever I'm away you and Joe will be in control.' I looked at Joe who winked. A huge smile on his face cemented an incredible friendship that was to last for no more than three years.

Joe established his regional office at Blyth, I took over an elaborate office complex at Middlesbrough. We each had a huge administrative office, an army of supervisors and were each responsible for sales of over £1 million per week.

Within a week of taking over, May and I were invited to a staff function at Marton Hotel and Country Club. We were to be guests of honour, no doubt replacing the redundant Alf and his wife. Still, I thought, it's a good start to meet all the managers (about 250) at a social occasion.

When we arrived we were greeted at the entrance to the club by the senior supervisor and his wife and ushered into a side room to meet all the regional supervisors and their wives over a welcoming drink. They all seemed to line up to be introduced as if we were royalty. I knew May would feel embarrassed beside me, making small talk to about 25 supervisors and their wives who were total strangers, all dressed in their finery, but this was nothing compared to what followed.

After about twenty minutes, everyone in the room jumped with startled surprise when a loud banging was followed by a deep voice announcing the time was near for the 'parade'. I turned towards the door to see an immaculate toastmaster in red coat and white bow-tie evening suit. Some 'staff do' this! We were ushered into line, May and I were at the rear and off we trooped into the main hall, which was absolutely packed, everyone standing at their table, clapping in unison as we marched to the top table. Everyone remained standing until May and I were seated. I've never felt so embarrassed in my life. May just didn't speak.

The meal was fabulous, but interrupted at intervals by the red-coated loud-mouth who seemed to hover over my left shoulder, taking every opportunity to bang his gavel on the table in front of me to announce toasts to the Queen, honoured guests, Uncle Tom Cobley, and all. It was the most formal occasion we had ever attended, and although the meal was excellent and we couldn't have been made more welcome, it wasn't the type of formality we enjoyed. If I had any say, we would never have so much formality again. (We never did.)

It was at this point in my career that I began to operate as a manager, (which may seem a strange thing to say after my extensive experience). It's a true saying that while you're doing things yourself you're not managing, and that management is doing things through other people. Until now I had tried to do far too many things myself, but now I would delegate. I had plenty of staff, ample facilities, and a huge business to control. I would be the regional figurehead, controlling people, and working with Joe and John, determining policy for the whole society food group.

NEW MANAGEMENT APPOINTMENTS

NEW APPOINTMENTS—

THE Society has re-organised its management structure from four areas into two regions, North and South. The re-organisation covers the trading, personnel, finance and administration groups. Most appointments within the new structure have been made; those remaining will be phased in over a period of months. Some new positions have been created.

There will be no change in the democratic organisation or the way members are represented on committees or the board of directors.

Up until now the North Eastern Co-op has divided its management organisation to cover four geographical areas—Northumberland, Tyneside, Durham and Teesside.

The new structure, which is designed to improve management efficiency and communication will be based on two regions—North, covering the former Northumberland and Tyneside Areas, and South covering Durham and Teesside. The word Regional no longer applies to Headquarters in Jackson Street, nor the managers who operate from there. In future the designation Regional will apply to either North or South.

Announcing the re-organisation the Chief Executive Officer, Mr. Harold Whitehead, said, "The four area structure was introduced in 1973 as part of the phased regionalisation plan following the merger of 33 societies into one North Eastern Co-operative Society. We have now completely transformed the co-operative societies in the North East into a single viable organisation with a £100m. turnover.

"The management tasks and problems in the years to come are going to be quite different from those we have known in the past. We believe that the new structure will be more efficient and more productive. While we are dispensing with some positions we are also creating new ones."

In cases where jobs are to be phased out over a period of time several long serving managers have chosen early retirement with generous severance payments against alternative positions offered.

FOOD GROUP:

Regional Manager North—Mr. Joe Brown. He was previously Area Food Manager for Northumberland. Mr. Brown lives in Blyth.

Regional Manager South—Mr. David Hughes. He was previously Area Food Manager for Tyneside. Mr. Hughes lives in Houghton-Le-Spring, Co. Durham.

Both regional managers will eventually operate from Headquarters in Gateshead, but are currently operating from Blyth and Middlesbrough respectively.

Mr. J. Brown

Mr. D. Hughes

14

CALM BEFORE THE STORM

The top man in any company decides the type of management, the discipline—or lack of it—and the atmosphere in which everyone works. Very often a hard, authoritarian manager is followed by one with a softer image, and vice-versa. The Co-op was no exception.

At the CWS, Philip Thomas had been a hard disciplinarian, and a quiet more amenable man was appointed to succeed. Harry Jennings, a tough manager, was followed by a very friendly man who would in turn be replaced by another disciplinarian. The food controller, who was a difficult man to like, let alone work for, was replaced by John Beer, a man it would be difficult to dislike.

Joe Brown and I had equal status as regional managers and the two men above us (the chief officer and the food controller) were similar characters: both enjoyed a social occasion and were determined to enjoy the fruits of their position. To our surprise, Joe and I were included in almost everything arranged.

With a multi-million-pound business dealing with a huge range of products, the competition among suppliers to get their products on to our shelves was intense. We were invited to and attended almost every trade presentation of new products, whether local, in London, or abroad. On most occasions our wives were invited and we soon became a regular quartet at these functions. Very few London hotels were missed in our annual circuit and usually the trip included the latest West End show.

We became experts at delegation. After so many years with my nose to the grindstone, I found this a new world and very enjoyable. We had a chief officer who not only encouraged social involvement but actually joined in. The four of us enjoyed playing golf, a hobby that soon became general knowledge among suppliers, many of whom produced teams of their own to challenge us. Of course the challenge included invitations to top courses such as Gleneagles, the Belfry, Sunningdale, etc., etc. The hospitality provided was fabulous. In addition, I was invited to Pro-ams which allowed me to play with professional golfers—that was beyond my wildest dreams: Sam Torrence, Bernard Gallagher, Mark James, to name a few. .

I had never worked in such a friendly atmosphere in senior management in my life. We were away from work, but still maintained close scrutiny in the business. Some of our business excursions were memorable, to say the least.

A trip to Monaco to see the Grand Prix was unforgettable for the huge crowds, roar of cars, smell of petrol and the sight of Grace Kelly sitting on the back of an open car with Prince Rainier at her side, waving to the crowds on the course.

A weekend in Paris to see Notre Dame, the Eiffel Tower, the Moulin Rouge, and actually stay at the Palace of Versailles.

John, Joe and I were invited to a trade presentation by a cosmetics company. Air tickets were provided and, on arrival at the hotel in Majorca, we met about 50 other guests, but no one from the company—they had forgotten to delegate anyone to do the presentation. Food, drinks and the hotel bill must have been huge, with nothing to show for it.

A trip to the champagne cellars at Rheims followed by a banquet at a French Chateau showed us a sample of affluence far beyond anything May or I had ever seen, particularly when we were told our hostess, a countess, was reputed to consume a bottle of champagne a day: it was her only form of liquid.

A company that produced floor cleaners invited Joe and me to Heidelberg to see a presentation of their new product. Heidelberg was quaint and beautiful, the hospitality was tremendous and the product rubbish. Joe and I returned home but didn't buy the product.

These were a small selection of a vast range of functions, excursions and activities that were provided by companies who did business with the North Eastern Co-op.

Meanwhile, the business continued to operate but I was getting concerned at the lack of growth and the increase in expenses. Raising it at our weekly meetings got me nowhere—the depth of our business discussions was very shallow. 'Where are we going to next?' was the most important topic.

I produced facts and figures to back my concern, but they thought I was over-critical. Joe couldn't care less. Like the others, I was enjoying the life, but I knew the business was sliding—and I could do little about it.

We hadn't opened one new shop, which was disgraceful for a business of our size, and eventually it was agreed we would build our first modern superstore. The site would be on my region. The old Co-op buildings at Ryhope would be demolished, the site cleared and the most modern food store built. I would have a free hand to decide the stock range, price policy and staffing. But first, Harold decided, we must get all the most modern methods of food retailing information available, to ensure we produced the best store possible.

Of course, where else were the most modern food stores, but in America? It was 'essential' we visit to see for ourselves. Ryhope would be the prototype for all future new stores. Harold put a case to the board that a 'fact-finding mission' should visit America. They agreed, on condition the chairman joined the party. The party would consist of eight and would last two weeks. My God, the cost would be enormous—who would underwrite such a cost? That was no problem, three companies would share our costs: Heinz, Campbell's and Johnson's Wax (three American-based firms).

In addition to the four of us, the party included the chairman, the greengrocery buyer, the provisions buyer and the shop fittings manager. I am certain the party was so big to give it the air of authenticity, otherwise Harold would never have got the board to agree. I felt that too many key people would be away from the Co-op at the same time. God knows what the staff would think, but why should I worry? If the board gave its approval—even the chairman was going—I'd go and enjoy a fortnight in America.

Although I enjoyed a gin and tonic I wasn't a regular drinker. Before boarding our plane at Gatwick a visit to the duty-free shop was considered a must, to buy the maximum spirits we were allowed to take into Kennedy Airport in New York. Harold was paymaster: he paid for everything. He delegated our greengrocery buyer to carry all the drink when we landed so that the rest of us could see to the luggage through customs.

'Has anyone seen Stan?' Harold asked as we cleared customs and were standing in a group with our luggage. No on had seen him, so after waiting almost twenty minutes John decided it was time to find him. After an hour John returned with an ashen-faced greengrocery buyer. He'd been stopped at customs for carrying an amount of spirits equal to eight people's allowance. We were nowhere in sight and he was given a grilling until John arrived and confirmed his story. Poor Stan, it was an unhappy start to the tour.

Campbell's were our host for the first part of the tour. Huge limousines transported us everywhere. Our first hotel was the Roosevelt, off Times Square—it was pure luxury. For the next five days we were taken out to modern stores, the like of which we'd never seen. We were given access to everything and everywhere. In the evenings we were taken to a race meeting, a Japanese restaurant and a banquet. No host could have been more generous.

We then moved to Chicago and Philadelphia, courtesy of Heinz. Between even more supermarket visits we were taken on a sightseeing tour of Chicago, where Al Capone lived, and to see the giant Liberty Bell at Philadelphia. Our lunch-time stop was at a road-side pub that boasted it could supply any drink in the world. Joe immediately requested a Newcastle Brown Ale. To everyone's surprise it was supplied without a raised eyebrow.

Johnson's Wax booked us into a hotel at a mid-west town called 'Racin'. It was as luxurious as any, and was proclaiming: 'Vote for Ronald Reagan'. Apparently our hotel was his hotel for the night during his presidential campaign. We got a glimpse of the future president as he swept out of the hotel the next morning, surrounded by an army of secret-service men.

By the time we arrived back home we were absolutely shattered. It had been an eventful, non-stop two weeks, but we had gained ample knowledge to create the blueprint of a modern food supermarket that would be the model for every future new store we built.

I hadn't been back very long when a supervisor vacancy occurred. I interviewed the six applicants and, without doubt, the most outstanding one was Lynn Allanson. Her record as a manageress was extremely good and I didn't hesitate to give her the job. I was aware that she would be the first female to be promoted to supervisor but I didn't expect the reaction it created. Even Joe Brown, the regional manager (north), phoned to ask what I was playing at, promoting a woman to field management!

Her life was hell in her endeavour to create her authority over store managers. She was aware of the problems at the outset but was determined to succeed.

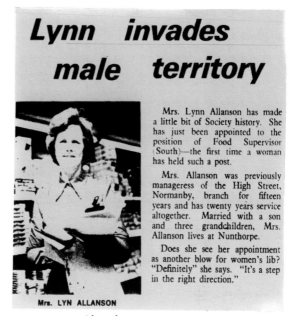

Lynn invades male territory

Mrs. Lynn Allanson has made a little bit of Society history. She has just been appointed to the position of Food Supervisor (South)—the first time a woman has held such a post.

Mrs. Allanson was previously manageress of the High Street, Normanby, branch for fifteen years and has twenty years service altogether. Married with a son and three grandchildren, Mrs. Allanson lives at Nunthorpe.

Does she see her appointment as another blow for women's lib? "Definitely" she says. "It's a step in the right direction."

Mrs. LYN ALLANSON

Ahead *magazine, 1976*

At least twice she was on the verge of resigning but battled on and eventually was accepted and respected by most managers.

Ryhope store opened in a blaze of publicity. Many American ideas on greengrocery, frozen foods, and other areas were introduced and it was an overwhelming success from the first day. Plans were laid for similar stores at Whickham, Newcastle, Middlesbrough and other areas, but our underlying problems continued.

Expenses were too high and needed unpopular measures. Profit was too low and needed some detailed analysis of our costings. I was frustrated, and decided to put my concern on record. In an eight-page report I analysed our position as I saw it, and gave details of action required as a matter of urgency. I had the report hand-delivered to the controller so he couldn't deny its existence. The report was never discussed or even acknowledged. We carried on as if we had no problem. I didn't know it then, but that report would one day save my job (I kept a copy).

At this time the chief executive officer decided to take early retirement. A new CEO was appointed and my career took yet another dramatic turn.

15

THE HARD MAN

The food controller John, the regional manager (north) Joe, and I were standing outside the new chief executive officer's office, waiting to be called into a meeting with him. We'd been kept waiting twenty minutes and were beginning to feel rather restless.

It was January 1979. Harold Whitehead had departed, to be replaced by Terry Norris, an ex-CWS man whom I knew from my CWS days. He was about four years younger than me and had a wide business experience outside the Co-op. He had already established his image by sacking two senior managers for gross inefficiency. As usual, a 'soft' man had been replaced by one with a 'hard' reputation. This was our first meeting as a food team with the man who would be responsible for the fortunes of the North Eastern Co-op for the next decade.

He didn't lift his head from his papers as we filed in to occupy the three seats in front of the chief officer's desk. When we were seated, he looked, but made no comment of greeting or recognition that he already knew me. Instead, he launched into a tirade against the whole food group, and us three in particular. He'd obviously rehearsed his speech, pointing out the weaknesses and problems of the food group and the stories he'd heard about the socialising. He was completely right of course. I'd have said the same if I'd been in his place, but when he began to question our ability and integrity it was too much. No chance was given to reply. We were dismissed with notice he intended to visit every single shop we controlled.

Outside his office John was ashen-faced and Joe was visibly shaken at such a blasting. I was foaming. No one had ever spoken to me like that in my life and I was damned if I'd let a guy question my integrity.

'I'm going back. He's not getting away with that,' I said to the other two, who didn't even respond. I'm sure they thought I was mad.

I knocked on his door without speaking to his secretary and entered at his request. With obvious surprise he said:

'Can I do something for you, David?'

'Just give me two minutes,' I answered, and continued without a pause: 'You're right in commenting about the socialising. You've no right to criticise, because it was your predecessor's policy. You've got no right to question my integrity unless you can back it up.'

'What about the other two?' he interrupted. 'I'm not here to talk about anyone else. And another thing'—I was aware my voice was raised but I was boiling with anger—'don't question my ability until you read this.' I pushed a copy of my eight-page report in front of him. 'That was completely ignored. Maybe you'll do something about it.'

'Why don't you sit down until I read this?' he said, I was still so mad I nearly refused, but thought better of it and sat while he read every word.

'David, I'm sorry I included you in that blasting, but you were part of the team.' He handed back my copy report and continued: 'I'll come down to your region next week and we can have a good chat.' I left his office, not sure whether I'd talked myself out of a job or not, but at 54 years old I wasn't prepared to buckle under to anyone.

A few days later Joe phoned me from Blyth in a terrible state. He had spent the whole day with the new boss and had faced criticism all day long. Every shop visited was criticised. Joe was absolutely fed up. On the Sunday I played golf with John Beer, who was unusually subdued throughout the game.

My turn will be next, but I'm not going to take it quietly, I thought; I would pack the job in first. Sure enough, a phone call on Monday morning from his secretary informed me the chief officer would meet me the next morning at 9 o'clock. Very quickly managers were notified of the impending visit with a clear understanding that I didn't expect any problems or complaints from the new boss.

Precisely at 9 o'clock the next morning he arrived and spent an hour at our regional office looking round and being very friendly with all the staff. After a cup of coffee, one of my supervisors drove the car for our visit to branches that I'd selected and had given ample advance notice to ensure the standards would be immaculate. We had visited six shops by the time we were ready for lunch. The managers had done us proud—the shops were a credit to the society. Terry was relaxed, complimentary to staff and congratulatory to managers. None of the hassle that Joe and John had experienced had come my way—yet.

'What about lunch David?' he enquired as we left the sixth shop.

'A table is booked at Marton Hotel.' I replied.

'I'd like to speak to you alone over lunch,' he said, to my surprise. I had no choice but to tell the supervisor to eat elsewhere and pick us up later.

As soon as we sat down he began his obviously prepared speech.

'David, I'm going to make some big changes, and I'd like your help to implement them.'

'After the other day I expected to be on my way out,' I replied.

'I'm sorry about that. I had to include you as part of the team responsible, but if you want to work for me I'd be pleased to forget the past few days.'

'Why me?' I asked. 'You and I haven't met for some years. You're right to criticise the business going down, and, as you say, I'm part of the team.'

'I know your reputation, I've seen the result of your experience and that eight-page report analyses the problems perfectly,' he replied.

I didn't answer and waited to see what was to follow.

'What I'm going to say is between you and me, for the moment,' he began. I nodded agreement. Harold Whitehead had eliminated four area managers and now the man sitting opposite was planning another reorganisation. The fact that he was confiding in me was a hopeful sign. His next few words took my breath away.

'I'm getting rid of the food controller,' was his first salvo.

'You're demoting him?' I asked.

'No, he's got to go.' I said nothing. He continued: 'Allan Griffin, the garages controller, is trying his best to find a job elsewhere so I'll give him a sideways move to food until he gets a new job.'

'He hasn't a clue about food retailing,' I answered.

'That's where you come in,' he said. 'Instead of two regional managers I want you to be operations manager to take full control of the whole food group. Allan Griffin will only be a figurehead until he gets another job.'

'What happens to Joe Brown, north regional manager?' I asked.

'Oh, he will be going, he's no good to us.'

I was staggered. Two of the top people of a two-million-pound-a-week business being dismissed without a second thought!

He hadn't finished. 'John will be going on holiday in four weeks' time. The reorganisation takes place while he's away, so you have four weeks to decide who you want rid of and who your team will be to control the business,' he continued. 'The controller will be dismissed when he returns from holiday.'

Thankfully he didn't want to visit any more branches. He returned to his office at Gateshead, I went back to Middlesbrough.

May was very upset on hearing the news. Over the past three years a good friendship had developed with our wives and she was concerned at the shock awaiting the wives of both Joe and John. The four weeks up to John going on holiday were hell. Obviously I couldn't tell managers what was happening, so tried to appear normal. While they talked about future plans, I was quietly planning a total reorganisation.

The day after John went on holiday the new chief officer sent for Joe and told him he was redundant. I phoned Joe later in the afternoon to tell him how sorry I was about the whole business, but he'd cleared his desk, gone home, never to return. My attempts to contact him at home were unsuccessful. We never had any contact from then on and, sadly, he died a few years later.

The four weeks of John's holiday in America was the time it took me to get established at an office in Gateshead, create and install my own team of merchandisers and supervisors, and at the same time make redundant several people I knew to be a dead loss. By the time John returned, everything had been changed. Within an hour of his return he'd been made redundant, cleared his office and was gone. I didn't even see him.

The whole of the food group had been turned upside down in a few weeks. Not only had I survived the carve up, I had ended up in charge of the whole operation. I was responsible for 260 stores within an area from the Scottish Border down to Scarborough and west to the Dales. The sales were £116 million a year. This was a bigger business than I'd ever handled in my career.

By such ruthless action, the new chief executive officer, Terry Norris, was now a man everyone was scared to cross. He had firm ideas and rarely listened to others. He concentrated most of his time with the non-food departments, with everyone from the controller down running round in circles. Meanwhile, I was allowed to get on with the job of improving the fortunes of the food group by some aggressive pricing and promotion activity.

Co-op introduces 'sweeping changes' in merchandising

The North-Eastern Co-op, whose profits slumped by nearly half last year, has taken a head office hard-line policy on merchandising.

It affects over 50 Price-fighter and Saver stores which account for 50 per cent. of weekly turnover and started to come into operation last month but continues until the end of the year.

The Co-op says it is a "radical, sweeping change to merchandising."

Retail operations manager David Hughes said: "After two years study, we have come up with a plan for every store which will detail how many facings and metre length of every product we sell."

Hughes said: "For years we have brought up managers with the idea that they have freedom to choose their own range of products from about 5,500 options.

"As a result, I have 260

By DENNIS STOKOE, Business Staff

managers with different choices and priorities, along with 820 supplier merchandisers and salesmen pushing their goods. So you could say there are over 1,000 people holding different opinions about what sells best and where."

Hughes added that as profit margins became increasingly squeezed he could not afford one area of a store not working well, either left unstocked or selling slow lines.

"Profit in the supermarket relies on the mix in the shopping basket. The wrong mix means a profitable store can quickly turn into a loss maker.

"Pricefighters and Savers stores account for 50 per cent. of our weekly turnover. Start getting the mix wrong in these by a slight error of buying judgment means thousands of pounds can be lost.

"How can 1,000 people

be experts in this delicate balancing act? Salesmen are interested in getting the maximum space for their product.

"A busy manager can be persuaded on a hectic morning to let the salesman or merchandiser have his or her own way in taking up too much space on the fixture."

Hughes said there would be no deviation from the plan. "It is not negotiable except at head office. All negotiations over space have taken place with suppliers, which have followed up by an intense period of training with every manager, deputy manager and section head. I have also given presentations on the new scheme to all major suppliers."

When the system is completed, there will be regular checks: "Some goods may need space allocation review or even seasonal space review, such as hot

David Hughes

cross buns at Easter, soft drinks in summer.

"This is where we are relying on market information to tell us if we need space for new products, or if the space is insufficient for existing products.

"Empty fixtures can spell disaster for the store and supplier alike, so it requires co-operation from suppliers and store manager at all times."

Hughes is asking management to "have a totally committed approach" to the scheme which, he said, was working smoothly and efficiently.

"I feel confident that this centralisation of merchandising control will contribute to a strengthened and more efficient operation."

North-Eastern turnover increased £11.6m. to £195m. in 1981 but profits fell to £944,000 compared to £1.7m. for 1980.

The Pricefighter group of supermarkets account for around 40 per cent. of food division sales.

Great care was taken to ensure our public relations created an image of efficiency, competitiveness and modernisation.

Steve Warren, our PR man, played his part by getting the right stories in the press. Doug Campbell was brilliant in designing press adverts.

Our image was enhanced tremendously by Terry Norris giving the authority to use Kathy Secker in our TV adverts. Already a star of radio and television, she was the ultimate professional. Her glamorous image completed a perfect advertising approach.

Kathy Secker with a group of butchery sales managers

In three years we opened eight new supermarkets and modernised well over 50 existing stores, adding another £50 million a year on the sales. Throughout my four years as an operating manager, I always spoke my mind. While everyone was afraid of Terry, the fact that he knew I always gave my opinion seemed to cement a bond of friendship that was to our mutual benefit.

Only once did we have a real clash of opinion. He had visited a branch, found things not to his liking, reprimanded the supervisor and sacked the store manager on the spot. The manager happened to be a union shop steward. The unions and personnel controller got nowhere with him. He was determined his decision would stand. I'd been tipped off that staff were incensed and talking of walking out.

'Can I talk about the manager you sacked?' I asked as I sat down in front of his desk.

'You can talk, but he remains sacked.' he answered bluntly.

'You know you're in the wrong,' I said. 'You've broken procedures, you'd lose at a tribunal and I reckon we'll have a strike on our hands.' No one spoke to him in such fashion, but he had to know the situation. 'Can I suggest you reinstate him, pending a review, then fine him a week's pay for negligence, which will be one week's holiday pay. He'll work and lose no money, and everyone is satisfied.'

He wasn't happy but accepted the idea. Union and staff were notified and everyone settled back to work. He never ever sacked anyone in such a fashion again.

The food group became a real professional operation, our 'pricefighter' image was created and projected by Kathy Secker from Tyne Tees TV. Our shop standards were as good as any and our prices were better than Presto, Tesco or Savacentre.

It was a period of my career I really enjoyed. I had ample resources to do a good job. The chief officer didn't interfere and the controller hardly got involved. Inevitably I had returned to working long hours. Once again I was trying to set an example to everyone else.

It nearly cost me my life. I was sitting at my desk having a cup of tea, when suddenly I had an unbelievable pain in my chest. It was excruciating and brought me out in a sweat. I was convinced I was having a heart attack. I wanted only one thing—to get home to May and my own bed. I wouldn't listen to talk about hospital and instructed a supervisor to take me home. I was sitting on the back seat of the car in absolute agony. By the time we reached Fence Houses the pain had eased considerably and on reaching home it was only a dull ache.

A specialist diagnosed heart muscle spasm. I had been lucky—I'd had a warning. For many weeks, every twinge of pain had me in a mild panic in anticipation of a reccurrence. I knew I had to take care.

It was 1983, I was 58 years old, and at long last the food controller's job was vacant. Allan Griffin had found another job. I waited to be informed the job was mine. It would be automatic; after all, I'd survived three major

New supermarket opening, 1982

re-organisations, modernised, streamlined and successfully controlled the group for the past four years. There was no one else.

Once again, the message was brought home to me that the expected doesn't happen and sentiment has no place in business.

Terry called me into his office to tell me I would not be controller of the food group for three reasons:

1. The recent heart spasm put my health in doubt;
2. I was 58 years old and too old for the job;
3. Members of the board were from societies I'd taken over when I worked for the CWS. Memories were long and they wouldn't agree to me getting the top job.

Of course I was disappointed, but once again I was presented with another challenge. Throughout my career I'd faced different problems and situations and now, in the twilight of my working life, I was being asked to turn yet another corner to a new job. The North Eastern Co-op was now so big it was considered that the time had arrived to have its own food buyer.

At the same time, the board had decided to recruit younger executives from Fine Fare and Presto as operational managers to control day-to-day activities and be the future executive management. In addition to buying I would also decide on the price policy and promotion activity. I would have a team of nine people and we would operate from a new block of offices at Birtley, next door

NEW GENERAL MANAGERS

MARKETING

HEADING the newly formed food marketing group is Marketing General Manager, David Hughes, 57, who lives in Durham Road, Houghton-le-Spring.

Based at the giant CWS complex in Birtley, Mr. Hughes and his marketing team are responsible for buying in all the grocery lines, wines and spirits, provisions and fresh food sold in the Society's stores.

The group plans the ranges, determines marketing strategy, sets prices, controls distribution, tests new products, analyses competitor activity, and arranges advertising in association with the Society's in-house advertising department.

David Hughes, Marketing General Manager.

Ahead *magazine, 1982*

to the CWS warehouse and only fifteen minutes from home.

On the Friday before starting the new job, I was sitting in the new office with Ted Foulger, who was to be my deputy buyer. Ted was the only general manager I hadn't made redundant when I took over his society at West Cornforth in my CWS days. Now we were to work closely together, and we were sitting talking about how we'd make it a pleasant job to take us to retirement (he was one year younger than me).

'Good night David, see you on Monday.'

Those were the last words Ted spoke to me. On the way home he had a heart attack and died.

BIG BUSINESS AT BIRTLEY

LAST YEAR the food group's sales were in excess of £112 million! It sounds like a lot of money but it's only when you actually convert the cash into the number of products sold that you really start to realise just how big the NECS food business is!

For example, during 1983 the group sold:
21,600,000 eggs...
273,600,000 cigarettes...
1,319,000 bottles of wine or spirits...
3,700,000 lbs of bacon...

The list of impressive statistics could go on and on.

Most of the products sold in our food stores come through the huge CWS distribution complex at Birtley where the Society's marketing team are based.

The team headed by **Marketing General Manager David Hughes** handle all the negotiations with suppliers, arrange test markets for new products, set the prices, monitor competitors' activity, arrange advertising and promotional activity for the group. Since January alone over 70 new products have been test marketed in the Society's stores.

David, 58, has held senior management positions for many years and is now using his expertise to develop a strong marketing strategy.

His marketing management team at Birtley consists of:
Christine Triggs, 25-year-old promotions co-ordinator, the

department's most recent appointment. Christine, who lives at Sunderland, is a former NECS management trainee, and is the main link between the marketing department and the stores, communicating promotional information to managers taking inquiries on supplies etc.

Don Etherington, 57, is the **Product Service Manager** responsible for establishing prices, profitability, analysing the results of the weekly surveys conducted by the Society in which 40 to 50 product prices are compared in competitors' stores. Don has been with the Co-op since he joined the former Middlesbrough Society as a 14 year old.

Harvey Smith, 49-year-old grocery products analyst is responsible for investigating the market background of the products, the terms, and competitiveness. He examines the ranges available, new product areas, analyses market research etc.

In the seven years he has been with the Society's food group Harvey has headed up the chain of 160 NECS off-licences and more recently the freezer centres.

GUARANTEE

One of the latest moves by the marketing department to ensure the Society obtains the best possible terms from suppliers is a new guarantee scheme scheduled to be introduced next month.

If a manufacturer will guarantee a cost price for at least 12 weeks, the NECS will guarantee a maximum retail price for the same period of time, distribution to the stores will be guaranteed, the products will receive a guaranteed place on the shelves and number of facings, and a shelf talker will also be guaranteed.

The Birtley Marketing team, left to right: Don Etherington, Chris Triggs, David Hughes and Harvey Smith.

Ahead *magazine, 1983*

16

THE POWER OF A BUYER

I began my new job as marketing manager by making a firm decision. The year 1983 was just in its infancy and I was 58 years old: I would work no longer than two more years. I would retire on my 60th birthday. I'd been in retailing from the age of 14 and had worked in nearly every capacity.

Little did I understand the world I was now entering. As the third biggest Co-op food buyer in England, the pressure would be greater than I expected. I'd been involved with reps to some degree most of my life, but now I was in a new ball game.

On my personal authorisation depended:

a) Whether a new product was accepted or not;

b) The retail price of every product;

c) Which products were promoted;

d) Which products were delisted or listed to be sold;

e) The quantity of every product sold.

We had over 10,000 products listed, but a large number required no involvement of mine. Sugar, tea, butter, etc., were automatically re-ordered by the warehouse. Most of my time would be involved in new products and organising promotions of existing products. However, the first priority was to decide on my schedule of seeing reps. From my first hour in the job they were queuing up to see me. With a buying budget in excess of £2 million per week, any rep would try to get a slice of that business.

I planned to see reps on three days of each week at fifteen-minute intervals, so I'd see almost 200 reps each week for a product range covering groceries, toiletries, frozen foods, paper products and medicines. Greengrocery and meat were bought by specialists. Within a few days I was booked six weeks in advance to see a different rep every fifteen minutes. The 'non rep' days were sheer bliss.

Companies were producing a new product every day of the week. Our society was the possible outlet for a major part of their production and it was fascinating to observe the different methods used to persuade me to accept their deals.

The major companies like Procter & Gamble and Heinz often sent young reps straight from university, armed with a video tape recorder and flip chart. They'd been programmed to tell a clear story, using their equipment without interruption. When I told them their 40-minute presentation had to be reduced to fifteen minutes they were in utter confusion. Very rarely were these young men seen twice. To them it was a stepping stone in a career. For me, it was a waste of valuable time. Almost twenty 'new' products were presented every week, and an abundance of samples were provided for testing. Staff and relations were bombarded with samples of every product imaginable to test. I was constantly invited to lunch or dinner, and usually refused, to avoid being compromised.

The individual reps had a variety of approaches when trying to get my custom:

Flash Harry—immaculately dressed, dripping with gold, and trying to create the image that he was doing me a favour by giving me his time.

Weepy Willie—I got all his personal problems and family troubles in an effort to get my sympathy and hence some business.

Director Dan—had an impressive title, was accustomed to talking down to his staff, and tried the same tactic with me.

Dolly Bird—rarely had a clue about selling and assumed the image alone would get an order.

Boss Man—accompanied the usual rep, did everything possible to make him look inferior and in need of Boss Man to hold his hand.

Money Man—always implied that money was no problem (in any form) so long as he had an order.

Confidential Ken—always had an offer available to me and no one else.

Boaster Ben—was the 'best' salesman, had the 'best' product and the 'best' price.

I could go on and on. All were different, which made the job fascinating.

I could count on one hand the reps I could trust, whose word was their bond. For everyone else a written agreement was not only desirable but absolutely essential.

The buying was on such a huge scale, it wasn't possible to make a little mistake. Even a one-per-cent error could be significant. Some of the buying quantities were staggering:

4 million pounds of bacon.

21 million dozen eggs.

2 million bottles of wine.

73 million packets of cigarettes.

I never refused to see a rep because the next one might have had an absolute winner. They needed me, but without their products we had no business. I wasn't always right in my decisions—when Bovril launched a cube, I thought they would never break the Oxo business. I was wrong. Procter & Gamble launched Vortex—I thought Domestos was invincible. I was wrong. I didn't think disposable nappies would be such a huge success. I was wrong.

Every single day it was a two-way discussion with suppliers about products, prices and promotions. The realisation of the power of a buyer in a large company came to the fore when dealing with a small company supplier. The size of an order or the closing of an account could mean the life or death of a small company. Some were so inefficient they had no future, others I was able to help to become a substantial organisation.

The atmosphere in the buying office was the happiest and most tranquil of my whole career: the staff were efficient; there was no hassle from anyone; it was the perfect way to wind down on my working life.

About nine months before my 60th birthday, the chief officer said he would appoint my successor so that I could help him to settle into the job and at the same time I could slowly become accustomed to being retired. It was the perfect arrangement and those few months passed so quickly, it was time to retire before I realised. An area general manager was retiring at the same time and we were invited to a 'small' function.

With amazement, I entered a room at the Five Bridges Hotel, accompanied by May and my daughter Sheila, to find it crowded with managers and reps from almost every major company I had dealt with. Some had travelled many miles to attend in order to say cheerio and wish me well. I was overwhelmed at such a gesture from so many people.

So this was the end of my life at the Co-op. I didn't feel sad. In fact, I was ready to retire. I'd had a career that couldn't have been more eventful. I could say there were things that could have been done better, but one thing was for sure: I never had a minute of boredom.

A big regret was the fact that the Co-op had taken a bigger slice of my life than my family. On my retirement May booked a table for two for a quiet celebration dinner. Entering the County Hotel, Durham, I was stunned and delighted to find the family waiting to share a glorious evening.

No matter what I'd achieved or how far I'd travelled, at the end of the day I was surrounded by the really important things in my life—May and our family.

Tomorrow?—It's the first day of the rest of my life. Maybe the best is yet to come!

Co-op says goodby to its Mr Cut Price

The Journal, 1985

A GROCER who became known as "Mr Cut Price" and changed the shopping habits of the North-East, leaves his job at the end of the year.

David Hughes, who lives in Houghton, is retiring as the North-Eastern Co-op's marketing manager.

Back in the 60s his innovations made him a household name. He introduced a remarkable number of "firsts."

These included cut-price bread, cut-price cigarettes, local TV advertising, and self-service-style shopping.

Mr Hughes rose from being shop boy at Hetton Downs Co-op 44 years ago, to mastermind the amalgamation of Co-op societies across the North-East.

His task was to go into areas where societies were in difficulties and put them right.

Local Co-ops eventually combined into the North-Eastern Co-op in 1970, when Mr Hughes was made an executive with special powers.

"Mr Cut Price" likes to recall those days when he led the trends. "There were a lot of regulations which had been necessary during the war, but by the 60s they had just become red tape," he said.

The cut-price tactics stirred a storm of protest among shoppers and traders, but resulted in newspaper headlines and "plugs" on television.

Mr Hughes said: "The formation of the NECS was one of the best things to have happened, and I believe it will continue to dominate as the region's leading retail operation in future."

DALEPAK

DALEPAK FOODS LIMITED,
AMEN HOUSE, NORTH END, BEDALE,
NORTH YORKSHIRE DL8 1XA.
TEL: (0677) 24111.

17th April 1985.

D. Hughes, Esq.,
Marketing General Manager.
North East Co-Operative Society Limited,
Birtley RDC
Drum Road.
Barley Mow.
Birtley.
Chester-le-Street,
Co. Durham.
DH2 1AA.

Dear David,

Just a line to wish you a Very Happy Retirement from everyone here at Dalepak. It will be difficult thinking of the NECS without associating it with you and I am perfectly certain you will be very sorely missed.

May I take this opportunity of extending sincere thanks for the support you have given to Bob Hird over the past years – I know he has appreciated your professionalism and co-operation at all times, together with the prompt and efficient way in which you have organised every aspect of business relating to Dalepak.

Michael Hughes (Managing Director) and the other Directors and myself, together with Bob Hird envy the amount of time you will now be able to spend on the Golf Course ! You now have no excuse for not getting your handicap down to scratch !!

Every Good Wish from us all and All the Very Best.

Yours sincerely,

John Kerwin
Sales & Marketing Director.

Bob.

Bob Hird.
National Account Manager

Retirement party, December 1985

EPILOGUE

'So this is the rest of my life'!

I was sitting all alone in our lounge, the TV full on, yet I hadn't a clue what programme was on.

May was out at the local WI meeting. I had been retired three months and was feeling sorry for myself.

If this was retirement I wasn't enjoying it. I'd finished a stressful career and should have been delighted to be free to do my own thing, but what? I couldn't, nor did I wish to, play golf every day, even if I'd been fit enough. I was driving May to distraction trying to help in the house and in the garden.

Of course she'd done things to suit herself for years and my half-baked attempts to help usually produced the remark:

'For God's sake, go for a walk'.

We made a pledge when first married never to go to sleep without making up from an argument. I know it took super-human effort on her part to keep the pledge.

May loved shopping. We visited shops of the very type I had just left, only to hear the remark: 'David, you've retired!' Without realising, I was straightening loose tins on shelves, the same as I'd done for the past 30 years when inspecting stores (except we were in Sainsbury's).

I had every reason on earth to be happy in retirement. After all, it was my decision to retire. Financially we were OK, we lived in a lovely house, and, apart from stupid little arguments, May and I were as much in love as ever.

Our David was married. Shirley and he had four daughters—Nicola, Zoe, Gemma and Laura—of whom I was so proud. They lived at a village near Nottingham and we saw each other as often as we could.

Our daughter Sheila and John had a son and daughter. They lived only a short walk away and May and I had the pleasure of babysitting Helen, who was four years old, and Gary, a toddler. We saw them regularly. So what on earth had I to be miserable about? I had as much and more than most retired men.

When you've been married 38 years, words are often unnecessary. As soon as she walked in the door she knew my thoughts: this wasn't what retirement was supposed to be.

She came over and kissed me on the cheek and said:

'Why don't you give Terry Norris a ring in the morning?'

'What do you mean?' I said with great surprise. She sat down with resignation in her voice, explained that she and my ex-boss had been talking on the night of my retirement, and he had said:

'David can't possibly switch off after all he's done. Give him a few weeks and when he's ready I have a part-time consultancy job waiting for him.

He knew, May and the family knew: I couldn't switch off completely. I'll be forever grateful to Terry Norris—no manager could have done more. He said I'd given the Co-op my life, it was the least he could do for me.

Those fifteen hours a week were a saviour. I worked in an office next to his, helping him to check the accounts and expenses of the food group, now under control of executives recruited from Presto. Naturally it wasn't popular, but Terry and I had never courted popularity, so I got on with the job and began part-time retirement. I was happier, May and I got back to normality.

After about six months, I received an invitation to join a firm in Newcastle part-time. I was asked to be one of the consultants to Entrust, who operated a government scheme to help people set up a business on their own.

'As long as it keeps you off my feet I'm all for it,' was May's response when I mentioned the offer. For the next eighteen months I helped people to set up all types of business (hairdressing, shops, door-to-door selling, driving instructors, etc., etc.). It was interesting and enlightening. Some hadn't a clue and, when told the pitfalls, packed in the idea there and then.

I hope many of the people I helped on the road to self-employment are still in business and successful. At least during my time at Entrust I could say: 'I've been there and know the problems.'

January 1987: I had now been semi-retired for two years. I woke up one morning and said to May:

'I'm ready to retire full-time.' I just knew I could settle down to a life away from business, 48 years almost to the day since I'd started working life as a butcher boy at Murton.

She turned round, gave me a cuddle and said:

'Thank God, maybe now we can enjoy some retirement.'

I left the Co-op, left Entrust, and finally said goodbye to business. It had been rewarding, fulfilling and exciting, but now it was time to give my life to May and the family. Both our parents had died. My brother Ted had taken up music and become a very successful clarinet player with Billy Ternent and his band. He toured with Frankie Vaughan and other celebrities and seemed happy living in London with his wife Joan.

Over the next few years May and I were completely happy in each other's company. If we'd spent time apart when I worked, we made up for it now. We did everything together, wanting only each other's company, shopping, gardening, and doing housework.

I now had time to watch the grandchildren grow up and although they will cringe at me saying it, I loved pushing them in the pram and hearing them say 'Granddad'.

We now took time to have some holidays without the thought of getting back to work. We both loved Switzerland and over the next few years visited almost every part of the country. We both agreed that a hotel overlooking Lake Lucerne was our ideal spot. We had a holiday in Cyprus where I was able to show her the places where I had done my army service and the sites of the Jewish camps. May and I went on regular short breaks in England with her cousin June and husband Roland. We had the time of our lives.

So we settled into a routine of retirement that suited us both. May had her WI and a small group of friends, I had my golf and I started to teach myself watercolour painting.

We were approaching our 70s and, except for a balance problem that

May had, our health was reasonable. We were happy, saw our family regularly and were still as much in love as ever.

May on holiday in Switzerland, 1991

As 1997 was getting near, it would soon be our Golden Wedding. How would we celebrate? It was the same year as the Queen's Golden Wedding, so our celebration began with a lovely letter signed by the Queen and Prince Philip offering their congratulations. This was followed by an invitation, along with other 'Golden Wedding' couples, to Sunderland Civic Centre, where we were wined and dined like royalty. May looked fabulous in her new outfit.

We invited the whole family to spend a weekend with us at the Oulton Hall Hotel near Leeds. It was one of the most wonderful weekends of our lives. May was radiant, so happy, and I loved her as much as I had on the day we married.

If anyone deserved this weekend, she did. Without her I could never have achieved what I did. We were celebrating fifty years of an incredible life together, surrounded by all that was dear to us. The weekend was marred by the news that Princess Diana had been killed (even our Golden Wedding had an incident).

It's taken four years for me to write this story. At the beginning I said: 'Read and enjoy.' I hope you've found it of interest and not too boring.

I've enjoyed living it.

May and me at our Golden Wedding, September 1997